Michael Teutsch

Moving Object Detection and Segmentation for Remote Aerial Video Surveillance

Karlsruher Schriften zur Anthropomatik
Band 18
Herausgeber: Prof. Dr.-Ing. Jürgen Beyerer

Eine Übersicht aller bisher in dieser Schriftenreihe erschienenen Bände finden Sie am Ende des Buchs.

Moving Object Detection and Segmentation for Remote Aerial Video Surveillance

by
Michael Teutsch

Scientific
Publishing

Dissertation, Karlsruher Institut für Technologie (KIT)
Fakultät für Informatik, 2014

Impressum

KIT Scientific Publishing

Karlsruher Institut für Technologie (KIT)
KIT Scientific Publishing
Straße am Forum 2
D-76131 Karlsruhe

KIT Scientific Publishing is a registered trademark of Karlsruhe Institute of Technology. Reprint using the book cover is not allowed.

www.ksp.kit.edu

Print on Demand 2015

ISSN 1863-6489
ISBN 978-3-7315-0320-0
DOI 10.5445/KSP/1000044922

Moving Object Detection and Segmentation for Remote Aerial Video Surveillance

zur Erlangung des akademischen Grades eines

Doktors der Ingenieurwissenschaften

von der Fakultät für Informatik
des Karlsruher Instituts für Technologie (KIT)

genehmigte

Dissertation

von

Michael Teutsch

aus Tuttlingen

Tag der mündlichen Prüfung:	01. Dezember 2014
Erster Gutachter:	Prof. Dr.-Ing. Jürgen Beyerer
Zweiter Gutachter:	Prof. Dr. Mubarak Shah

Abstract

Mobile platforms such as Unmanned Aerial Vehicles (UAVs) equipped with video cameras are a flexible and efficient support to ensure both civil and military safety and security. Some prominent potential applications include the detection of criminal or terroristic activities, traffic monitoring, search and rescue, disaster relief, or environmental monitoring. However, analyzing aerial surveillance video data is a difficult task for human operators due to fatigue resulting from the large amount of visual data. Appropriate computer vision algorithms such as image stabilization, image stitching, automatic object detection and tracking, or activity and behavior recognition can assist the operator. In scene understanding and situation awareness, moving objects play a key role and have to be detected and tracked as accurately and precisely as possible. This can be a challenging task due to the large distance between camera and objects, simultaneous object and camera motion, low contrast due to weak illumination, or shadows. As a result, small-sized objects in the image often cannot be detected and tracked reliably. In scenarios where vehicles are driving on busy urban streets, this is even more challenging and often results in merged or missing detections. Although many approaches for moving object detection in aerial video surveillance data exist in the literature, state-of-the-art methods are often lacking reliability, robustness, transferability, or real-time capability.

In this thesis, a video processing chain is presented for moving object detection in remote aerial video surveillance with a moving camera. In contrast to wide area surveillance or wide area motion imagery, remote aerial surveillance videos provide a smaller observation area but higher frame rate. Novel approaches are proposed that improve the performance and robustness of multiple object detection, segmentation, and tracking. Compensation for camera motion is achieved by image registration. Subsequently, motion is detected that is independent of the camera motion and can thus originate from objects. In contrast to most existing approaches, a Track-Before-Detect algorithm is applied for detection and clustering of independent motion instead of difference images. Image stacking is a preprocessing step considering temporal information at a level between independent motion detection and object detection to remove the stationary background from the motion clusters. In this way, short occlusions or street texture disturbing the detection and segmentation process can be handled. Due to the small size of objects in the image which can be as small as 5×10 pixels per object, three novel or modified algorithms are presented for detection and segmentation of such small objects. The first one implements clustering of edge pixels that are determined with a novel approach for noise resistant gradient calculation based on Local Binary Patterns (LBP). The second approach uses clustering of relative connectivity that can be interpreted as a simple hand designed object model. Finally, the third one is a modification of the popular sliding window approach. Significant search space reduction is achieved and therefore the robustness for object detection is improved. In top view videos, the sliding window clearly outperforms the other two methods while clustering of edge pixels performs best in case of a variable camera angle. Multiple object tracking is introduced in order to utilize temporal information and reach higher reliability and robustness for object detection. By fusion of independent motion and object detection, effective split and merge handling is achieved and both detection accuracy and precision are improved.

In summary, the standard Track-Before-Detect algorithm taken as baseline is improved significantly by the proposed methods. Furthermore, existing approaches for object detection and segmentation taken from the literature are outperformed with respect to detection accuracy and precision. This is demonstrated in a quantitative and qualitative evaluation for sample videos coming from different aerial surveillance datasets.

Zusammenfassung

Der Einsatz mobiler Videokameras, die von unbemannten fliegenden Plattformen (UAVs) getragen werden, kann eine flexible und daher effiziente Unterstützung dabei darstellen, sowohl zivile als auch militärische Sicherheit zu gewährleisten. Bereits bestehende und potentielle Anwendungsgebiete umfassen beispielsweise die Entdeckung krimineller oder terroristischer Aktivitäten, Verkehrsüberwachung, Suche und Rettung, Katastrophenhilfe oder Umweltüberwachung. Die Analyse von Überwachungsdaten luftgetragener Kameras ist für den Menschen jedoch ein schwieriges Unterfangen, da Aufmerksamkeit und Konzentration bei einer derartig großen Menge an Bilddaten binnen Minuten nachlassen. Videoverarbeitungsalgorithmen wie beispielsweise Bildstabilisierung und Bildmosaikierung sowie automatische Verfahren zur Detektion und Verfolgung von Objekten oder zur Erkennung von Aktivitäten und Verhalten können den Menschen bei seinen Aufgaben unterstützen. Eine Schlüsselrolle für das Verständnis und Einschätzen bestimmter Situationen spielen sich bewegende Objekte. Sie müssen daher so präzise wie möglich detektiert und verfolgt werden. Dies kann aufgrund von hoher Distanz zwischen Kamera und Objekten, simultaner Kamera- und Objektbewegung, schwacher Beleuchtung oder Schattenwurf eine herausfordernde Aufgabe darstellen. Vor allem kleine Objekte im Bild können aus diesen Gründen oftmals nicht zuverlässig detektiert und verfolgt werden. Eine noch größere Herausforderung stellen verschmolzene oder fehlende Detektionen dar, wie sie oft bei dichtem städtischen Straßenverkehr auftreten können. Obwohl ein umfangreicher Literaturbestand über die Detektion sich bewegender Objekte in Überwachungsdaten luftgetragener Kameras existiert, fehlt es Methoden, die dem Stand der Technik entsprechen, oft an Zuverlässigkeit, Robustheit, Übertragbarkeit oder Echtzeitfähigkeit.

Im Rahmen dieser Arbeit wird eine Videoverarbeitungskette für die Detektion sich bewegender Objekte zur Fernüberwachung mit einer luftgetragenen, sich bewegenden Kamera präsentiert. Im Gegensatz zur weiträumigen Überwachung bieten Fernüberwachungsvideos einen geringeren Beobachtungsbereich, dafür aber eine höhere Bildwiederholrate. Neue Ansätze werden beschrieben, die sowohl Leistung als auch Robustheit von Detektion, Segmentierung und Verfolgung sich bewegender Objekte verbessern.

Durch Bildregistration wird die Kamerabewegung kompensiert. Im Anschluss wird Bewegung detektiert, die von der Kamerabewegung unabhängig ist und daher von Objekten stammen kann. Im Gegensatz zu den meisten existierenden Ansätzen wird anstelle von Differenzbildern ein Verfahren zur Objektverfolgung vor der eigentlichen Detektion genutzt, um unabhängige Bewegung zu detektieren und zu gruppieren. Zwischen der Bewegungs- und Objektdetektion werden zeitlich gefilterte Bildstapel eingesetzt, um kurzzeitige Verdeckungen zu überrücken oder Straßentexturen zu entfernen, die den Detektionsprozess beeinträchtigen können. Aufgrund der geringen Objektgröße von bis zu 5×10 Pixeln werden drei neue Algorithmen zur Detektion und Segmentierung derartig kleiner Objekte präsentiert. Der erste Ansatz basiert auf der Gruppierung von Kantenpixeln. Diese werden mit einem neuartigen und rauschresistenten Verfahren mit lokalen Binärmustern, den sogenannten Local Binary Patterns (LBP), berechnet. Beim zweiten Ansatz wird anhand von Expertenwissen manuell ein einfaches Objektmodell erstellt, das auf der Berechnung relativer Konnektivität aufbaut. Der dritte Algorithmus schließlich nutzt eine Modifikation des sogenannten gleitenden Fensters oder auch sliding window. Hierbei wird durch signifikante Einschränkung des Suchraumes die Robustheit des Verfahrens bei der Objektdetektion erhöht. Das gleitende Fenster erreicht die höchsten Detektionsraten für Videos in Draufsicht, während die Gruppierung von Kantenpixeln bei variablem Kameraaufnahmewinkel die beste Leistung erzielt. Die Robustheit und Zuverlässigkeit der Objektdetektion kann über die Berücksichtigung temporalen Kontextes mit Multiobjektverfolgung zusätzlich verbessert werden. Durch die Fusion von Bewegungs-

und Objektdetektion kann zudem eine effektive Behandlung zerfallener und verschmolzener Detektionen und damit eine Verbesserung der Detektionsgenauigkeit erreicht werden.

Der Standardansatz zur Objektverfolgung vor der Detektion dient als Vergleichsbasis und kann durch die vorgeschlagenen Verfahren signifikant verbessert werden. Des Weiteren können gängige Verfahren zur Objektdetektion und -segmentierung aus der Literatur in ihrer Detektionsgenauigkeit übertroffen werden. Dies wird anhand von Beispielvideos verschiedener Überwachungsdatensätze im Rahmen einer quantitativen und qualitativen Evaluation gezeigt.

Acknowledgments

I would like to express my sincere thanks to my advisor Prof. Dr.-Ing. Jürgen Beyerer for giving me the opportunity to work at the Vision and Fusion Lab (IES) at the Karlsruhe Institute of Technology (KIT). Thank you for always taking time out from your busy schedule as director of IES and Fraunhofer IOSB to discuss my ideas and problems. This thesis would not have been possible without your guidance and support.

I thank my second advisor Prof. Dr. Mubarak Shah for hosting me as a visiting researcher at the Center for Research in Computer Vision (CRCV) at the University of Central Florida (UCF) for three months. Despite this relatively short time, I learned a lot and discovered a new point of view towards my research. Thank you for travelling to Karlsruhe in order to serve on my committee.

I am grateful to Prof. Dr.-Ing. J. Marius Zöllner and Jun.-Prof. Dr. rer. nat. Dennis Hofheinz for serving on my committee.

This dissertation was conducted in close cooperation with the Fraunhofer Institute of Optronics, System Technologies and Image Exploitation (IOSB) in Karlsruhe. I thank everyone at the department Video Exploitation Systems (VID) and, in particular, Dr. Wolfgang Krüger, Günter Saur, Michael Grinberg, and Norbert Heinze. Your experience and your willingness to share your knowledge with me in many discussion sessions greatly helped me to shape the path of my research.

I thank Dr. Marco Huber for many helpful discussions to generate and refine new ideas, Volker Gabler for assisting me in collecting and preparing my experimental data, Arne Schumann, Michael Grinberg, Dr. Wolfgang Krüger, and Dr. Alexey Pak for proof-reading my thesis, and everyone at IES for great coherence and support.

I thank the WTD81 for their support and the Karlsruhe House of Young Scientists (KHYS) for funding my research visit at the CRCV at the University of Central Florida (UCF).

I thank Dr. Haroon Idrees, Dr. Amir Roshan Zamir, Dr. Enrique G. Ortiz, Afshin Dehghan, Shayan Modiri Assari, Shervin Ardeshir, and Salman Khokhar for a great time at the CRCV in Orlando.

Finally, I would like to thank Janine, my parents Alexander and Erika, my sister Christine, and my close friends Hubert and Konstantinos for their patience and their encourangement during the preparation of this thesis.

Contents

1 Introduction **1**
1.1 Motivation . . . 1
1.2 Challenges . . . 4
1.3 Contributions . . . 10
1.4 Outline . . . 11

2 Related Work **13**
2.1 Compensation for Camera Motion . . . 17
2.2 Independent Motion Detection . . . 18
2.3 Object Detection and Segmentation . . . 23
2.3.1 Object Segmentation . . . 24
2.3.2 Vehicle Detection . . . 25
2.3.3 Person Detection . . . 28
2.4 Multiple Object Tracking . . . 29

3 Concept **33**

4 Independent Motion Detection **39**
4.1 Concept . . . 39
4.2 Approach . . . 40

5 Object Detection and Segmentation **47**
5.1 Motivation . . . 48
5.2 Concept . . . 50

5.3 Image Stacking . . . 51
5.3.1 Image Stack Initialization . . . 54
5.3.2 Association of Motion Vectors to Image Stacks . . . 56
5.3.3 Image Stack Update . . . 57
5.3.4 Replacement of Motion Clusters by Image Stacks . . . 60
5.3.5 Discussion . . . 61
5.4 Detection and Segmentation Algorithms . . . 64
5.4.1 Gradient Based Object Segmentation . . . 66
5.4.2 Object Segmentation using Relative Connectivity . . . 77
5.4.3 Object Detection using Local Sliding Window . . . 85
5.5 Outlier and Duplicate Removal . . . 96
5.5.1 Rejection of Duplicate Detections . . . 97
5.5.2 Rejection of Outlier Detections . . . 98

6 Multiple Object Tracking 101
6.1 Concept . . . 102
6.2 The Association Problem . . . 103
6.2.1 Association between Detections and Tracks . . . 104
6.2.2 Association between Motion Vectors and Tracks . . . 105
6.3 Split and Merge Handling . . . 106
6.4 Track Management . . . 109
6.5 Tracking Algorithm . . . 109

7 Evaluation of the Proposed Methods 111
7.1 Evaluation Measures and Methods . . . 111
7.1.1 Evaluation Measures for Object Detection . . . 112
7.1.2 Evaluation Measures for Object Tracking . . . 116
7.2 Datasets . . . 118
7.3 Parameter Estimation and Optimization . . . 124
7.3.1 Gradient Based Object Segmentation . . . 124
7.3.2 Object Segmentation using Relative Connectivity . . . 128
7.3.3 Object Detection using Local Sliding Window . . . 129
7.3.4 Image Stacking . . . 133
7.3.5 Duplicate and Outlier Removal . . . 136
7.3.6 Multiple Object Tracking . . . 137

7.4 Experiments and Evaluation 139
7.4.1 Object Detection and Segmentation 139
7.4.2 Image Stacking 148
7.4.3 Multiple Object Tracking 154
7.5 Processing Time and Optimization 159
7.6 Summary 161

8 Conclusions and Outlook 165
8.1 Conclusions 165
8.2 Outlook 167

Bibliography 169

Publications 201

List of Figures 205

List of Tables 209

Acronyms 211

1 Introduction

1.1 Motivation

The global threat of asymmetric warfare was raised to a new level during the last decade. In spite of significantly different relative military power, novel strategies of the weaker belligerent can cause severe damage to the stronger one [Ste08] leading to more and more conflict victories [AT01]. In recent years, the networks behind such attacks became even more organized with advanced hiding, communication, and planning methods [Kyd06, Pol10]. As a result, well-conceived assassination attempts, hostage-taking, or terrorist arracks threaten civil, military, and economic security. In order to prevent such criminal activities in the future, their preparation has to be detected as early as possible. Electronic eavesdropping [Lan11], computer surveillance, or social media analysis [Fuc09] are popular methods nowadays for early detection during the planning stage. But even if these methods fail, mobile surveillance and reconnaissance platforms and devices can still help to detect and immediately avoid criminal or terroristic activities right before or during their execution.

Surveillance data can be acquired by a variety of sensors such as acoustic, laser, radar, ultrasonic, or imaging sensors. Each sensor type has its advantages and disadvantages. Hence, it depends on the specific application to decide which sensor or sensor combination should be used [Hal08]. However, analyzing the acquired surveillance data is a difficult job for human operators due to fatigue or boredom as a result of the large amount of information in the data [Gar07]. Appropriate algorithms for automatic data processing can assist the operator, but in most applications it is still a challenge to guarantee low error rates and high confidence of the algorithms and at the same time meet real-time capabilities.

This thesis focuses on analyzing video data coming from airborne visual-optical (VIS) cameras. In particular, it deals with detection, segmentation, and tracking of moving objects. These signal processing steps are necessary in order to pave the way for automatic scene understanding and situation awareness. By using higher level information fusion methods, abnormal behavior of or suspicious interaction between persons or vehicles can be modeled and detected to recognize criminal activities earlier and more reliably [Kim10]. This could be a driving vehicle deviating from the dominant traffic flow, a car chase in dense traffic, a digging person, or a person walking in a restricted area. Image and video based methods offer high potential to cope with such tasks since many properties of detected objects can be derived directly from the data such as object position, size, shape, appearance, motion, or class.

In most modern applications, surveillance is performed with stationary cameras near the ground. Buildings, public places, private properties, or restricted areas are to be protected against criminal activities. However, this also means that only a limited area is observed and it can be difficult to determine the situation context. The solution is to use either stationary camera networks [Col01, Uki01, Mon11] or cameras with small focal length for large area surveillance. In the first approach, single objects can be analyzed well as they appear larger in the images but the network of cameras has to be arranged and organized. In the second, the context can be determined well since many objects and their interactions are captured by one camera. Surveillance of a wide area is difficult to achieve with stationary cameras due to the limited field of view, the large number of cameras needed to enlarge this field of view, and the required infrastructure for their installation and operation. Thus, moving platforms such as Unmanned Aerial Vehicles (UAVs) as shown in Fig. 1.1 are a beneficial support. A single UAV can perform tasks such as detection of changes in an infrastructure or along a road, observation of restricted areas, single object tracking, or tracking of multiple objects in a large area for several minutes or hours in a flexible and efficient way. At the same time, no ground personnel is needed in the observed area and data can be acquired safely. As a result, the fields of application for UAVs outside surveillance and reconnaissance are growing rapidly. Search and rescue [Rud08, Mor10], disaster relief [Net12, Eze14], traffic monitoring [Hei07a, Pur08], environmental monitoring [Arn10, Arn13], or archeology [Lin11] are among the applications where UAVs have proven themselves as useful support. The terms *Wide Area Surveillance (WAS)* [Rei10a] and *Wide Area Motion Imagery (WAMI)* [Pro13] denote aerial video surveillance with coverage of several square kilometers per image usually at a low frame rate of 1–2 Hz. This thesis, however, focuses on *remote aerial video surveillance* which is defined by analyzing videos with a high frame rate of 15–30 Hz and coverage of up to 0.5 km^2 per image. Since only a limited amount of data can presently be processed in real-time, there exists a tradeoff between coverage and frame rate.

In order to process data from a moving camera, one needs a chain consisting of several modules for different subtasks to solve the main task. There are many different ways to design such a processing chain, but the common aim is to solve the main task as reliably and precisely as possible, often with the additional constraint of short processing time. The processing chain proposed in this thesis is not novel with respect to its design but several novel approaches are introduced to the separate modules in order to improve existing methods with respect to object detection rates, confidence, and runtime.

Figure 1.1: Luna UAV with a VIS camera and one example for an acquired aerial image.

1.2 Challenges

Remote video surveillance with moving cameras to detect, segment, and track moving objects is a challenging task especially when small UAVs with strictly limited payloads are used. These challenges can be categorized with respect to the occurrence time and processing step:

1. Image/video acquisition
   - **Limited quality** of the image material can originate from the application of light-weight sensors. Such sensors have to be used since limited payload of small UAVs leads to strong constraints on sensor size and weight.
   - **Shaking videos** can be the result of missing active hardware sensor stabilization due to weight or cost constraints. Hence, especially small and light UAVs are affected by engine vibration or winds during flight.
   - **Sensor/image noise** is a random deviation from optimal image pixel intensity values. Depending on the sensor, noise can be modeled in most cases either as additive, multiplicative (speckle), or impulsive (salt-and-pepper) deviation from the expected pixel value [Bro05].

- **Weak contrast** is mainly the result of environmental conditions. This can be weather effects such as mist, fog, or clouds as well as weak illumination during dawn, dusk, or night.
- **Blurred images** can occur due to fast sensor/object motion. This is especially occurring in case of weak illumination leading to longer camera exposure times.

2. Image/video transfer
   - **Strong artifacts or even missing images** can be caused by a disturbed wireless connection.
   - **Compression artifacts** such as typical block-like appearances as result of MPEG compression [Wat04] can significantly decrease the image and processing quality.
3. Image/video processing and exploitation
   - **Independent camera and object motion** can be challenging for object detection and segmentation. Image registration and warping [Zit03] is widely used to compensate for camera motion. Then, moving objects can be detected as they move relative to the stationary background. However, stationary objects closer to the camera such as tall buildings or towers appear to move faster than the more distant ground plane. Such kind of apparent motion is the result of a continuously changing line of sight of the camera and can be mistaken for object motion if a planar ground is assumed. This displacement in the apparent position of an object viewed along different lines of sight is called *parallax* [May12].
   - **Small object size of only few pixels** is the result of the large distance between camera and object. Object detection and classification becomes very difficult under such conditions since there is only little information available about object appearance or shape. In aerial surveillance videos, there can be hundreds or even thousands of objects in one image with only about 50 pixels per object [Sal13]. When objects move spatially close to each

other, merged detections are likely to occur where several small objects are mistaken for one large object.

- **Object shadows** appear due to sunlight from the side mainly during morning or afternoon hours. This can lead to imprecise object boundary determination especially in gray-value aerial images where objects and shadows often have a similar appearance and, thus, merge together. Effective shadow handling or removal is possible even in gray-value images [Fin06] but in aerial videos it has been done only for color images up to now [Tsa06, Chu09, Li14].
- **Utilization of temporal information** in videos can provide important and helpful context knowledge about object motion, appearance change, or the stationary background. Furthermore, short-term occlusions of moving objects due to trees, buildings, or bridges can be handled. However, it is challenging to find a suitable way of utilizing this information for given applications.
- **Generality and transferability** of the algorithms enable higher robustness against variations in the data. One example application in which this robustness plays a key role is the determination of an object's class such as *vehicle*. Machine learning approaches [Mit97] can be used to learn the appearance of vehicles in contrast to non-vehicles from given samples. The learned model should be able to distinguish between these two classes for new, previously unseen samples. However, there are many variations of vehicles regarding color, shape, or size. Generality is the ability of the model to compensate for this intra-class variability while still being specific enough to reject non-vehicles [Hal06]. Intra-class variability in the context of this thesis is mainly caused by changes in camera perspective, illumination, or environmental conditions. Transferability denotes the robustness to dataset biases in case of machine learning where training data looks different than test data [Tor11].
- **Real-time requirements** have to be met in many applications. While new images in a video sequence are acquired, the processing of one image has to be finished before the next image arrives.

A typical frame rate is 25 Hz. Thus, about 40 ms are available to extract and process the current image information.

The overall task of detection, segmentation, and tracking of moving objects is difficult due to many challenges such as those summarized above. This thesis only addresses the challenges of image/video processing and exploitation, excluding the problem of object shadows. Image noise, weak contrast, motion blur, or compression artifacts are difficult problems in image processing, too, since decreasing image quality directly impairs the performance of image/video processing algorithms. Image denoising [Sha14], image deblurring [Che08, Zha13], image restoration [Wei98, Por03], temporal filtering [Mül10], and superresolution [Far04] are common methods to explicitly handle the mentioned problems. In this thesis, poor image quality is handled only implicitly by considering and incorporating noise resistance during algorithm development.

The typical problems in image/video processing and exploitation are illustrated in Fig. 1.2. Each image comes from an aerial VIS video. The task of detecting moving objects in spite of a moving camera is visualized in Fig. 1.2 (a). The red vectors represent the displacement of single points in the stationary background between two consecutive images. Since the camera is turning, the vectors have a higher magnitude in the left half of the image compared to the right one. This local displacement is used to estimate the camera motion. After the sequence is compensated for camera motion, objects which are moving independently of the camera can be detected. Again, this is done by considering the displacement of selected object points between the two images. The resulting vectors of this *independent motion* are depicted in yellow color. Some object vectors have similar magnitude and direction as some of the background vectors. This makes it difficult to detect them reliably. In Fig. 1.2 (b), the challenge of large distance between camera and objects is presented. The red square shows a zoomed area of five vehicles driving on a street. Since the camera is at the distance of approximately 400 m, each vehicle only covers between 50 and 200 pixels in the image. Modeling the appearance of vehicles at this scale is tough as there is only little texture information. During overtaking, the vehicles drive close to each other in the same direction. In such situations, the detection of individual vehicles is difficult as object boundaries become blurred. Object shadows are visualized in Fig. 1.2 (c). As the shadows of moving objects are moving, too, it is probable that they are detected and misleadingly treated as part of the objects or even as individual objects, also known as *False Positive (FP)* detections. This can be a problem especially when multiple vehicles are driving in a group one behind the other with shadows between them. The detection algorithm may interpret this group of objects moving in-line as a single object. The potential benefit of temporal information is shown in Fig. 1.2 (d). Two trucks are driving next to each other. At time step t, a tree next to the street is partially occluding the right truck. A missed detection, also known as *False Negative (FN)* detection, is likely to occur in this situation. There is no occlusion at time step $t-20$ and both trucks are clearly visible. Learning this information can help to handle the occlusion situation in time step t. While five of the images (a, b, c, d, and f) come from datasets collected by the Luna UAV, Fig. 1.2 (e) originates from the VIVID dataset [Col05]. In this sequence, six vehicles drive one behind the other on a runway. Significantly different altitude and camera view angles lead to large deviations in vehicle appearance. A vehicle detection algorithm is supposed to be general enough to compensate for this intra-class variability while still being specific enough to reject non-vehicles [Hal06]. Transferability is then given by applying the same method with good performance for both Luna and VIVID videos. Finally, in Fig. 1.2 (f), a scene is shown with 17 vehicles driving on a busy urban street. Each vehicle is manually labeled with a red bounding box. Such kind of manual labeling is called *Ground Truth (GT)* and can be used to evaluate automatic detection approaches. In order to meet real-time requirements, all vehicles have to be detected and tracked in parallel with a processing time of less than 40 ms per image. Consequently, a multiple-step processing chain solving these tasks must therefore employ very efficient algorithms.

Several approaches that have been proposed to meet these challenges are discussed in the literature review in Chapter 2. However, there is high potential to enhance existing methods regarding reliability, robustness, and processing time.

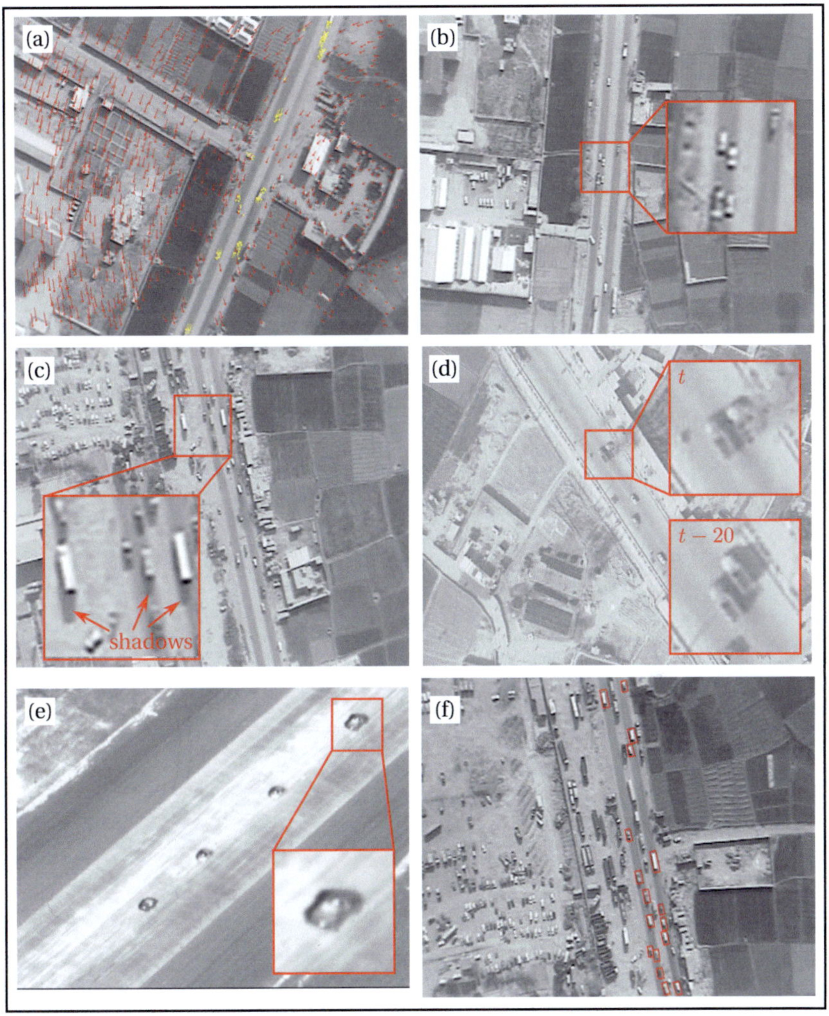

Figure 1.2: One example for each mentioned challenge of moving object detection and tracking with a moving camera: (a) camera and object motion, (b) large distance to objects, (c) object shadows, (d) utilization of temporal information, (e) generality and transferability, and (f) real-time processing.

1.3 Contributions

The aim of the work presented in this thesis is the design of a video processing chain consisting of individual modules for detection, segmentation, and tracking of moving objects with a moving airborne camera. The video data is coming from a single camera with no color information but only gray-value images at a frame rate of 25 Hz. The principal dataset for evaluation was collected by Luna UAV in top camera view as seen in Fig. 1.2. The main contributions are made in the areas of object detection and segmentation:

- *Image stacking* [Teu12b] utilizes temporal information in a novel manner. Occlusions or nearby stationary structures such as parked vehicles or buildings can disturb the detection and segmentation of moving objects, and are handled before object tracking is applied.
- Two new approaches for object segmentation are introduced. They are based on clustering of object edge pixels. While the first method uses noise resistant *Local Binary Pattern (LBP) gradient calculation* to determine edge pixels [Teu13a], the second approach uses *relative connectivity* [Teu11e]. The two algorithms are especially designed to detect small objects covering only few pixels in the image and achieve better performance compared to existing approaches in both aerial VIS surveillance data [Teu12a, Teu14a] and spaceborne Synthetic Aperture Radar (SAR)[1] surveillance data [Teu11d, Teu11c].
- The popular *sliding window* approach for object detection is improved by considering object motion [Teu14a]. The search space for this algorithm can be reduced significantly and thus both processing time and the amount of detection errors are reduced compared to the traditional approach.
- A novel *object classification algorithm* is introduced to detect objects across different datasets despite of partial occlusions [Teu14b]. This

1 SAR is an active radar sensor used for wide area surveillance with airplanes and satellites [Sau10, Bru11, Sau11]. Metallic objects and structures can be detected from large distances nearly independent of environmental conditions such as clouds or illumination.

classifier outperforms existing approaches with respect to generality and transferability across several ground-level infrared (IR) surveillance datasets [Teu13b, Teu14b].

- A new approach to *fuse position, size, and motion information* of objects is introduced to improve multiple object tracking [Teu11a]. As it is challenging to separately detect moving objects overtaking each other due to blurred boundaries, temporal information can be used to detect individual object in such situations. With the proposed improvement for multiple object tracking, many objects can be tracked in parallel more reliably compared to existing approaches. This approach proved to work well with both ground-level IR surveillance data [Teu11a] and aerial VIS surveillance data [Teu12a].

Better performance in the context of this thesis generally means the capability of an algorithm to detect more objects and produce less FPs and FNs compared to other applicable methods.

1.4 Outline

This thesis is organized as follows: existing literature and related work is reviewed in Chapter 2. There are articles either covering whole processing chains or improving only selected modules. In the interest of greater clarity, the chapter is subdivided in sections covering single modules of a potential processing chain and all articles are integrated into this structure. In Chapter 3, the concept of the processing chain is introduced. Similarities and differences compared to other concepts are identified and discussed. The three single modules independent motion detection, object detection and segmentation, and multiple object tracking are described in detail in Chapters 4, 5, and 6, respectively. In Chapter 7, all modules are evaluated individually and in context of the entire processing chain. The data for the experiments mainly comes from Luna UAV, but also a subset of the VIVID dataset is used. The comparison between the proposed algorithms and existing methods is performed by a quantitative and qualitative evaluation. While the aim of the quantitative evaluation is to analyze the performance of the processing chain with respect to certain measures from the literature, the qualitative evaluation shows the effectiveness directly in the images by visualizing the results of different methods. Conclusions and an outlook to potential future work are given in Chapter 8.

2

Related Work

This chapter covers related work on similar processing chains or single modules applied to similar surveillance datasets and facing the same challenges as in this thesis to analyze moving objects in large distance with a moving camera. The focus of the literature review will be on aerial imagery, while the considered tasks will be limited to detection, segmentation, and tracking.

Aerial image and video data considered in the literature under review are coming from UAVs or airplanes flying at different altitudes and equipped with VIS cameras. The camera angle varies between perpendicular top view [Lav10, Cao11a, Xia10, Luo12] and oblique front view [Yao08, Cao11b, Che12d, Sia12a] for remote surveillance, wide area surveillance [Per06b, Rei10a, Sal13], or surveillance in low-altitude aerial videos [Kan05, Yua07]. Many authors use their own collected datasets [Kum01, Sha05b, Li09a, Ibr10, Lav10, Cao11a, Xia10, Luo12] since only few public datasets exist for aerial surveillance. The Defense Advanced Research Projects Agency (DARPA) VIVID dataset [Col05] is widely used for remote surveillance [Yal05, Yao08, Xia08, Yu09, Cao11a, Che12c, Che12d, Mun12, Sia12a] with less than 10 objects per scene and high frame rate of 15–30 Hz. The Columbus Large Image Format (CLIF) dataset [USA06, USA07] and the Wright-Patterson Air Force Base (WPAFB) dataset [USA09] are often evaluated for wide area surveillance [Rei10a, Lia12, Pel12, Pol12, Pro12, Shi12, Kec13, Sal13, Pro14] with

Figure 2.1: Example images taken from the VIVID dataset [Col05] (left) and the WPAFB dataset [USA09] (right). While remote aerial video surveillance (VIVID) covers about 0.5 km^2 with an image size of 640×480 pixels and a frame rate of 30 Hz, wide area aerial surveillance (WPAFB) covers several km^2 with about $30{,}000 \times 23{,}000$ pixels and 1.2 Hz.

thousands of vehicles per image in dense traffic and low frame rate of 1–2 Hz. Several example images taken from the VIVID and the WPAFB dataset are shown in Fig. 2.1. Few authors process satellite images [Wan11, Zhe13] for vehicle detection which look very similar to top view high altitude aerial image data.

Processing chains as discussed in this thesis can be subdivided in several modules which do not necessarily have to be arranged in a sequence as presented here. The structure of this subsection is based on this sequence of modules and organized as follows: compensation for camera motion is discussed in Section 2.1, independent motion detection is presented in Section 2.2, object detection and segmentation is covered in Section 2.3, and multi-object tracking is presented in Section 2.4. Table 2.1 and 2.2 give an overview of the reviewed literature. Except for Xiao et al. [Xia08], no article covers all modules but, without loss of generality, each article can be integrated into the mentioned structure.

Table 2.1: Related work overview (first part).

publication	compensation for camera motion	independent motion detection	object segmentation	object detection	multi object tracking
Kumar et al. [Kum01]	×	×			×
Zhao & Nevatia [Zha01]				×	
Jones et al. [Jon05]	×	×	×		×
Kang et al. [Kan05]	×	×			×
Shastry & Schowengerdt [Sha05b]	×	×			×
Yalcin et al. [Yal05]	×	×	×		
Perera et al. [Per06b]	×	×			×
Tanaka & Saji [Tan06]			×		
Nguyen et al. [Ngu07]				×	
Tanaka & Saji [Tan07]			×	×	
Xiao et al. [Xia08]	×	×	×	×	×
Yao et al. [Yao08]	×	×			×
Li et al. [Li09a]			×	×	×
Lin et al. [Lin09]	×	×	×	×	
Wu et al. [Wu09]					×
Yu & Medioni [Yu09]	×	×	×		
Ibrahim et al. [Ibr10]	×	×	×		×
Iwashita et al. [Iwa10]				×	
Lavigne et al. [Lav10]			×	×	
Oreifej et al. [Ore10]			×	×	
Reilly et al. [Rei10a]	×	×			×
Reilly et al. [Rei10b]				×	
Xiao et al. [Xia10]	×	×	×		×
Cao et al. [Cao11a]	×	×	×		×

Table 2.2: Related work overview (second part).

publication	compensation for camera motion	independent motion detection	object segmentation	object detection	multi object tracking
Cao et al. [Cao11b]				×	×
Gaszczak et al. [Gas11]			×	×	
Gleason et al. [Gle11]			×	×	
Prokaj et al. [Pro11]	×	×			×
Cheng et al. [Che12c]			×	×	
Cheraghi & Sheikh [Che12d]	×	×			
Liang et al. [Lia12]		×		×	
Luo et al. [Luo12]	×	×	×		
Mundhenk et al. [Mun12]	×	×	×		×
Pelapur et al. [Pel12]				×	×
Pollard & Antone [Pol12]	×	×			×
Prokaj et al. [Pro12]	×	×			×
Shi et al. [Shi12]				×	×
Siam & ElHelw [Sia12a]	×	×			×
Siam et al. [Sia12b]	×	×			×
Keck et al. [Kec13]	×	×			×
Saleemi & Shah [Sal13]	×	×			×
Shen et al. [She13a]			×		
Shen et al. [She13b]			×		×
Türmer et al. [Tür13]	×			×	
Zheng et al. [Zhe13]			×		
Prokaj & Medoni [Pro14]	×	×			×
Zhu et al. [Zhu14]			×	×	

2.1 Compensation for Camera Motion

Before moving objects can be detected, segmented, and tracked, the camera motion has to be compensated. This is necessary since not only the moving objects but the entire scene seems to move in videos recorded during a UAV flight. Registration of one or more images to a reference image is a suitable approach to estimate the relative motion between the camera and the static scene background [Kum01]. Since the variation of the scene elevations is small relative to the distance of the observing camera, the scene can be approximated by a ground plane [Har04]. The processing steps for image registration can be characterized as follows: local image features such as corners or edges are detected and tracked. Kanade-Lucas-Tomasi (KLT) feature tracking [Luc81, Tom91, Shi94] is the most commonly used method [Jon05, Sha05b, Yal05, Per06b, Cao11a, Che12d], but also Harris corners [Rei10b, Luo12, Pol12, Sia12a], Scale Invariant Features Transform (SIFT) [Low04] or Speeded Up Robust Features (SURF) [Bay06][Ibr10, Rei10a, Shi12], and other optical flow based approaches [Kum01, Xia08, Yao08, Yu09, Sia12a] are widely used. Usually, sparsely distributed local image features [Yal05] are sufficient to estimate the parameters of a global motion model (homography) [Har04]. Affine transformations [Jon05, Kan05, Sha05b, Yal05, Xia08, Yao08, Yu09, Shi12] described by six parameters or projective transformations [Sia12a, Mül07] described by eight parameters are most frequently applied. Outliers in local image feature tracking are produced by moving objects or parallax effects and disturb the estimation of the global motion model. These outliers can be removed using Random Sample Consensus (RANSAC) [Jon05, Yal05, Yu09, Ibr10, Rei10b, Pol12] or Least Median Of Squares (LMedS) [Yao08, Sia12a]. Further detection and removal of parallax effects can be achieved by the introduction of epipolar constraints [Kan05, Sia12a] or structural consistency constraints [Kan05].

It should be mentioned, that the presented methods work well, if the overlapping area of the considered images is large enough and mainly covered by stationary background. Further improvement and refinement is necessary in presence of strong parallax effects [Kan05, Per06b, Yua07] caused by tall buildings or when the UAV is moving at a relatively low altitude. Using a 3D model as additional information can improve image registration significantly [Tür13]. Further applications of image registration can be found in image stabilization [Cen99, Hei08], image stitching or mosaicking [Hei08, Rei10a], superresolution [Far04], or 3D model estimation with Structure From Motion (SFM) [Dou10].

2.2 Independent Motion Detection

After the camera motion has been compensated for, one may proceed to the detection of motion that is independent of the camera motion. This can be achieved either by calculating difference images, background learning and foreground segmentation, or clustering of moving local features.

Difference images are the most popular approach [Kum01, Sha05b, Xia08, Yao08, Ibr10, Xia10, Cao11a, Che12d, Pol12, Sal13]. The intensity value difference D at pixel (x,y) in the overlapping area A_o of two registered images I_1 and I_2 is calculated by

$$D(x,y) = \begin{cases} |I_1(x,y) - I_2(x,y)|, \text{ if } (x,y) \in A_o \\ 0, \text{ else.} \end{cases} \tag{2.1}$$

High difference values D stand for strong local appearance changes caused by either moving objects or imprecise image registration. Depending on the moving object velocity, the camera frame rate, and the UAV velocity and altitude, it can be expedient to use two or more registered images to calculate the difference image. In case of low camera frame rate of 2 Hz and high UAV altitude, two consecutive images are sufficient since object motion produces prominent motion blobs in the difference image and noise due to parallax effects can be minimized [Sal13]. Even in medium UAV altitude videos with higher frame rate of 25 Hz, two images can be sufficient [Yao08, Cao11a, Che12d] but slowly moving objects may not be distinguishable from noise in the difference image. More prominent motion blobs can be reached by dropping some frames of the image sequence and considering only every n-th image for difference image calculation [Sha05b]. A general problem when using only two images for independent motion detection is *ghosting*. This means that each moving object produces two motion blobs in the difference image: one at its position in the first and one at its position in the second image. Ghosting can be handled implicitly by the registration of three images [Kum01, Xia10, Kec13] or explicitly by rejecting motion blobs with low gray-value intensity standard deviation and low average gradient magnitude [Sal13]. According to Keck et al. [Kec13], difference image D can be calculated for three consecutive registered images I_1, I_2, and I_3 with overlap area A_o by

$$D(x,y) = \begin{cases} \min(|I_1(x,y) - I_2(x,y)|, |I_2(x,y) - I_3(x,y)|), \text{ if } (x,y) \in A_o \\ 0, \text{ else.} \end{cases} \tag{2.2}$$

Additional reduction of parallax errors is achieved by using blurred images for the difference image calculation [Ibr10] or using optical flow to detect parallax areas and subtracting them from the difference image [Xia08]. Pollard et al. [Pol12] additionally propose to use minimum differences of pixel values in small neighborhoods to suppress registration errors. Strong parallax is handled by weakening the assumption of a planar ground surface and using a set of evenly spaced planes parallel to the ground. In a final processing step, detected motion is verified by implying temporal consistency.

Background learning and subtraction to detect foreground objects was originally developed for video surveillance using stationary cameras [Pic04, Bou08, Bou11]. The approach works well, if as many images as possible with a large overlapping area are available to learn the background and only few moving objects are present during the learning process. However, the camera is moving and there can be hundreds of moving objects in UAV video data. So, well-known algorithms such as Stauffer-Grimson probabilistic background modeling [Sta99] are difficult to apply since either the background model contains foreground objects if only few images are used for modelling or the overlapping area becomes progressively smaller if many images are used. Furthermore, parallax effects and imprecise image registration impair the quality of the background model. In the task of observing the same highway junction for several minutes, Perera et al. [Per06b] use 30 successive images for Stauffer-Grimson background modeling. A similar approach in Hue Saturation Value (HSV) color space is implemented by Jones et al. [Jon05]. To avoid impreciseness of the learned background due to large number of moving objects, the pixelwise intensity median of 10 consecutive images [Rei10a, Lia12] or 16 subsequent images [Pro11, Pro12] can be used instead. Since the camera is moving and background learning is only possible in the overlap area A_o of all considered images, a larger number of images causes a smaller background model. Motion blobs are detected by registration of the current image I and the learned background I_{BG}, and then by the pixel-wise subtraction which is similar to the calculation of difference images:

$$D(x,y) = \begin{cases} |I(x,y) - I_{BG}(x,y)|, \text{ if } (x,y) \in A_o \\ 0, \text{ else.} \end{cases} \tag{2.3}$$

The noise in the difference image coming from parallax effects in the background model can be reduced by subtracting the background gradient magnitudes from the difference image [Rei10a]. In addition to difference images, background subtraction can be used to detect stopped vehicles [Xia10]. Fig. 2.2 depicts the comparison of 10-frame background learning [Rei10a], 3-frame difference image [Xia10], and 2-frame difference image with explicit handling of ghosting [Sal13]. The example image which covers only a 350×350 pixel image section of the $30{,}000 \times 23{,}000$ pixel full image shows a busy intersection originating from the WPAFB dataset [USA09]. The green dots visualize the manually labeled GT moving vehicles while the red areas represent the overlay of the difference image in the red color channel of the original image. Even slowly driving vehicles can be detected with background learning. Ghosting cannot be fully avoided when using 3-frame compared to 2-frame difference images and can lead to FP detections. In contrast, explicit handling of ghosting avoids FP detections but is prone to produce FN detections.

Clustering of moving local features is a completely different method to detect motion areas. Outliers removed during image registration by RANSAC or LMedS are usually coming either from moving objects or originate from the parallax. If the tracked local features for image registration are not sparsely distributed, each moving object is expected to produce several moving local features. Tracking and clustering of these moving local features together with spatial and motion constraints can be used to extract motion areas in the image [Yal05, Cao11a, Luo12, Sia12a]. While object detection

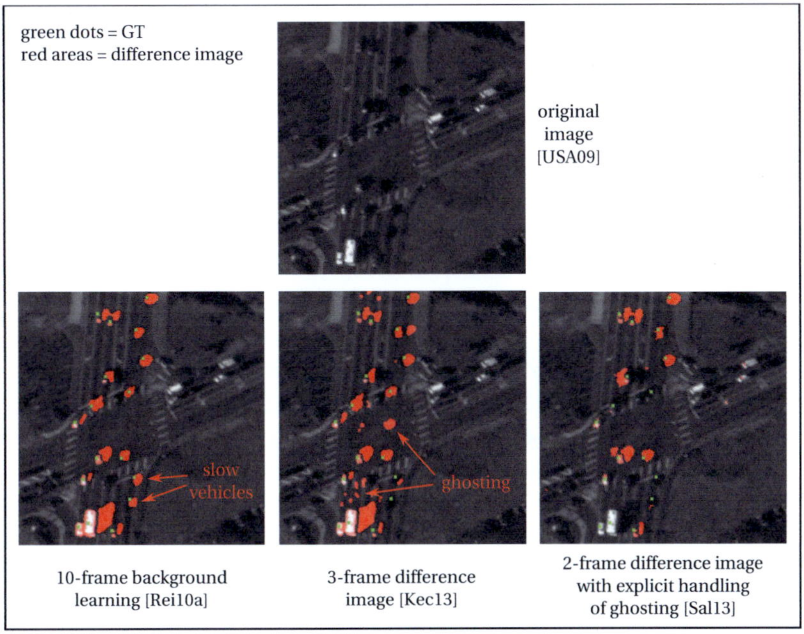

Figure 2.2: Comparison of background learning and difference images for moving object detection. Background learning needs several seconds to calculate the background model but is able to detect even slowly driving vehicles. 2/3-frame difference images can be calculated much faster and are less affected by parallax effects but produce more FP or FN detections.

in difference images and subsequent tracking is a typical example for a *Detect-Before-Track (DBT)* algorithm [Liu05, Bug08], clustering of moving local features is a *Track-Before-Detect (TBD)* approach [Dav08, Taj09]. TBD is the concept of simultaneous detection and tracking and was originally developed for object detection and tracking in radar data in order to handle the presence of strong noise and clutter which usually dominate the radar signals [Bla99, Ris04]. This is exactly the motivation why TBD is used in visual tracking with moving cameras where the entire scene seems to be in motion and object motion is only a minor part [Fra05, Hos12, Pap13]. Some advantages compared to difference images are the avoidance of ghosting due to temporal information of the tracked local features and less processing time for clustering. As potential disadvantages, one may point out the longer processing time in order to densely detect and track local features and missing features leading to imprecisely segmented motion areas. In particular, the need for densely distributed tracked local features makes this approach impractical for wide area surveillance videos with thousands of vehicles per image and a usual image size of 30,000 × 25,000 pixels. However, remote surveillance such as in the VIVID dataset is a good field of application for this method. This can be seen in Fig. 2.3 in an example taken from Siam et al. [Sia12b]. Slowly moving objects create blobs in the difference image that are difficult to separate from noise coming from parallax effects or inaccuracies in image registration. In this case, tracking and clustering of moving Harris corners performs better. The same effect was discovered by Heinze et al. [Hei08].

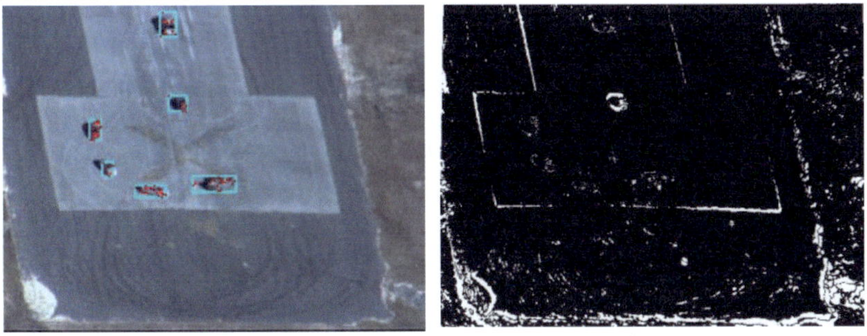

clustering of moving local features — difference image

Figure 2.3: Comparison of motion vector clustering and difference images [Sia12b]. While motion clustering is able to detect all objects, slowly moving objects can hardly be seen in the difference image.

2.3 Object Detection and Segmentation

The detection of independent motion areas does not necessarily imply the detection of single moving objects. One motion area can contain exactly one moving object. This is the desired case. However, it can also contain only a part of an object, multiple merged objects, or no object at all, if the motion area is the outcome of imprecise image registration or parallax effects. Although *object segmentation* and *object detection* are two different topics in computer vision, they can be used to solve the same problem in the context of this thesis: improved object localization and object boundary determination. The motion areas define the search space in the image.

Segmentation subdivides an image into connected sets of pixels [Gon08]. The connection of pixels inside the same segment is determined based on criteria such as similar intensity, similar color, or similar geometrical structures [Aza07, Bey12]. Segments are found either by clustering or by fitting a model [For03]. Clustering can be performed by grouping of edge pixels or pixels with high intensity values in difference images. Model fitting is usually done with rather simple models such as line segments, curve segments, or Hough transform [Dud72]. Object segmentation and object detection converge as soon as machine learning is introduced in order to learn a more sophisticated model and separate objects from the background. In object detection, the image is usually scanned for one specific object class such as vehicle and all positions in the image where matches occurred are marked by bounding boxes [Sze11]. The terms object detection and *object recognition* are often used as synonyms [Jai95, dS01, Gon08, Tre10]. Few authors, however, equate object recognition with *object classification* [Shr12]. Machine learning approaches are applied in object classification, too, but only to determine the presence of a specific object and not its position in the image. While the challenge in object detection is to find all positions of a specific object class as precisely as possible, the challenge in object classification is to distinguish between a large number of different classes or categories. *Multiclass object detection* tries to solve both problems simultaneously [Tor06]. Classification should not be mistaken with object *identification*. The aim of identification is to re-identify one specific individual object or a specific group of objects. Especially re-identification of persons across different cameras and environments is a challenging problem [Gon14].

Motion clusters can be considered as a search space reduction since only a part of the image has to be processed inside a few small regions. Search space reduction is important since it can reduce the processing time and the number of FP detections significantly [Fer08]. Based on the assumption that vehicles drive on roads, some authors limit the search space for vehicle detection by automatic road detection [Tan07, Li09a, Lin09, Rei10a, Luo12] or using context knowledge about road positions such as Geographic Information System (GIS) [Xia10, Zhe13].

2.3.1 Object Segmentation

One typical way to *segment* moving objects is to cluster independent motion pixels coming from difference images or background subtraction and consider clusters as single object hypotheses. The latter can be tracked or verified by object classification. In order to separate moving and stationary pixels, several different methods are applicable such as simple pixel intensity thresholding [Sha05b, Per06b, Ibr10, Cao11a], Otsu's method [Ots79] used by Cheraghi and Sheikh [Che12d] and Saleemi and Shah [Sal13], Gaussian Mixture Model (GMM) learning [Lee05] in combination with graph cuts [Boy01] for shape estimation as proposed by Ibrahim et al. [Ibr10], graph cuts [Xia08], or mean shift kernel density estimation [Com02] used by Mundhenk et al. [Mun12].

In case of object segmentation without preceding independent motion detection, color based segmentation algorithms and clustering of local features such as corners and edges are used for initial detections. Image based road or background segmentation is usually achieved by color histograms [Tan07, Li09a, Lin09, Che12c]. If roads are straight, the Hough transform [Dud72] can be used for lane detection [Luo12]. Road markings which are potential FPs can be detected and removed using connected component labeling [Dil92] of edge pixels [Tan07] or morphological operations in difference images [Li09a]. In order to detect vehicles, Tanaka and Saji [Tan06] propose parallelogram detection with Hough transform assuming that vehicles have a rectangular appearance in top view UAV images. Li et al. [Li09a] detect object pixels based on color value deviation from the background pixel values. Zheng et al. [Zhe13] propose to use the black and white tophat transform [Dou92] in road areas and Otsu's thresholding method to detect objects. Shen et al. [She13a, She13b] extract spatiotemporal saliency for object detection in street regions. Cheng et al. [Che12c] detect and cluster Harris corners and Canny edges [Can86] in areas of foreground color. Finally, Gleason et al. [Gle11] apply clustering of densely distributed Harris corners and refine the cluster areas using color segmentation. It should be mentioned that in contrast to independent motion detection no temporal context is used. So, moving and stationary objects can be segmented with the presented approaches.

The resulting moving and stationary object blobs can be refined by applying morphological operations to fill holes [Per06b, Yao08, Cao11a, Che12c] and by applying additional constraints such as color [Lin09, Ibr10], size [Tan07, Xia08, Lin09, Cao11a, Sal13, Zhe13], shape [Per06b, Xia08, Ibr10], or eccentricity [Ibr10, Sal13].

2.3.2 Vehicle Detection

Object classification is a good way to verify segmented areas since the assumption that all moving blobs of acceptable size, shape, or eccentricity are vehicles can be violated. The segmented object could come from parallax effects or birds flying between the UAV and the ground. Usually, appearance features of objects such as color, shape, or texture are learned in a training stage and stored in a model which is then applied in the operating stage by classifiers such as the Support Vector Machine (SVM) [Vap98], Random Forest (RF) [Bre01], or boosting [Fre97]. Classification starts as soon as any kind of model knowledge such as blob motion [Che12d], blob size or shape [Ibr10, Zhe13], object edge orientations [Li09a], or shape template matching [Tan07] is used to verify detections or tracks even without machine learning algorithms. Instead of a training stage, expert knowledge can be used to set up the parameters of a Bayesian Network (BN) to recognize vehicles. However, human experts may not consider every part of the problem domain due to the complexity and the high number of examples [Zha01].

There is no strict separation between detection, tracking, and classification. Lavigne et al. [Lav10] use machine learning before vehicle detection: local SIFT features are detected, classified with an SVM for being part of a vehicle or not, and clustered with an Unsupervised Affinity Propagation Clustering (UAPC) algorithm [Fre07].

A very common combination of detection and recognition is the sliding window approach [Pap00, Wei10], which has been applied successfully to face detection [Vio04] and human detection [Dal05]. A search window of certain size is shifted across the entire image. At each window position, features are calculated and a classifier returns a decision value representing its certainty that the image area inside the window contains an object. In order to detect objects at different scales, either the window size is varied or the image is rescaled between the minimum and maximum expected size of an object in the image. The naïve approach uses no image rescaling and N different window sizes with one separately trained classifier model for each size. This is time-consuming and requires many training samples. The traditional approach takes one fixed window size with one classifier model at N different image scales [Dal05, Dol09], where N is usually around 50 [Ben12]. In order to achieve a high speed-up with similar object detection performance, either nearby image scales are approximated while using one classifier model [Dol10] or classifier decisions can be approximated across scales using few classifier models and only one image scale [Ben12]. After the calculation of all decision values, objects are detected by applying Non-Maximum Suppression (NMS) to the decision values and using a minimum classifier certainty threshold. In contrast to part based models such as Implicit Shape Models (ISMs) [Lei08] or Deformable Part Models (DPMs) [Fel10] which search for object parts and combine them to whole objects, the sliding window approach uses a holistic object representation by modeling the object in its entirety. Holistic representation is usually better for small objects in the image since it is difficult to detect even smaller object parts reliably.

Similar to Dalal's method [Dal05], Türmer et al. [Tür13] apply the sliding window approach with Histogram of Oriented Gradients (HOG) features and SVM to find stationary and moving vehicles. Gaszczak et al. [Gas11] detect vehicles using sliding window with Haar features und cascaded AdaBoost which is very similar to the Viola-Jones [Vio01] approach. Since vehicle orientation may vary, four discretized orientations are specified and one classifier is trained for each orientation. Nguyen et al. [Ngu07] use sliding windows with Haar features, orientation histograms, and LBP as vehicle decriptors and Discrete AdaBoost [Fre97] for classification. Since multiple detections appear for each object due to the sliding window shift, kernel density estimation and mean-shift clustering [Gra05] are applied to suppress them. Cao et al. [Cao11b] propose a boosting light and pyramid sampling histogram of oriented gradients (bLPS-HOG) feature extraction method together with a linear SVM. Pelapur et al. [Pel12] use sliding window to generate likelihood maps for vehicle presence in order to introduce a TBD approach [Boe08, Dav08]. In this way, sliding window is not applied to make a hard decision (vehicle or non-vehicle) but a soft decision (likelihood).

Sliding window object detection is an exhaustive search also referred to as *brute force* approach as the entire image has to be scanned at different scales. Applying the sliding window only to areas where independent motion was detected can reduce the search space and, thus, shorten the processing time and reduce the number of FPs significantly. After the detection of independent motion areas, Lin et al. [Lin09] use scale normalization, Haar features, and cascaded AdaBoost to classify vehicles in these areas. In areas with detected local features such as corners or edges, Cheng et al. [Che12c] suggest to perform a color transform [Tsa07] and use an SVM to distinguish between vehicle and nonvehicle colors. Vehicles are then recognized with a pixelwise Dynamic Bayesian Network (DBN) [Rus03], morphological operations, and connected component labeling. Shi et al. [Shi12] propose a two stage SVM using size features in the first and HOG features in the second stage. The FP rate is reduced by road estimation from object trajectories. After initial detection and tracking, Xiao et al [Xia08] separate vehicles and persons using HOG features and view-pose-based SVM classifiers. Gleason et al. [Gle11] extract HOG features and histograms of Gabor coefficients [Zeh06] from initial detections and test three different classifiers: SVM, RF, and k-Nearest Neighbors (k-NN). The combination of Gabor coefficients and RF works best. Liang et al. [Lia12] calculate HOG and Haar features in independent motion areas detected by short-term background subtraction. A Generalized Multiple Kernel Learning (GMKL) that combines these features outperforms single HOG or Haar features.

2.3.3 Person Detection

In contrast to ground imagery [Enz09, Ger10, Dol12], only few authors detect persons specifically in aerial imagery. One reason is that with an oblique camera view the same methods can be applied for ground and aerial imagery since person appearance does not change significantly. Another reason is that with a top camera view persons can hardly be detected or recognized since usually their appearance is not only very small (e.g., less than 10 pixels) but also very similar to the appearance of shadows as seen in Fig. 2.4.

Zhu et al. [Zhu14] extract Multi-Scale Intrinsic Motion Structure (MIMS) features from walking persons' motion patterns. These features contain location, velocity, and motion trajectory and are integrated into an AdaBoost classification algorithm. Xiao et al. [Xia08] use HOG features and view-pose-based SVM classifiers to classify persons after Regions of Interest (ROIs) have been extracted with difference images and graph cuts. Oreifej et al. [Ore10] aim to identify persons and initially detect them with a sliding window approach using HOG features and an SVM classifier. Precise segmentation is achieved with joint foreground background kernel density estimation. Iwashita et al. [Iwa10] detect persons only by their shadows. Obviously, shadow based approaches are applicable only if good lighting and weather conditions are given. After background subtraction, shadow silhouette normalization is performed using metadata such as time, sun position, and camera position. Shadow features are calculated and analyzed.

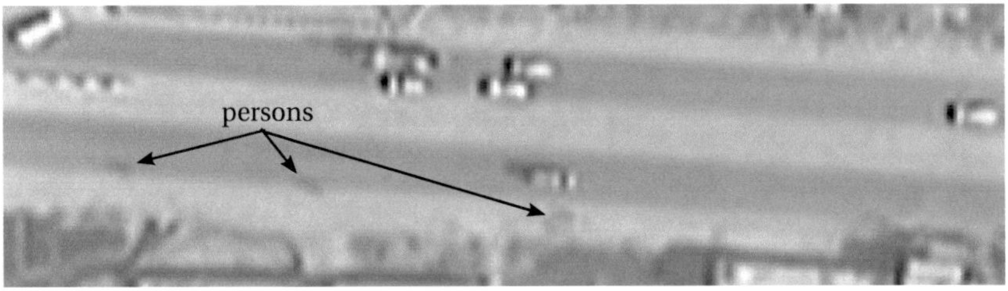

Figure 2.4: Appearance of persons in top view aerial videos.

Finally, Reilly et al. [Rei10b] use gradients, geometric constraints (metadata), and the object shadow relationship for initial detections. In order to verify these detections as humans, Haar features are calculated and used for SVM classification with a Radial Basis Function (RBF) kernel.

2.4 Multiple Object Tracking

Object tracking is the process of using sensor measurements to determine the location of one or more objects over time [Mag11]. It is an essential requirement for surveillance systems to interpret the environment [Bla99]. Sensor measurements in the context of this thesis are the resulting bounding boxes of object detection and segmentation. Besides the location, further object characteristics such as path, positions, velocity, and other features can result from object tracking [Cha11]. Furthermore, temporally and spatially stable tracks confirm object detection and segmentation results, while the rejection of instable tracks can reduce the number of FP or FN detections [Mag11]. A good survey of different tracking approaches is provided by Yilmaz et al. [Yil06] and a more recent survey together with a comprehensive experimental study is given by Smeulders et al. [Sme13]. In addition to video surveillance, robot vision [Che12b] and driver assistance [Sun06] are important fields of research and application for multiple object tracking with a moving camera. The typical components of object tracking are (1) object representation such as point, bounding box, ellipse, contour, or silhouette, (2) tracking features such as color, edges, optical flow, or texture, (3) object detection based on approaches discussed in the previous section, and (4) an object tracking algorithm such as point tracking, kernel tracking, or silhouette tracking [Yil06]. After the association, optimal filter methods such as Kalman filter [Kal60] or particle filter [Kit87] are usually applied to update the tracks with the associated detections. One big challenge in tracking multiple and extended objects is the association of multiple, potentially split or merged detections to multiple already existing tracks [Cha11]. A detection is split if there is more than one detection for one object and, vice versa, a detection is merged if there is more than one object for one detection. Tracking of extended objects represented by bounding boxes or silhouettes can be further improved by additional split and merge handling [Kum06].

The complexity of tracking algorithms depends on the complexity of the processed data. If for example less than about 10–20 objects are visible and only few split and merge situations occur, rather simple tracking approaches can be used. One simple but effective and fast approach is to assign tracked and clustered KLT features to detected motion blobs [Cao11a]. This way, motion (KLT features) and spatial (blobs) information is fused. If motion areas are considered as local features per se, they can be tracked using KLT feature tracking [Sha05b, Xia08].

If point tracking is desired, extended objects can be converted to a point-like representation [Jon05]. The position of the object center or centroid in combination with object velocity are commonly used features for point tracking [Per06b, Sia12a, Sal13]. In extended object tracking, vehicles are usually represented by bounding boxes [Li09a, Wu10, Cao11b], ellipses [Wu09], or blobs [Ibr10]. Contour tracking is less popular since vehicles are rigid objects and rectangles usually represent vehicle shape in top view images well.

Depending on the scene complexity, the association problem for point-like representation can be solved by simple nearest neighbor [Per06b], graph matching [Sha05a], Multiple Hypothesis Tracking (MHT) [Sal13], or Joint Probabilistic Data Association Filter (JPDAF) [Kan05, Wu09], if multiple point representations are possible for a single object. For extended objects, the association problem can be solved by checking the overlap of bounding boxes [Sia12a]. In the literature, this criterion is also known as Intersection over Union (IoU) or Jaccard index (JI) [Gri13]. Further approaches to solve the association problem for extended objects include feature based object re-identification between two time steps using similarity measures, or graph matching. While blob appearance similarity can be checked with graph cuts [Xia08], color and spatial similarity is evaluated by Yao et al. [Yao08] and Cao et al. [Cao11b]. Ibrahim et al. [Ibr10] take blob centroid, area, orientation, eccentricity, and color composition as object representation and similarity measures for these blob features in order to associate current detections to existing tracks. Mundhenk et al. [Mun12] propose to use spatial entropy and color features represented by a Generalized Linear Model (GLM) [Nel72] to associate detections to tracks with Kullback-Leibler divergence (KL) [Kul51]. Xiao et al. [Xia10] model color, appearance, spatial, and shape features in a graph framework and associate detections with tracks by joint probabilistic relation graph matching [Zas08]. Prokaj et al. [Pro11] use blob position and appearance to generate tracklets which are combined to multiple object tracks. This approach is extended in a later article [Pro14] by a regression tracking algorithm that is used to learn the object appearance simultaneously to the detection based tracking algorithm. Pollard et al. [Pol12] combine kinematic information (position, velocity) and appearance (shape, pattern).

Handling of occlusions or split and merged detections can be achieved by template based normalized cross correlation [Sia12a], object fingerprinting and re-identification [Guo05, Ali07, Mun12], or modeling bipartite graphs [Yao08, Rei10a, Sal13] and solving them with Hungarian algorithm [Kuh55]. Bipartite graphs are suitable especially for complex scenarios in wide area surveillance with several hundreds of objects. Association probabilities are propagated over time and decisions are made at a specific time step with maximum a posteriori probability (MAP) estimation. Usually, constraints reduce the complexity of such decisions to distinct one-to-one decisions [Yao08, Rei10a]. Furthermore, road constraints and driver behavior constraints can be used including road orientation and object context [Rei10a], motion patterns [Pro12], object-to-object distance and traffic flow distributions [Xia10], or the tendency of drivers to follow each other and to avoid lane changes [Sal13].

After the association problem is solved, the tracks can be updated using tracking algorithms such as Kalman filter [Per06b, Sia12a] or particle filter in case of point-like representation and mean shift [Li09a, Zhu10, She13b] or Expectation Maximization (EM) algorithm solving a MAP estimation for object representations with motion, appearance, and shape [Kum01] for extended objects. Yao et al. [Yao08] use the Kalman filter to predict the motion of occluded objects with no detection.

An approach that significantly deviates from the previously mentioned ones is TBD [Yu09]. Moving local features coming from optical flow are tracked for a long time to calculate motion flow represented by 4D vectors consisting of point position and velocity. Tensor voting [Tan01] is performed as local, nonparametric estimation of the geometric structure at each sample position. Finally, motion patterns are segmented in this 4D space using a flood fill algorithm. Pelapur et al. [Pel12] introduce a Likelihood of Features Tracking (LoFT) system for single object tracking. Likelihood maps are calculated with a sliding window using histogram and correlation features. A weighted sum Bayesian fusion is used to implement a TBD scheme.

Further topics in tracking which will not be discussed here are track linking [Per06b, Xia08, Sal13], object speed estimation [Sha05b, Li09a], and behavior recognition [Red12].

3

Concept

The overall concept of the developed processing chain is visualized in Fig. 3.1. It consists of three modules, implementing *independent motion detection*, *object detection and segmentation*, and *multiple object tracking*. Rounded rectangles denote data types and straight rectangles represent algorithms. Each module has its specific color that will be used in all subsequent visualizations of concepts (Fig. 3.1 upper row) or image examples with bounding boxes (Fig. 3.1 lower row) in this thesis. Furthermore, each module with its concepts and algorithms will be described in detail in the following chapters of this thesis.

Image sequences are the input data of the processing chain. These sequences are coming from one visual-optical camera in top view that produces 25 gray-value images per second. The typical UAV flight altitude is approximately 400 m and the *Ground Sampling Distance (GSD)* is about 0.3 meters per pixel. GSD is the size of an area in the scene that is mapped to one pixel in the image and is given by meters per pixel. This means, that a standard car covers only about 15×6 pixels in the image. Usually, there are no more than 30 moving objects per image. Independent motion detection is used to compensate the image sequence for camera motion and to generate motion clusters as initial object hypotheses. Pixels that exhibit motion inconsistent with that of camera are visualized in yellow vectors and cyan

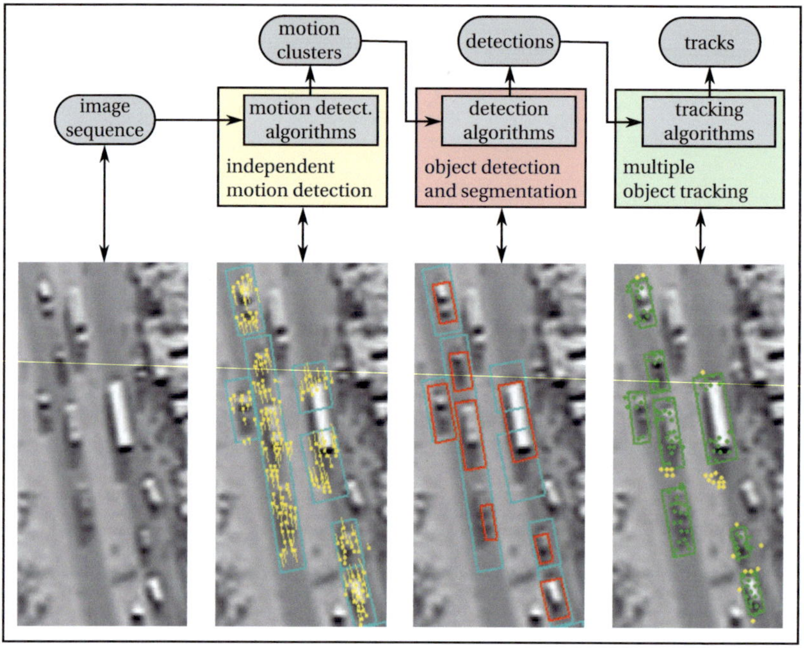

Figure 3.1: The overall concept of the processing chain.

bounding boxes depict motion clusters which are the result of clustering vectors with similar position and motion. The calculation of these motion clusters is fast but can be imprecise since split and merged detections are likely to occur. Object detection and segmentation is introduced to find object boundaries and to handle split and merged detections.Three different novel methods for object detection and segmentation that exploit object contour and shape features are presented and discussed. These approaches range from simple edge pixel clustering to rather complex object detection technique using machine learning. Figure 3.2 shows the difference between the two mentioned methods. The red bounding boxes represent the resulting detections. While object detection uses an object appearance model with a trained classifier, object segmentation algorithms usually avoid making assumptions about object appearance. Instead, clustering of pixels with similar gray-value or prominent gradients is applied as well as simple thresholding of object blob features such as size or eccentricity. Therefore, the classifier only detects objects fitting to its appearance model. Additionally, object detection with machine learning can be applied to reject FP detections coming from parallax effects or to determine the object class such as vehicle, motorcycle, or person. Since the classifier in Fig. 3.2 (c) is trained for vehicles only, bicycles or motorcycles are not detected although their motion has been detected and clustered. Finally, multiple object tracking is used in order to take advantage of the temporal context between consecutive images. Split and merged detections can be avoided by fusing motion vectors (green and yellow dots in Fig. 3.1) and tracks (green boxes in Fig. 3.1).

This kind of concept is not new for moving object detection and tracking. Other authors have also pooled similar tasks in well-isolated modules [Kum01, Ali06, Lin09, Ibr10, Mun12, Pel12, Shi12]. However, there are two significant differences between most of the cited concepts and the proposed one:

1. Nearly all authors use difference images in order to detect motion. This method works well for wide area surveillance data with high UAV altitude and low frame rate such as 1 Hz, where the same ground area is surveilled for at least several seconds and object motion is fast enough to produce prominent motion blobs in the difference image. For lower altitude UAVs with higher camera frame rate such as 25 Hz, this may not be an appropriate approach since each local area is surveilled for only a few seconds or less and slow object motion might not be prominent enough to be detected [Teu14a]. Furthermore, due to parallax effects and misalignment during image registration, distinguishing between motion and noise in the difference image becomes even more difficult [Sia12b]. While object detection in difference images and subsequent tracking is a typical example for a DBT algorithm, motion clustering as proposed by a few authors [Cao11a, Luo12, Sia12b] and the author of this thesis is a TBD approach. The yellow motion vectors in Fig. 3.1 are the result of short time tracking of local image features such as corners [Shi94]. Tracking

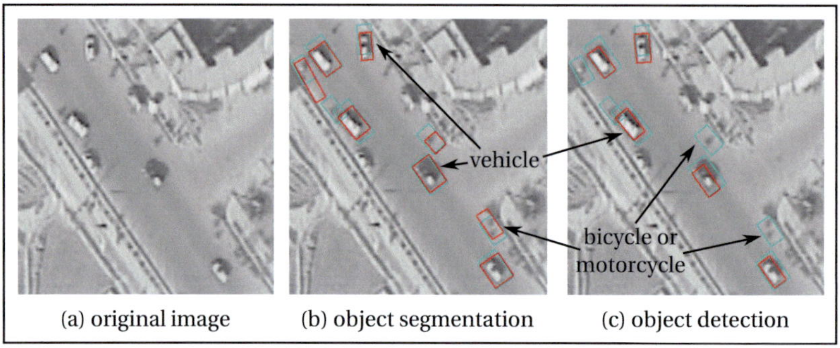

Figure 3.2: Difference between object segmentation and detection. Since object detection uses an appearance model trained for vehicles only, bicycles or motorcycles are ignored.

of those features starts simultaneously or even before the related moving object is detected. Compared to using difference images, a TBD approach (1) produces less noise, and (2) delivers additional information such as object's orientation and motion. The main disadvantage is the increased processing time. Since all objects in the scene are to be detected, a very large number of motion vectors has to be calculated to ensure that there are enough vectors for each object. This is possible for low altitude UAV data as usually no more than 30 moving objects are visible at the same time. For wide area surveillance with hundreds or thousands of objects per image, this can be very time-consuming. However, parallax effects are still a problem for both difference images and TBD. The presented processing chain in this thesis is built on this TBD approach and utilizes certain properties of the motion vectors.

2. Moving object detection in aerial videos is a difficult task due to the small object size, strongly varying object velocities, and potentially dense traffic. Independent motion detection is usually not sufficient to reliably detect moving objects and avoid missed, split, and merged detections at the same time. A common solution to this problem is multiple object tracking. Point tracking of blob centroids coming from

difference images [Per06b, Rei10a, Sal13] can have good performance in general but bad detection performance cannot be fully compensated by tracking. Another way to solve the problem is clustering of motion vectors [Cao11a, Sia12a, Sia12b] to introduce a spatial object representation such as bounding boxes before tracking. As seen in the example image for independent motion detection in Fig. 3.1, this does not work in dense traffic due to merged detections for objects driving one behind the other. Thus, additional object detection and segmentation algorithms are introduced in this thesis to determine a more reliable spatial object representation. Some authors propose to use machine learning to verify motion clusters [Xia08, Lin09, Lia12, Shi12]. However, the fusion of motion clusters and the sliding window algorithm as proposed in this thesis is a novel approach.

The order of the modules in the processing chain is not fixed. Especially in the module providing object detection and segmentation, submodules can be skipped, permuted, applied sequentially, or even combined by using the sliding window approach. Object classification after object tracking is possible, too, but does make sense only if (1) a model is trained for each specific object for advanced tracking using online learning [Gra08, Bab11] or persistent tracking [Pel12, Pro14], or (2) if objects change their appearance during motion such as walking pedestrians [Vio05]. In this thesis, advanced tracking is not considered and mainly rigid objects such as vehicles are observed in top camera view.

Just as in most implementations described in the reviewed literature, the data flow of the proposed processing chain is unidirectional. Few authors use feedback of information to update parameters of background learning [Xia08], update classification parameters [Shi12], or support track management in multiple object tracking [Pel12]. Feedback between modules is not considered here but can help to reduce the search space for independent motion detection, or adapt algorithm parameters such as in reinforcement learning [Sut98].

4

Independent Motion Detection

Independent motion detection is used to detect image regions that move independently of the camera. These regions usually represent moving objects such as vehicles or persons. Parallax effects or inaccuracies in image registration can be detected as independent motion as well. However, they originate from the stationary background and are thus considered as noise or FP detections. In order to detect independent motion, it is crucial to compensate the image sequence for camera motion first. In the context of this thesis, this is done by using the images of the video sequence only and without additional meta-information such as camera calibration parameters, Digital Elevation Models (DEMs), or UAV flight parameters. This chapter will be kept short since the module has not been developed by the author of this thesis. Hence, the performance of independent motion detection is evaluated with respect to object detection accuracy only and the precision of image registration is neglected. The remainder of this chapter is mainly based on the work of Krüger et al. [Kru99, Mül07, Hei08, Teu11b, Teu12a].

4.1 Concept

The structure of the independent motion detection module is shown in Fig. 4.1. Local image features also referred to as *keypoints* or *local interest*

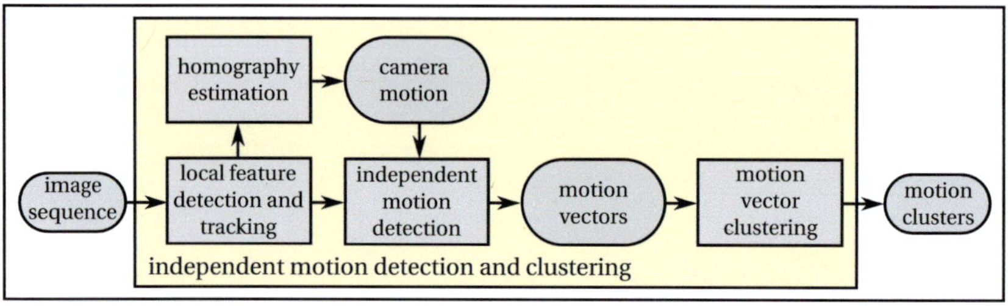

Figure 4.1: Concept of independent motion detection and clustering.

points [Mik05, Hei12, Bek13] are detected and tracked. These local features are used to estimate the frame-to-frame homographies and the respective camera motion. Local features which do not fit to the homography are assumed to be part of moving objects. Since these features have been tracked for a few frames, they can be represented not only by their positions but by motion vectors. Similar motion vectors are grouped to motion clusters. As its output, the independent motion detection module delivers a set of motion vectors and motion clusters.

4.2 Approach

The image sequence is compensated for camera motion by the application of image registration [Zit03]. Förstner-Harris corners [För87, Har88] are detected with sub-pixel accuracy and tracked over time [Shi94]. A corner is defined by an image position with two dominant and different edge directions in a local neighborhood. Two large eigenvalues of the structure tensor indicate the existence of a corner [Bla10]. In order to track corners, each corner has to be retrieved in the subsequent images. Therefore, gradient descent is applied in a local search area [Shi94] in contrast to feature matching using descriptors such as SIFT or SURF [Rei10a]. This is possible since the displacement of a corner between two consecutive images is typically not larger than a few pixels in UAV videos with high frame rate. Corresponding corners between subsequent images are used to estimate homographies as global image transformations to register images [Har04]. Therefore, a projective transformation with eight parameters is estimated using the corresponding corners between subsequent images. Outlier correspondences are removed by applying RANSAC [Fis81] with subsequent refinement. Using homographies is possible since the depth differences in the evaluated scenes are small compared to the distance of the observing camera and the scene can therefore be approximated well with a ground plane. For higher precision of image registration and to avoid the assumption of a planar ground, plane and parallax decompositions with multiple-view geometric constraints [Har04, Kan05, Yua07] can be used. After compensation for camera motion, velocities relative to the static background of the observed scene are detected for each corner track. Relative velocities exceeding a certain threshold are assumed to originate from moving objects and are considered as independent motion vectors. The final step of independent motion detection is to group these motion vectors. Single-linkage clustering is performed based on position and velocity of the motion vectors. The choice of distance thresholds is based on the known GSD and the expected size of objects. This approach does not require camera calibration and is largely independent of object appearance.

For the evaluated UAV video data with medium UAV altitude and high frame rate of 25 Hz, motion vector clustering is a better choice than background learning [Sta99, Rei10a] or difference images [Xia10, Sal13]. Figure 4.2 shows the comparison of motion vector clustering (a) and difference images (b-d). Three options of difference images are considered: 2-frame difference with a small gap of three images (b) and a large gap of six images (c) as well as 3-frame difference (d). Therefore, the images I_{t-3} and I_{t-6} at time $t-3$ and $t-6$ are registered to I_t and warped. Areas outside of the common overlap area of the warped images are visualized in red color. Bright vehicles with high contrast to the background produce prominent blobs in the difference image (b). These blobs are even stronger if the time gap between the two images is increased (c). Concurrently, noise in the difference image coming from parallax effects and registration mistakes becomes stronger as well. In such difference images, it is difficult to distinguish between noise and moving objects with low velocity or weak contrast. So, further processing is necessary in order to suppress parallax effects and inaccurate image registration [Rei10a]. However, there is another source of noise in this example that cannot be suppressed: the parked vehicles in

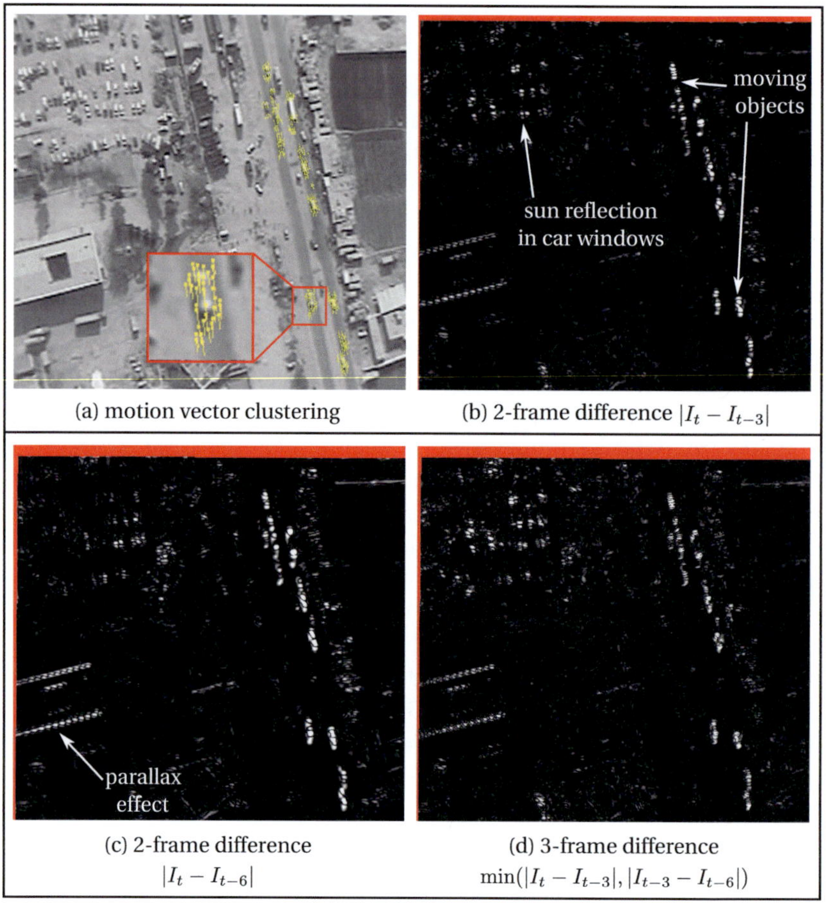

(a) motion vector clustering

(b) 2-frame difference $|I_t - I_{t-3}|$

(c) 2-frame difference $|I_t - I_{t-6}|$

(d) 3-frame difference $\min(|I_t - I_{t-3}|, |I_{t-3} - I_{t-6}|)$

Figure 4.2: Comparison of motion vector clustering and difference images. While motion clustering detects all moving objects (yellow vectors), parallax effects and sun reflections cause strong noise in the difference images. The offset between the frames is visualized in red color.

the upper left image corner produce blobs of similar brightness as some moving vehicles. The reason is that sun reflections in the car windows cause wide variations of the pixel intensity between two images. Since these local brightness changes belong to the stationary background and, hence, are not moving, no independent motion vectors appear. By contrast, motion vector clustering detects all moving vehicles and motorcycles correctly (a). As already mentioned, object detection in difference images is a DBT approach while motion vector clustering is TBD. For a moving camera, the entire scene seems to be in motion. After compensation for camera motion, noise can occur in the difference image due to parallax effects or inaccurate image registration as seen in Fig. 4.2. As the noise level increases, independent motion detection becomes more and more challenging. This is the motivation to use TBD in in the context of this thesis in order to detect small moving objects despite of potentially inaccurate image registration. One drawback of motion vector clustering is the necessity to perform short-term tracking of corners. Each corner has to be tracked for a certain amount of time such as 5 subsequent images. Then it is considered to be stable and used for clustering. This leads to a short delay of about 0.2 seconds for object detection. However, additional information such as motion magnitude and direction can be used in further processing steps.

Figure 4.3 shows example images for the estimation of camera motion as well as independent motion detection and clustering. Each red vector in Fig. 4.3 (b) visualizes the displacement of one detected and tracked corner between two consecutive images. The red dots in Fig. 4.3 (c) depict stationary corners used for homography estimation while independent motion vectors are visualized in yellow color and scaled by factor 5 for better visibility. Motion vector clustering is visualized in cyan bounding boxes in Fig. 4.3 (d). The clustering algorithm based on motion direction, motion magnitude, and motion vector distances works well here since nearly all moving objects have an adequate distance between each other or significant relative velocities. In total, there are 6,934 tracked corners. From these tracks, 283 are correctly classified as coming from moving objects. Tracked corners at parking vehicles are correctly classified as part of the static background. The histogram in Fig. 4.4 (b) shows the distribution for the magnitudes of the relative velocities estimated for the 283 motion vectors in Fig. 4.4 (a). The measuring unit of the velocities is pixels per frame. It can be seen that independent motion detection is able to reliably estimate and classify subpixel relative motion. The mean object velocity is approximately 1.4 pixels

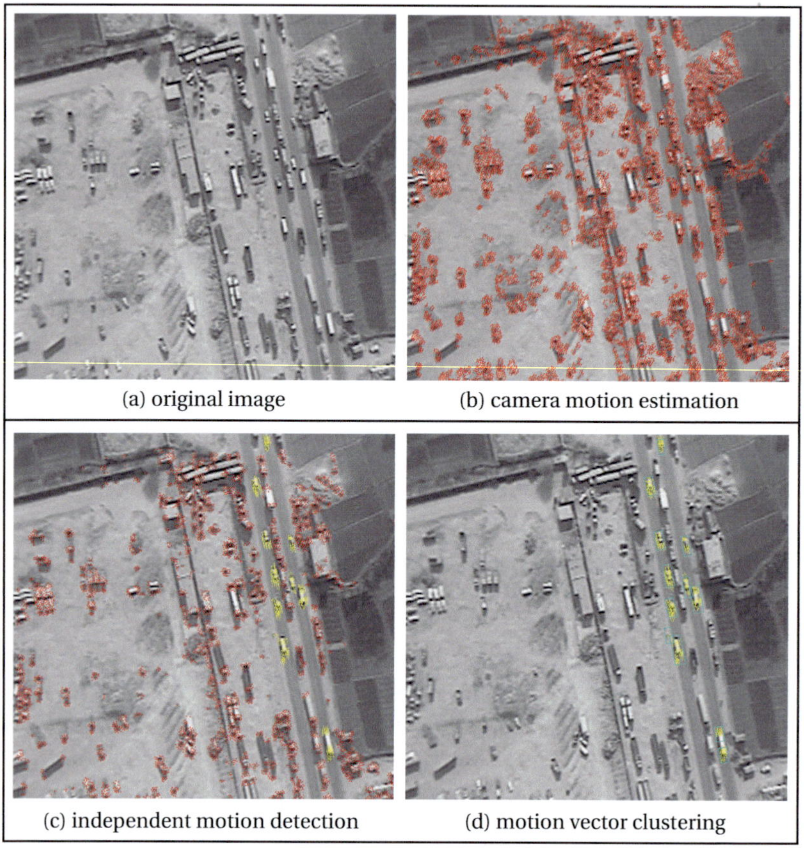

(a) original image (b) camera motion estimation

(c) independent motion detection (d) motion vector clustering

Figure 4.3: Examples for independent motion detection and clustering. Stationary corners are visualized in red color and motion vectors moving independently of the camera motion are displayed in yellow. Motion clusters are depicted as cyan boxes.

per frame. For a GSD of 0.345 meters per pixel and a frame rate of 25 Hz, this corresponds to a mean velocity of approximately 43 kilometers per hour. For urban traffic this is a plausible value.

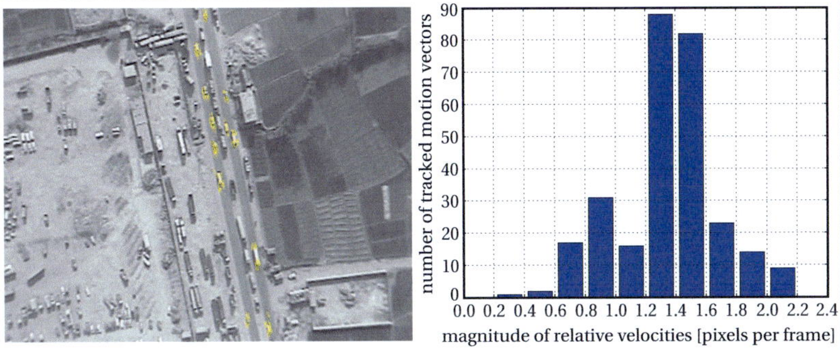

(a) independent motion (relative velocities) (b) histogram of relative velocities

Figure 4.4: Distribution of motion vector magnitudes (velocities relative to camera motion) for an example image in pixels per frame.

Current state-of-the-art approaches stop here [Luo12, Sia12a] since object detection is sufficiently solved for videos with low traffic such as in the VIVID scene. However, motion vector clustering can lead to a large number of merged and split detections for more challenging scenes with dense traffic as seen in Fig. 4.5. The GT objects in this scene are shown in Fig. 4.5 (a), while Fig. 4.5 (b) depicts the result of motion clustering. Merged detections appear for vehicles driving with the same velocity in the same direction closely one behind the other. Split detections can occur for example for long vehicles such as trucks or buses since there is a large distance with no image texture between the corners found in the front and in the back of the vehicle. In Chapter 5, solutions are presented to improve the performance of object detection by object segmentation and machine learning. Object detection by motion vector clustering as described in this chapter is the baseline algorithm for the evaluation of the proposed algorithms presented in Chapter 7.

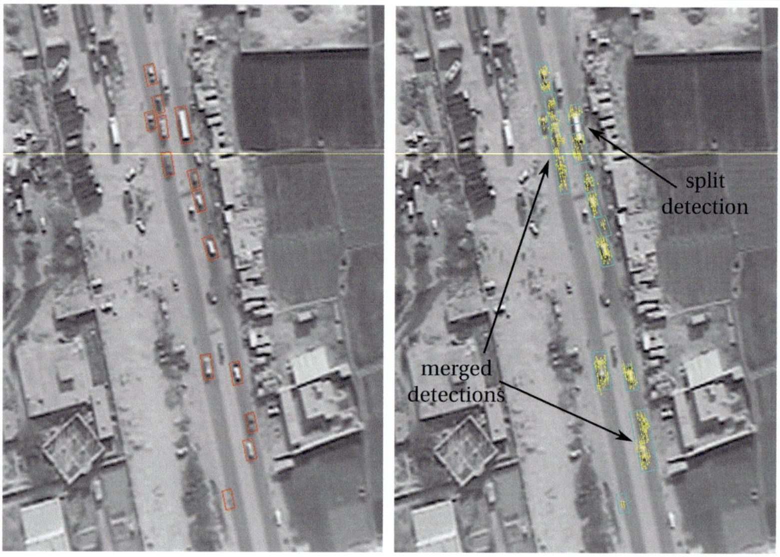

(a) ground truth objects (b) motion clusters

Figure 4.5: The main problems of independent motion detection and clustering are merged and split detections for objects moving one behind the other or overtaking each other.

5

Object Detection and Segmentation

As already mentioned, independent motion detection and clustering is not sufficient to reliably detect and segment moving objects that drive on busy streets in aerial videos. While some authors try to solve this problem by transferring it to multiple object tracking [Per06b, Sia12b, Sal13], the author of this thesis proposes to improve detection before tracking by introducing a separate object detection and segmentation module. The main motivation is that not all problems of object detection can be solved by object tracking. Missing, merged, or split detections can decrease the tracking performance and, usually, tracking performance increases with a better detection performance. The aim is to handle merged, split, partial, and FP detections by the implementation of separate object detection and segmentation algorithms. Multiple objects in one motion cluster are separated while single objects with multiple split detections are fused. Motion clusters are considered initial object segmentation hypotheses and define the search space. Appearance features such as edges are analyzed. Before object detection and segmentation is applied, the motion clusters are extended in motion direction in order to handle split and partial detections. The content of this chapter is mainly based on the work of Teutsch and Krüger [Teu12b, Teu12a, Teu14a].

5.1 Motivation

Why do we need to develop new approaches for object detection and segmentation for the UAV video data analyzed in this thesis? Why are existing methods not sufficient? The main reason is the image quality. Due to the large distance between the camera and the observed objects and due to variable illumination, several challenges have to be faced such as weak contrast, blurry object edges, image noise, or compression artifacts. When considering an average object size of only 10×20 pixels in the image, such deterioration in the image quality is even more significant. Many approaches for detection and segmentation exist in the literature, but only few of them are applicable to the analyzed video data. In order to illustrate the challenging task of contour detection and segmentation, two state-of-the-art image segmentation methods have been applied to an example motion cluster as seen in Fig. 5.1. Three vehicles are driving one behind the other and, hence, are grouped in a merged detection. The size of the motion cluster is 15×100 pixels. Next to the original image the manually labeled GT and the result of the proposed local sliding window approach are depicted. The two state-of-the-art approaches for image segmentation are *global Probability of boundary (gPb)* [Arb11] and *Simple Linear Iterative Clustering (SLIC) superpixels* [Ach12]. gPb detects contours by calculating multi-scale local cues of difference in local image brightness, color, and texture channels for different orientations followed by spectral clustering. Segmentation is performed by Oriented Watershed Transform (OWT) and Ultrametric Contour Map (UCM) [Arb06]. k is a scale parameter that can be used to set a preference for component size. Superpixel segmentation partitions an image into a set of equally sized, non-overlapping and homogeneous regions called superpixels. The segmentation of the image is guided by a similarity measure by which the pixels are grouped [Sch14]. One of the most important properties is that superpixels should adhere well to image boundaries [Arb11]. SLIC superpixels is one of the most popular approaches. SP is the desired number of superpixels in the image, but the actual number may be lower as seen in Fig. 5.1.

Superpixels have already been used successfully for vehicle segmentation in aerial images with color information [Sah11, Meu13]. However, none

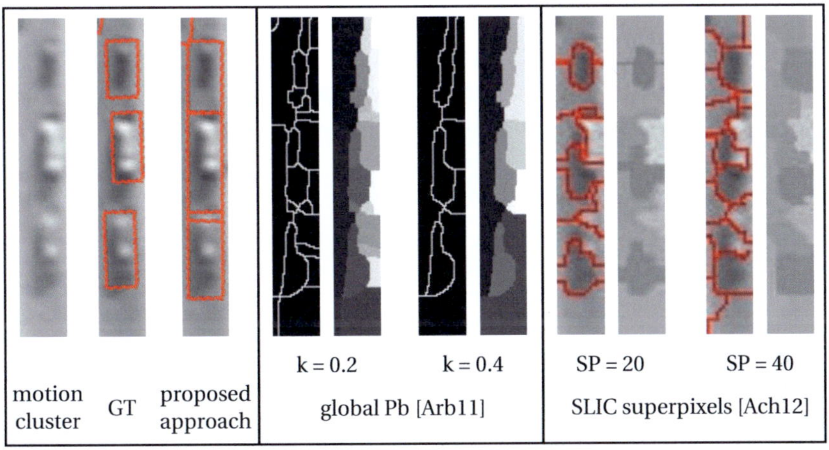

Figure 5.1: Motivation for object detection and segmentation. Neither gPb nor superpixels achieve a sufficient result for object segmentation.

of the two methods is able to capture the boundaries of all three objects well. There are cuts through the objects and object areas are merged with the background. In the example image, this happens since parts of the object contour are blurry either due to direct sunlight for bright objects or due to shadows for dark objects. Other well-known methods such as watershed segmentation [Roe00] or graph cuts [Boy01] have to deal with the same problems. Especially for the uppermost object in Fig. 5.1, it is nearly impossible even for a human to separate the object from the shadow. In general, shadows or curbs can have even more prominent edges than the objects. However, shadow handling or removal [Tsa06, Chu09, Guo13, Li14, Son14] is very difficult since (1) shading varies severely during the day, (2) each object casts a shadow of different shape, (3) reliable shadow detection is nearly impossible in gray-value images but necessary for removal, and (4) the appearances of dark objects and shadows are very similar.

Among the few methods that are able to handle the mentioned problems are edge based approaches such as parallelogram detection with Hough transform [Tan06] or Canny edge detection [Che12c], blob based approaches such as Maximally Stable Extremal Regions (MSER) [Mat02] or the tophat transform [Zhe13], and machine learning approaches such as sliding window [Gas11, Tür13]. The proposed method presented in Section 5.4.3 is a modified version of the sliding window approach.

5.2 Concept

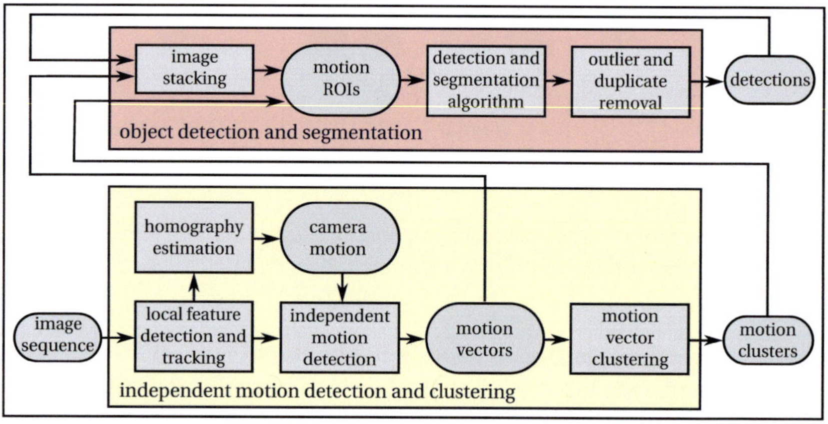

Figure 5.2: The concept of object detection and segmentation.

As seen in Fig. 5.2, the concept of independent motion detection and clustering module (indicated with yellow color on the scheme) has been extended by a new layer for object detection and segmentation (depicted in red color). Inside this layer there are three main modules: *image stacking, detection and segmentation algorithm,* and *outlier and duplicate removal.* Image stacking is an optional pre-processing step to improve the motion clusters coming from independent motion detection by a deeper analysis of the motion vectors. The resulting motion ROIs are analyzed with three different detection and segmentation algorithms in order to handle merged and split detections. Since each object can have multiple detections after these processing steps, duplicate detections have to be discovered and removed.

Furthermore, detections at stationary objects inside the motion ROIs are considered as outlier detections and are rejected, too.

5.3 Image Stacking

Object segmentation aims at determining object boundaries in the image. Therefore, pixels with large gradient magnitudes can be used. However, there are three effects that can change the object appearance and decrease the segmentation performance by either inaccurate object boundaries or even producing FP or FN detections: (1) partial occlusions by trees, power supply lines, or buildings, (2) stationary objects close to the observed object such as parked vehicles or buildings, and (3) street textures such as cobblestones or road markings. In order to suppress these effects, image stacking is introduced to mask and blur the stationary background around a moving object. Several motion ROIs of the same object in several subsequent images are registered and aligned using motion vectors. Each aligned motion ROI is a layer of the image stack. By calculating the pixelwise mean or median pixel value, the stationary background and even other moving objects with a non-zero relative velocity compared to the observed object are blurred. The gradient magnitudes at blurred image areas decrease and the observed object becomes more prominent for the segmentation algorithm. At the same time the focused object must be well-registered to avoid blurring of its own appearance. This idea is not entirely new since image stacking is also applied for temporal median filtering [Kle94, Mül10], moving object detection using background models [Mig05, Rei10a], or superresolution of small moving objects [Let08, van10]. However, to the author's best knowledge, so far there is no published approach where image stacking is proposed to improve moving object segmentation with a moving camera.

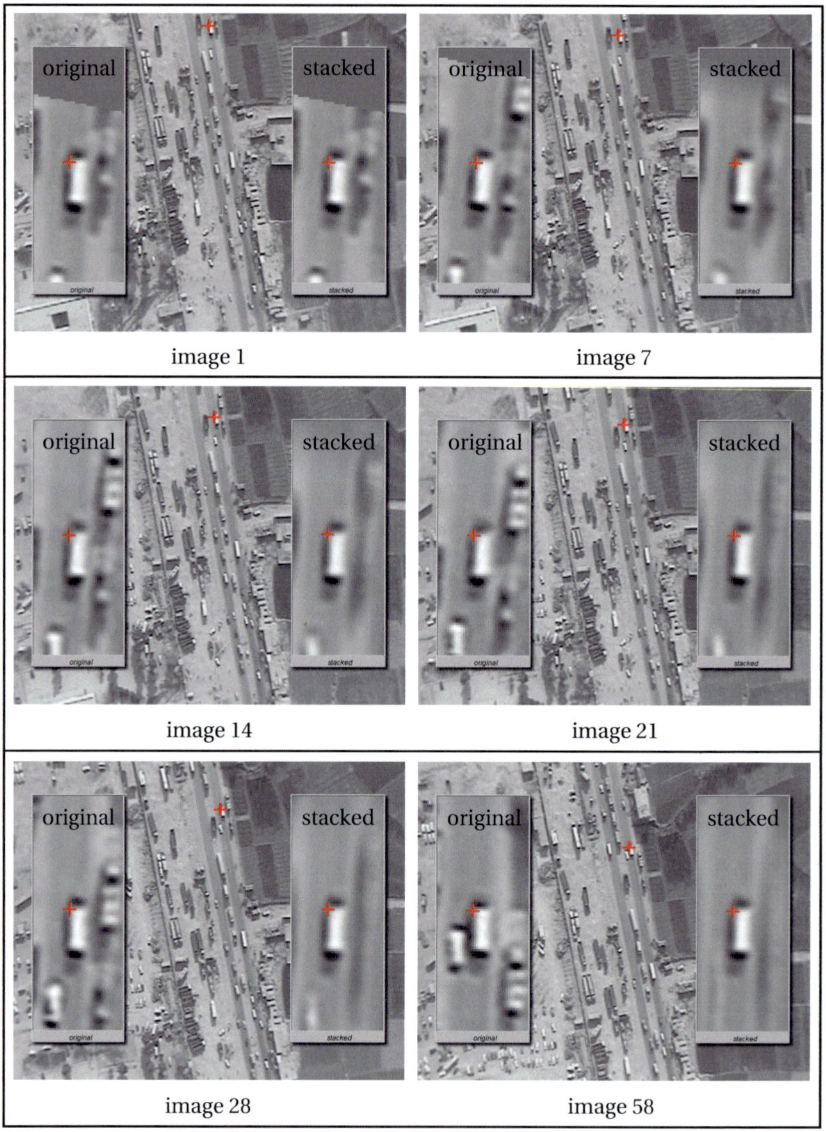

Figure 5.3: Motivation for image stacking. The left part of each image shows the zoomed original area around the red cross rotated upright and the right part shows the stacked image.

Tracked moving corners (motion vectors) are used to generate an image stack as seen in Fig. 5.3. The red cross is a moving corner that is tracked for 250 consecutive images. The image region (*stack region*) used for stacking is specified by the motion direction and predetermined values for width and length of the stack area. This stack region is zoomed and visualized without stacking in the left and with stacking in the right area of each image. The center of the stack region is fixed by the position of the moving corner (red cross). After that, the stack region, which is oriented in the motion vector direction in the original image, is rotated upright and added to the stack. Visualized in Fig. 5.3 is the pixelwise mean image of the whole stack. For a pixel position (x,y) in the stack S and in each aligned image I_h with $h \in \{1,\ldots,H\}$, the corresponding pixel value $S(x,y)$ is given by

$$S(x,y) = \frac{\sum_{h=1}^{H} I_h(x,y)}{H}. \tag{5.1}$$

H is the total number of stack regions added to the image stack and is called the *stack height*. Since the motion direction of single motion vectors fluctuates slightly, the direction of each motion vector can be smoothed by using the direction of the related motion cluster. This is important to avoid blurring of the edges of the observed object. After 28 images the stationary background is fully masked while the overtaking vehicle disappears later after 58 images due to its smaller velocity compared to the observed object. Parked vehicles or buildings can be very close to the observed object as seen in image 28, but image stacking successfully masks the building and thus facilitates the segmentation of the object.

The implementation of image stacking in a fast and efficient way is not easy. In a feasibility study [Teu12b], it was demonstrated that generating a stack for each motion vector in the image can lead to hundreds of detections per object, but adequate duplicate removal of sufficiently overlapping bounding boxes improves the performance of object segmentation with respect to detection rate and precision. However, this method is highly ineffective with respect to processing time and needs to be improved for implementation. Therefore, the concept depicted in Fig. 5.4 is proposed. The main difference between the feasibility study and the concept is the introduction of *master vectors* as representatives for clusters of motion vectors.

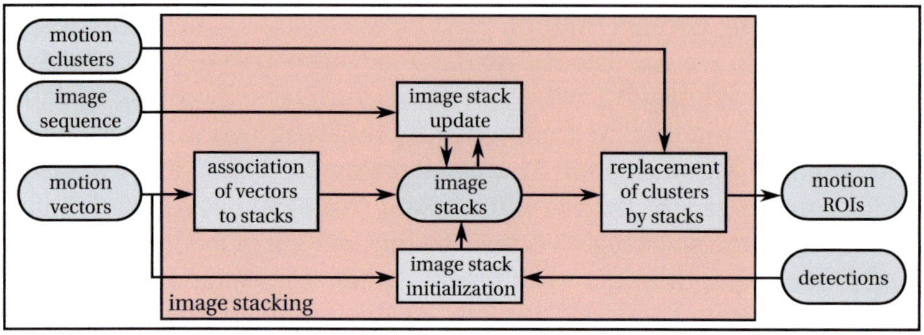

Figure 5.4: The concept of the image stacking module.

Each master vector is a virtual motion vector and owns exactly one image stack. Thus, the total number of image stacks decreases from several hundred to less than 50. The master vector lies in the center of its image stack. New image stacks are initialized either by using motion vectors or detections. New motion vectors are associated to existing stacks based on position and motion. Image stacks are updated by adding the corresponding image area of the current image to the stack. Finally, image stacks are associated with motion clusters and replace them for the application of the object detection and segmentation algorithms. The result is called motion ROIs and replaces the motion clusters to provide better image information for object detection and segmentation.

5.3.1 Image Stack Initialization

In order to initialize an image stack, one has to detect a cluster of similar motion vectors. This cluster can be different from the motion clusters which are the result of independent motion detection and clustering. The reason is that moving objects driving with a small relative velocity close to each other may be clustered together in the same motion cluster while image stacking aims at initializing at least one stack per object. Only in this way it is possible to benefit from the blurring effect since the first object is assumed to be focused and sharp in the first stack while the second object gets blurred over time due to its velocity difference and, vice versa, the second object

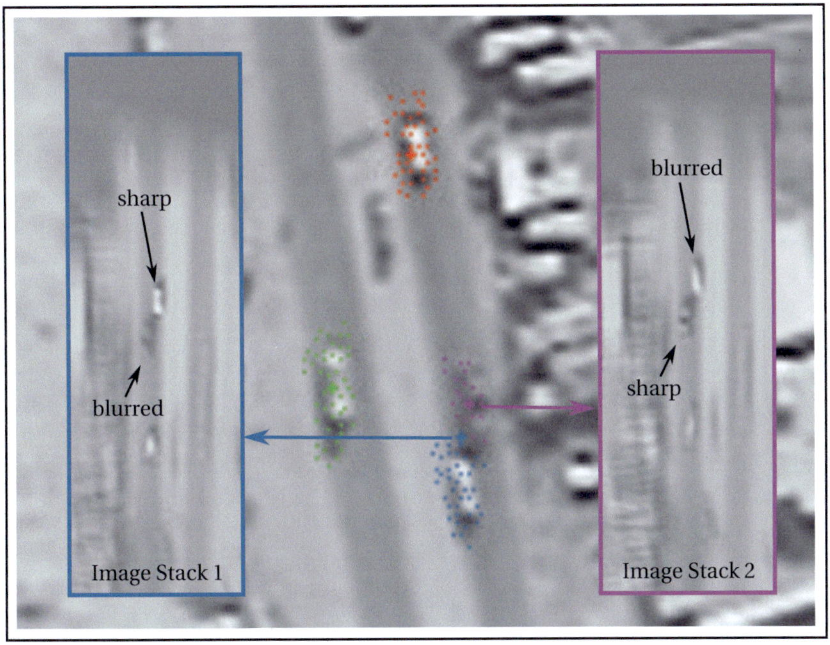

Figure 5.5: Image stacks for two vehicles with small relative velocity of about 10 km/h (about 0.4 pixels per frame). The first vehicle is sharp and the second is blurred in the first stack while the first vehicle is blurred and the second is sharp in the second stack.

stays sharp in the second stack while the first object is blurred. If only one stack is initialized for two objects, the blurred object may be missed by the detection and segmentation algorithm. This effect is visualized in Fig. 5.5 with two vehicles overtaking each other. Each master vector is visualized with a colored cross and has between 3 and 50 related motion vectors. These related motion vectors are represented by dots in the same color as their master vector. The blue master vector is not in the center of its cluster since it was initialized while both objects were merged in one large bounding box. In contrast, the magenta master vector was initialized later when both objects were detected separately. After one second or 25 stacked images, the pixelwise mean image shows that usually only one object stays sharp per stack. Two strategies have been implemented for image stack initialization:

1. The results of object detection and segmentation are called *detections*. These detections are assumed to have a higher detection rate compared to the motion clusters. By using them as feedback information to initialize stacks, the ratio of stacks to objects is close to 1 which is most efficient. Even for merged detections there will be separate image stacks, if each single object has been correctly detected at least once. Immediately after that, the individual stacks are initialized. This is the case in Fig. 5.5. The blue master vector is not in the center of its cluster as it was initialized while both objects were merged in one large bounding box. The magenta master vector was initialized later when both objects were detected separately for at least one time step. In order to avoid any information loss, the blue master vector is kept and not reinitialized. However, objects that cannot be detected and segmented separately at all end up in a common image stack. In such a case, the blurring effect is assumed to be weak for each object and detection performance is similar to using no image stacks.

2. A weak detection performance can lead to the initialization of image stacks for merged detections. In this way, image stacking may even decrease the overall detection performance. In order to use the motion vectors and motion clusters instead of the detections, *k-means clustering* [Har75, Bra00] is introduced. k is the number of clusters after clustering and can be chosen based on the known standard vehicle size and the size of the related motion cluster. Then, the motion vectors are grouped using position and motion. This approach is less efficient since usually more stacks than objects are initialized and the calculation of k-means is time-consuming.

Both approaches will be evaluated in Chapter 7.

5.3.2 Association of Motion Vectors to Image Stacks

Due to occlusions or varying object appearance, existing motion vectors can disappear and new motion vectors can appear at any time in the image sequence. A master vector is deleted if it loses all related motion vectors. While each master vector can have many related motion vectors, each motion vector can be related to only one master vector. A new motion vector is associated to a master vector by applying a k-NN algorithm [Eve11]. k-NN is a voting algorithm searching for the k nearest motion vectors in the image area around the new motion vector. Each neighbor votes for its master vector and the new motion vector is associated to the master vector with the most votes. The search space can be significantly reduced by only considering motion vectors in the same motion cluster. A typical value for k is 3. This process is shown in Fig. 5.6. Each master vector (image stack) is visualized with a cross in a different color. The associated motion vectors are displayed as dots in the same color as their related master vectors. After k-NN using the motion vectors and clusters, the new motion vectors are associated to master vectors.

5.3.3 Image Stack Update

With each new incoming image, image stacks are updated in two steps: (1) the position of the master vector is updated and (2) the current stack area is added as a new layer to the image stack. Since the master vector is a virtual motion vector, its position and orientation can only be updated by its related motion vectors. Each related motion vector stores its relative position and orientation to the master vector right after it has been associated. This way, it can suggest a position and orientation of its related master vector in the current image. The final master vector position and orientation is determined by calculating the median of all suggested positions and orientations. Hence, even few incorrectly tracked related motion vectors will not affect the final master vector.

The stack area surrounding the updated master vector is rotated in upright position and added to the image stack as depicted in Fig. 5.7. There are two considered strategies to arrange the image stack:

1. **Accumulation image:** One image with the size of the rotated stack area is initialized. Each pixel value is zero. In order to append a new stack area, it is rotated in upright position and each pixel value of the rotated stack area is added to the accumulation image. The

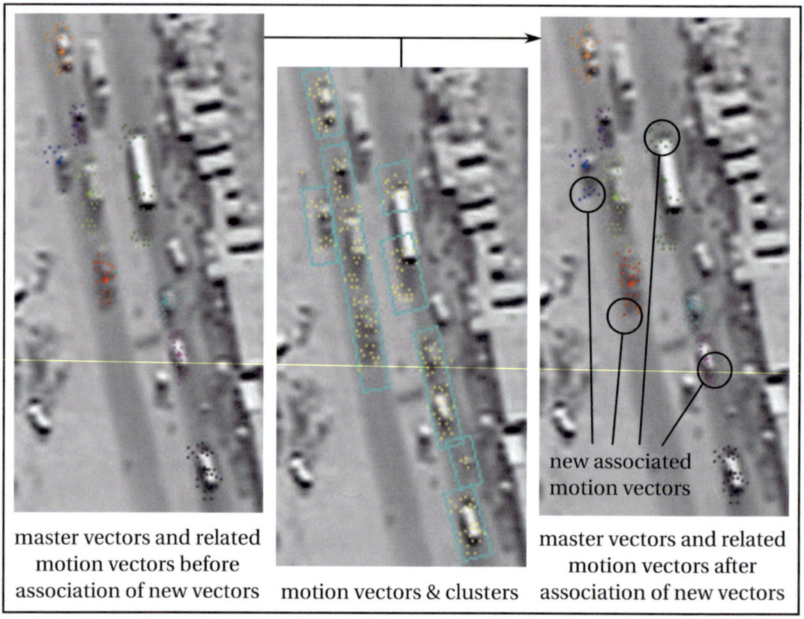

Figure 5.6: Association of new motion vectors to master vectors (colored crosses). Associated motion vectors are visualized as dots in the color of its master vector.

stack height is stored by incrementing a counter variable with each appended stack area. The accumulation image is a very efficient way to arrange the image stack since only one image has to be kept in the memory and new layers are simply added to this image. The motion ROI can be calculated very fast by dividing each pixel by the stack height. This is the mean pixel value of all stack areas appended to the stack just as described by Eq. 5.1. The main disadvantage of this approach is that a slightly varying object appearance due to changes in the camera angle or UAV altitude will strongly affect the resulting motion ROI by blurring the observed object.

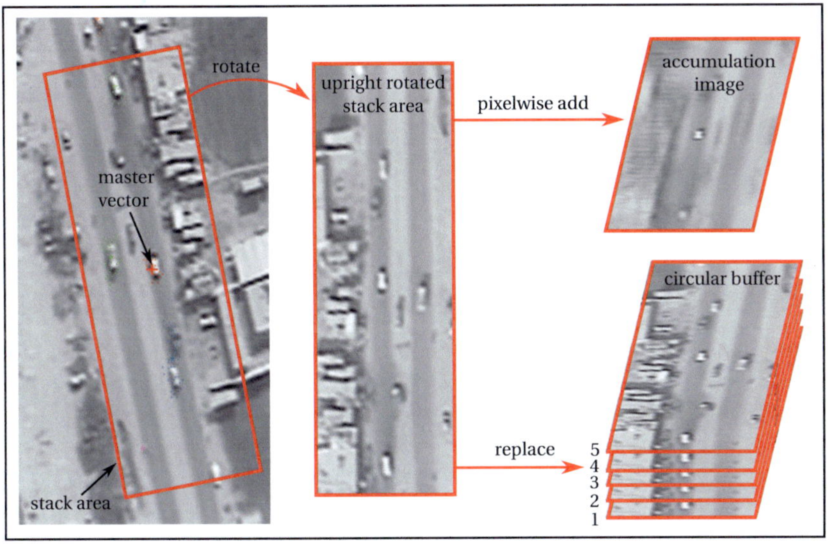

Figure 5.7: Image stack update and stack arrangement either as accumulation image or circular buffer.

2. **Circular buffer:** In order to avoid this self-blurring effect, old stack areas can be replaced after a certain time and, hence, the stack can be arranged as a circular buffer. The size of the circular buffer directly corresponds to the stack height. It is fixed and determined a priori. In this way, the maximum number of stack areas in the stack is limited. New stack areas are added to the buffer and as soon as the buffer is full, the oldest stack area is replaced by the new one. The motion ROI is calculated either by the pixelwise mean or median pixel value of all stack areas. This is much more time-consuming than the first approach with the accumulation image. Figure 5.7 shows a circular buffer with stack height $H = 5$ and where the stack area at position 4 is replaced. The standard buffer size used in this thesis is $H = 50$ since all stationary objects and most objects moving relative to the observed object disappear in the motion ROI.

The comparison and evaluation of both approaches will be presented in Chapter 7. An image stack is initialized as soon as the master vector is initialized. Hence, a region of the stack area can be outside of the image borders. In order to add the whole area to the stack but minimize the influence of the outer region for the calculation of motion ROIs, the pixels in these regions are set to the mean of the gray-value range. In the context of this thesis, this value is 127.

5.3.4 Replacement of Motion Clusters by Image Stacks

The replacement of motion clusters by motion ROIs that are provided by image stacking is optional. Motion ROIs are used, if suitable stacks are available, and motion clusters are used otherwise. A suitable image stack has to fulfil the following four criteria:

1. The velocity and the direction of the master vector have to be close to the velocity and the direction of the motion cluster.
2. The extended motion cluster has to be fully inside the stack area.
3. The master vector has to be inside the motion cluster.
4. The stack height has to exceed a minimum threshold H_{min}.

This process of finding suitable image stacks is shown in Fig. 5.8. Image stacks shall be found for the lower motion cluster (cyan rectangle). The extended motion cluster is visualized with a dashed cyan rectangle. There are two vehicles inside the motion cluster and for each vehicle an image stack has been initialized (shown in magenta and blue color). For both stacks all four criteria are fulfilled, so two suitable image stacks have been found. These image stacks replace the original motion cluster by replacing the original image with the stacked image. This stacked image can be calculated using the pixelwise mean of all images in the accumulation image or all images in the circular buffer as described in Eq. 5.1 or the pixelwise median of all images in the circular buffer using the equation

$$S(x,y) = \underset{h \in H}{\mathrm{median}}(I_h(x,y)), \tag{5.2}$$

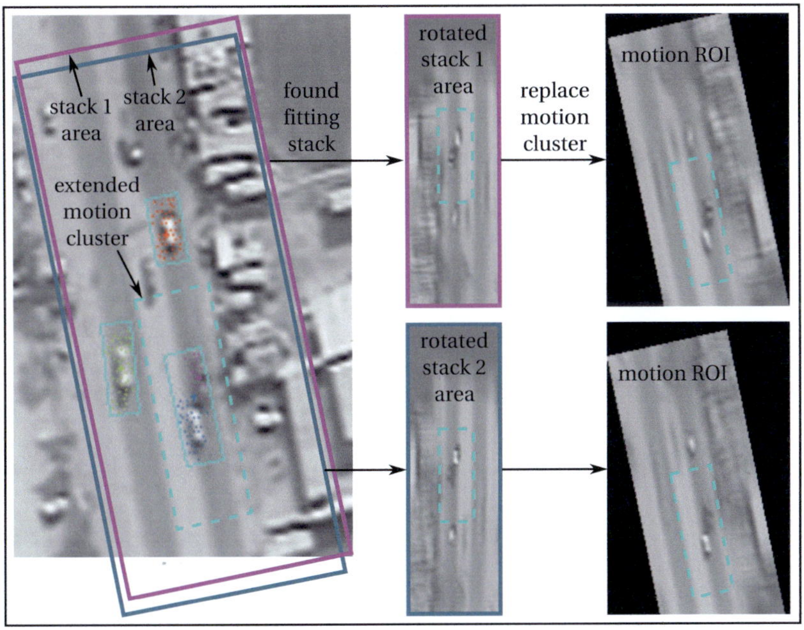

Figure 5.8: Replacement of motion clusters by image stacks (motion ROIs). Two suitable image stacks are found for the extended motion cluster (dashed cyan recangle) and replace the original image of the motion cluster.

where S is the stacked image and I_h the h-th original image in the stack at pixel position (x,y). H is the size of the circular buffer with $h \in \{1,\ldots,H\}$.

5.3.5 Discussion

Image stacking is introduced to improve the object detection performance by considering temporal context. Since only motion vectors and no object representations are used, image stacking takes place on feature level *before* multiple object tracking is applied on object level. Object detection and segmentation is applied to each motion ROI (stacked image) separately and the original image motion cluster is discarded, if suitable image stacks have been found. As soon as a motion cluster has been replaced by suitable image stacks, the aim is to detect only the sharp object in each stack and, thus, avoid a potential merged detection containing background structures or several moving objects. If a blurred object is detected, too, this detection should be suppressed by the outlier and duplicate removal module. In contrast to the first implementation of image stacking [Teu12b], the approach presented here can be processed in real-time. The runtime will be analyzed in detail in Chapter 7.

Figure 5.9 shows examples for each of the three situations where image stacking improves object detection as mentioned in the beginning of Section 5.3. This is (1) partial occlusion by a tree in Fig. 5.9 (a), (2) a parked vehicle close to the observed moving vehicle in Fig. 5.9 (b) and (c), and (3) disturbing street textures in Fig. 5.9 (d). The observed object is located in the center of each image. Since image stacking will improve object detection and segmentation only in such situations, no significant improvement of detection performance is expected. Furthermore, image stacking can even cause additional false detections if moving objects with small relative motion merge due to blurring. This effect becomes apparent in Fig 5.5.

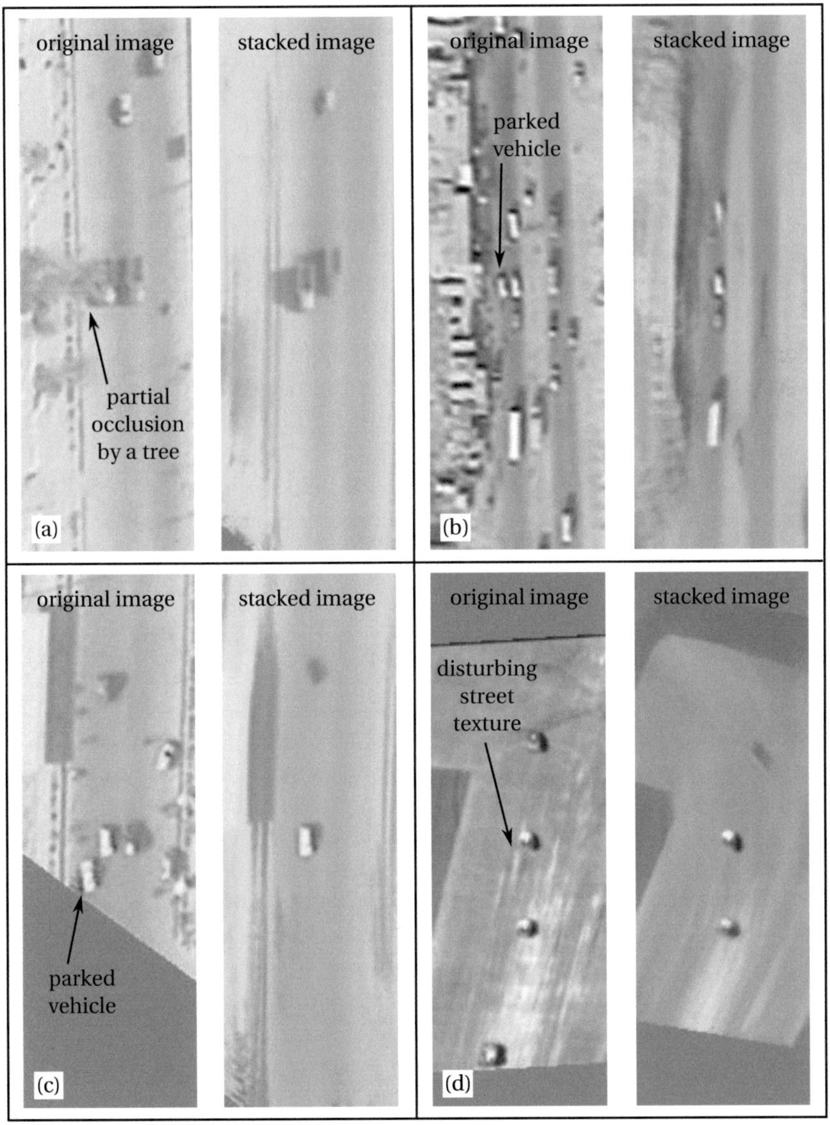

Figure 5.9: Examples for successful application of image stacking. The observed object is located in the center of each image.

Important parameters for image stacking are the size of the stack area A, the minimum stack height H_{min}, and the stacking strategy. A has to be chosen large enough so that the stack region fully covers even large objects such as trucks. H_{min} is the threshold of stack height H that has to be exceeded before a stack is returned as motion ROI. This is important since small stacks of $H = 10$ or less are prone to cause objects merging due to blurring. If H_{min} is too large (e.g., 50 or 100), fewer image stacks are used and potential benefit decreases as objects may already be outside of the camera view before H_{min} is exceeded and the motion ROI is returned. Good results have been achieved with $A = 100 \times 300$ pixels, $H_{min} = 25$, and circular buffer instead of accumulation image. The influence of varying these parameters for object detection and segmentation is analyzed in Chapter 7.

There are several potential applications for image stacking besides improved object detection. Among these applications is superresolution for moving objects, generating appearance templates without background for object tracking or re-identification, or temporal filtering to suppress image noise, compression artifacts, or artifacts of a disturbed wireless connection.

5.4 Detection and Segmentation Algorithms

Clustering of motion vectors works well in scenes with a few moving objects and sufficient spatial distance between them as seen in the VIVID dataset for example [Sia12b]. However, merged detections in particular are likely to occur in situations where objects drive in groups on busy streets. Not only similar motion of these objects makes it difficult to separate them, but also the presence of object shadows. The shadows of moving objects are moving, too, and the moving corners appear also in shadow areas, enlarge the motion clusters, and may even cause their merge. Although these enlarged motion clusters are correct results of independent motion detection, the shadow area belongs to the background and causes object *undersegmentation*, i.e. a situation when a bounding box is significantly larger than the object inside. If shadows appear right between moving objects, the spatial distance between these objects becomes even smaller due to the larger motion clusters. Shadow handling is challenging as dark objects and shadows have similar appearance and, hence, cannot be distinguished reliably. Image stacking cannot remove shadows for objects that move along straight paths but only for turning objects where the relative position of object and shadow varies.

Since standard object segmentation approaches such as superpixels, gPb, watershed, or graph cuts do not work well with the UAV video data analyzed in this thesis, new methods need to be proposed. Furthermore, split detections can occur for weakly textured objects such as buses or trucks. Corners are detected and tracked at the front and the back of the objects but not in the center area. In this case, two separate motion clusters appear: one in the front and one in the back. In order to handle split detections, each motion cluster is extended by factor 2 in motion direction and by factor 1.25 in the direction perpendicular to the motion direction. The proposed methods in this section work best, if two basic assumptions are met:

1. The object motion direction corresponds to its orientation. Thus, orientation normalization is achieved by rotating the motion ROI upwards based on the motion direction. If this assumption of corresponding motion direction and object orientation is not valid, the orientation of object and bounding box will be different and the bounding box can be oversized.

2. The object background is homogeneous. This is usually fulfilled since vehicles mostly drive on streets. Furthermore, image stacking can be used to remove road markings or partial occlusions by trees. If this assumption of a homogeneous object background is not valid, the bounding box can be oversized and merged detections are likely to occur since all approaches presented in this section are based on gradient information.

In the remainder of this section, different methods based on gradient and edge information are analyzed. These approaches are assumed to work better than methods based on blob detection [Mat02, Zhe13] since objects with inner texture occur regularly and do not appear as prominent blobs. The remainder of this section is based on five publications of the author of this thesis [Teu11e, Teu13a, Teu12b, Teu14a, Teu14b].

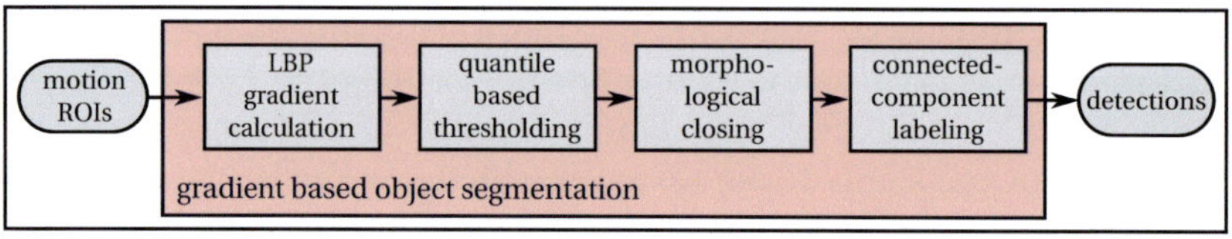

Figure 5.10: Concept of gradient based object segmentation.

5.4.1 Gradient Based Object Segmentation

Gradient calculation and edge detection are topics still worthy of a discussion since many image processing applications such as surveillance and reconnaissance have to deal with input images affected by noise or blur. Although not all object edges may be clearly visible and detectable due to weak contrast, gradients are promising features. The Canny edge detector [Can86] is a common method for gradient based edge detection. After noise reduction using a Gaussian filter, gradients can be calculated with the well-known Sobel filter for example. In order to get edges with a width of one pixel, directed NMS is applied in the dominant gradient orientation of a local pixel neighborhood. Finally, edge pixels are detected and edges are traced by hysteresis thresholding. The first two steps, noise reduction and gradient calculation, can be combined by using the first derivative of a two-dimensional Gaussian function. The variance σ^2 is used as parameter for noise reduction. Cheng et al. [Che12c] propose to use clustered Harris corners and Canny edges followed by foreground color classification for object segmentation. This method will be evaluated in Chapter 7 without foreground color classification since the UAV videos considered here do not provide color information.

In this thesis, a slightly different approach is proposed. It is visualized in Fig. 5.10. Gradients are calculated with a novel approach using LBP in order to achieve higher robustness to noise and blur compared to existing methods [Teu13a]. The gradient magnitudes are separated in object and non-object pixels by quantile based thresholding. Finally, morphological closing and connected-component labeling are applied to determine the object's bounding box.

LBP Gradient Calculation

The application of LBP is widely used in image processing research. Some examples are texture classification [Oja02, Guo10], face detection [Had04], face recognition [Aho06], background modeling [Hei06], or designing a SIFT descriptor [Hei09]. LBP describe a unique encoding for local pixel neighborhood. They are easy to implement, fast to compute, and characterized as high-performance and robust features in the abovementioned approaches [Pie11]. Furthermore, they are well-suited for implementation on a Graphics Processing Unit (GPU) in order to achieve significant speed-up in processing time [Teu13c]. In Fig. 5.11 (a), the typical way of LBP computation is shown. The gray-value of the central pixel is compared to each of the eight neighbors. In case of a higher or equal gray-value, its position will be indicated with 1 and, thus, considered for the LBP computation. LBP encoding is calculated by multiplying all indicated positions with their related weights and summing them up afterwards. The result is a value between 0 and 255 describing a specific neighbor constellation. There are two basic design parameters: number of neighbors P and radius R, since neighbors are ordered circularly around the central position c. This leads to the equation

$$LBP_{P,R} := \sum_{p=0}^{P-1} s(g_p - g_c)2^p, \text{ where } s(g) := \begin{cases} 1, \text{if } g \geq 0 \\ 0, \text{if } g < 0. \end{cases} \tag{5.3}$$

A specialization of LBP, which is important for edge detection, is the set of rotation invariant, uniform LBP

$$LBP_{P,R}^{riu2} := \begin{cases} \sum_{p=0}^{P-1} s(g_p - g_c), \text{ if } U(LBP_{P,R}) \leq 2 \\ P+1, \text{ otherwise,} \end{cases} \tag{5.4}$$

where

$$U(LBP_{P,R}) := \sum_{p=0}^{P-1} |s(g_p - g_c) - s(g_{p+1} - g_c)|. \tag{5.5}$$

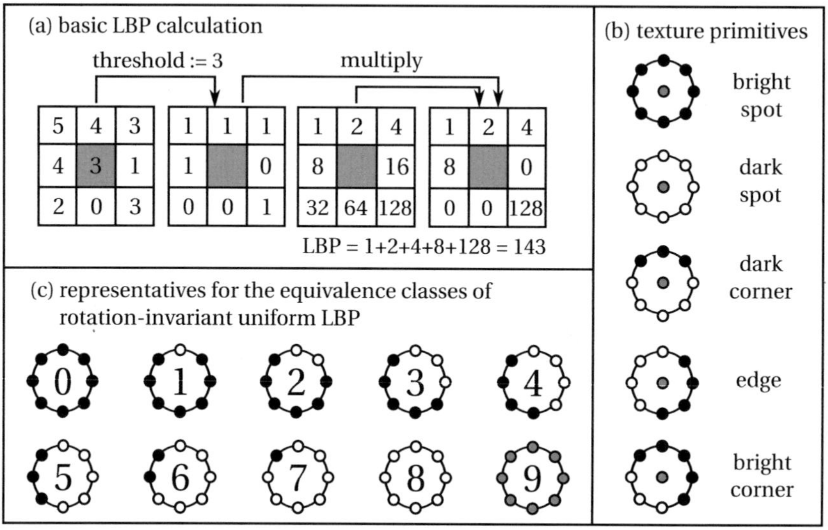

Figure 5.11: Calculation and interpretation of LBP [Mäe03].

According to Mäenpää [Mäe03], $LBP^{riu2}_{P,R}$ can be interpreted as texture primitives as seen in Fig. 5.11 (b). The description *riu2* stands for rotation invariance and uniformity measure U of 2 or less. U is the number of bitwise 0/1 and 1/0 transitions in an LBP. With $P = 8$ and $U \leq 2$, only the 58 texture primitives among the 256 LBP are considered.

Rotation invariance is achieved by assigning all potential rotations of a uniform LBP to the same equivalence class, for example *edge*, *bright corner*, or *dark corner*. As seen in Fig. 5.11 (c), there are nine equivalence classes (class 0-8) and eight LBP in each class, each LBP corresponding to a rotation in steps of 45°. An exception is given by the classes *bright spot* and *dark spot*, each having only one representative. The tenth class (class 9) contains all 198 LBP which are not texture primitives. LBP are gray-scale invariant [Oja02] as only the sign of the gray-value difference is considered.

More information is available in the neighbor's gray-values. To extract this information, the rotation invariant variance measure *VAR* is introduced by

$$VAR_{P,R} := \frac{1}{P}\sum_{p=0}^{P-1}(g_p-\mu)^2, \quad \text{where } \mu := \frac{1}{P}\sum_{p=0}^{P-1} g_p. \tag{5.6}$$

Ojala et al. [Oja02] point out that the combination of LBP and VAR is a powerful descriptor for texture classification. Thus, gradient calculation and edge detection using LBP is a crossover between texture analysis and edge detection. But why should LBP be suitable for gradient calculation? The answer is given in Fig. 5.12 and 5.13.

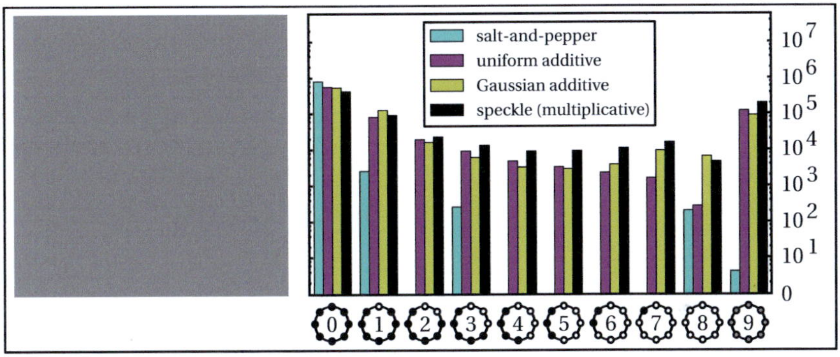

Figure 5.12: Motivation to use LBP for gradient calculation: image noise models visualized by LBP distributions. In a synthetic image without any texture, mainly $LBP^{riu2}_{P,R}$ classes 0, 1, and 9 appear in presence of noise.

In particular, image areas with low illumination and weak contrast are expected to be affected by image noise. The two most common ways to model noise are additive and multiplicative [Bro05]. In Fig. 5.12 left, a synthetic image without any texture or edges is visualized and artificially impaired by four different kinds of noise: Gaussian additive, uniform additive, speckle multiplicative, and salt-and-pepper. The right side shows the histogram of the appearing rotation-invariant uniform LBP. For additive and multiplicative noise, the classes 2–8 have significantly lower probability to appear in presence of noise compared to the classes 0, 1, and 9. In Fig. 5.13, three images are artificially impaired by Gaussian additive noise which is probably the most frequently occurring noise [Bro05]. Besides an image coming from the UAV video data in the lower row, a synthetic image with edges and well-known *Lena* image are analyzed. Gaussian noise in three different levels is added to the original images. The Peak-Signal-To-Noise Ratio (PSNR), which is widely used to calculate the difference between original and noisy image in decibel (dB) [Hou02], is approximately 38 dB for weak, 28 dB for moderate, and 22 dB for severe noise. In natural images, the amount of texture primitives such as corners or edges is much larger compared to the synthetic image. Since the spot-like LBP classes 0, 1, 7, 8 represent flat image areas, gradients should not be calculated there. Instead, the remaining corners and edges of LBP classes 2-6 can be used since they contain prominent edge information and a significant amount of them remains even in presence of severe noise.

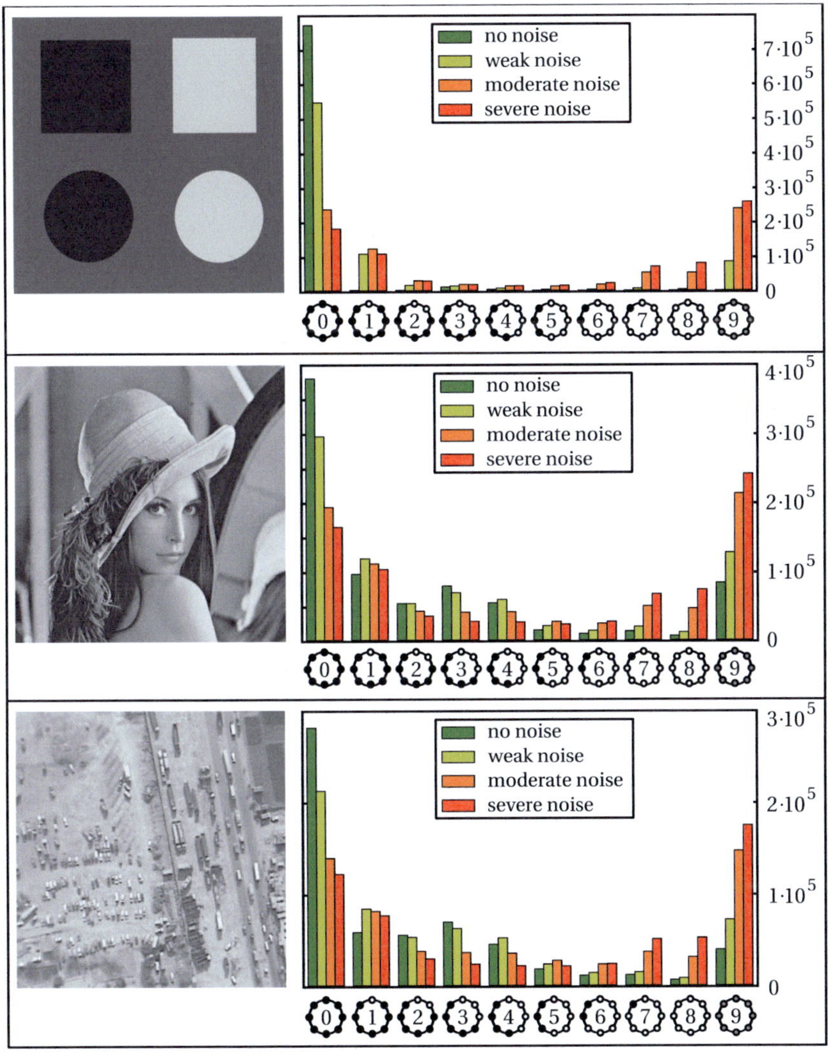

Figure 5.13: $LBP_{P,R}^{riu2}$ of classes 2–6 contain prominent edge information and many of them remain even in presence of severe noise. Hence, noise resistance can be achieved by calculating gradients only at their pixel positions.

Therefore, the basic idea in using LBP for gradient calculation is to generate a filter rejecting pixel positions which are either irrelevant for gradient calculation or likely to be produced by noise. After that, gradient magnitudes are calculated only for pixel positions assumed to be noiseless by using the local variance measure VAR. The first step to design such a filter is to enhance the robustness of the standard LBP. Following Heikkilä et al. [Hei06], the gray-value threshold T is introduced in order to modify Eq. 5.3 by

$$LBP_{P,R,T} := \sum_{p=0}^{P-1} s(g_p - g_c - T)2^p. \tag{5.7}$$

In this way, weak noise is suppressed especially in flat image areas with similar gray-values.

At that point, the contribution of the author of this thesis begins: a binary decision function d is defined and applied pixelwise to all image pixel positions $c = (x, y)$. d only accepts pixels with related LBP, which fulfill the three criteria

$$U(LBP_{P,R,T}) = 2, \tag{5.8}$$

$$LBP_{P,R,T} \neq 2^p,\ p \in \mathcal{P} = \{0, \ldots, P-1\}, \tag{5.9}$$

$$LBP_{P,R,T} \neq 2^P - 1 - 2^p,\ p \in \mathcal{P}. \tag{5.10}$$

This means, only $LBP_{P,R}^{riu2}$ of classes 2–6 are accepted, which are not spots (5.8) or spotlike (5.9), (5.10). The assumption is that all non-uniform LBP and all uniform LBP violating one of the three criteria are the result of noise. Thus, they should be suppressed before gradients are calculated. This leads to the following formulation of d for each pixel position c:

$$d(c) := \begin{cases} 1, \text{if } (5.8) \text{ and } (5.9) \text{ and } (5.10) \\ 0, \text{otherwise.} \end{cases} \tag{5.11}$$

Only pixel positions with $d(c) = 1$ are considered for the calculation of gradient magnitudes. A similar filter function can be used to emphasize object contours in SAR imagery [Teu11d, Teu11c] and to adapt the size of a Gaussian filter for edge preserving image smoothing [Teu13c].

The convolution of the image with Sobel, Prewitt or other filters is an approximation of partial derivatives. Here, $VAR_{P,R,T}$ and $LBP_{P,R,T}$ are used instead. The gradient magnitudes $G(c)$ for each pixel position c are calculated by

$$G(c) = \begin{cases} \sqrt{VAR_{P,R,T}}, & \text{if } d(c) = 1 \\ 0, & \text{otherwise.} \end{cases} \tag{5.12}$$

Since variance tends to focus too much on bright objects, standard deviation is used instead of variance as it produces more homogeneous edge images.

The robustness against noise can be increased significantly using multi-resolution LBP [Oja02]. In the literature, they are also known as multi-scale LBP. For the same pixel position c, several LBP are calculated varying the parameters P and R. In this thesis, only the variation of radius R is considered and P is fixed to $P = 8$. For each LBP accepted by d, $VAR_{P,R,T}$ is calculated and accumulated by

$$\tilde{G}(c) = \begin{cases} \sum_{r=R_1}^{R_n} \sqrt{VAR_{P,r,T}}, & \text{if } d(c) = 1 \\ 0, & \text{otherwise.} \end{cases} \tag{5.13}$$

This approach can be embedded to the Canny edge detection processing chain. The Gaussian filter for noise reduction is replaced by filter function d and gradient magnitudes are calculated using function $G(c)$ or $\tilde{G}(c)$. It is also possible to use LBP for a directed NMS since the LBP encoding implicitly includes the local orientation. This modified processing chain shows similar results as the Canny edge detector for images with high PSNR but performs better in presence of noise [Teu13a].

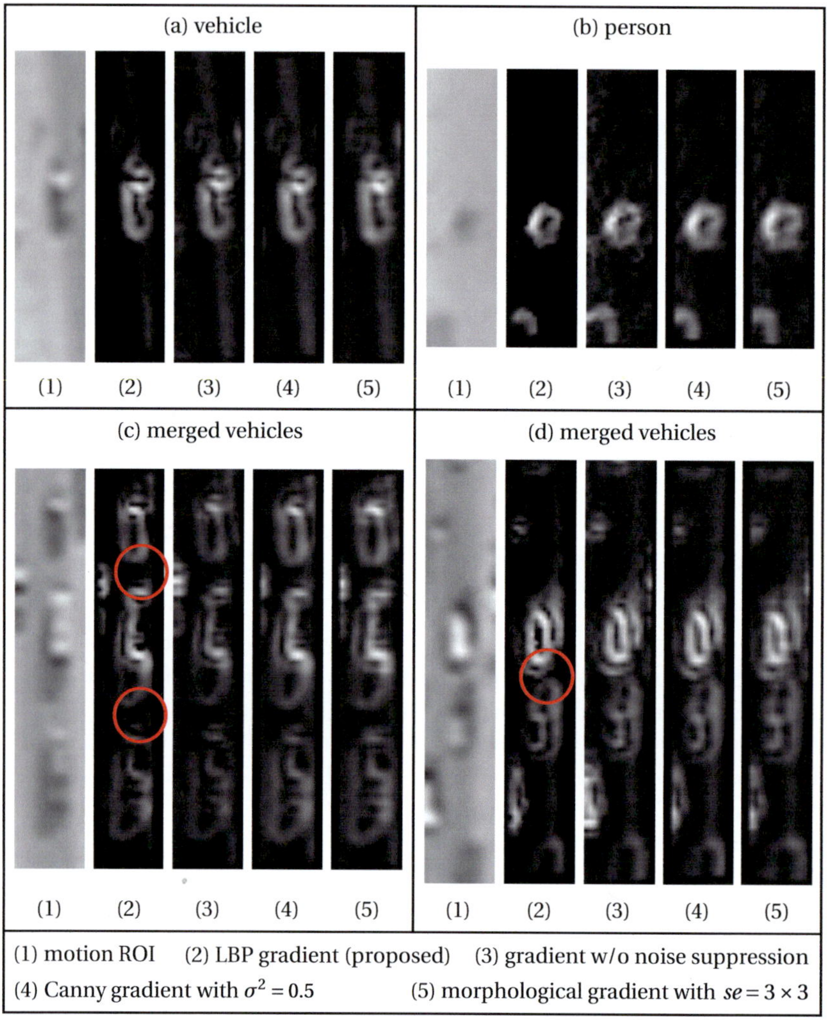

Figure 5.14: Comparison of four different gradient calculation approaches for object segmentation embedded to the processing chain in Fig. 5.10. LBP visually work best for object separation in all four examples. This is highlighted by red circles for the merged vehicles in the lower row.

One reason of this behavior is that the LBP approach is prone to produce FN edge pixels while the original Canny algorithm produces FPs. For the considered UAV video data with an object size as small as 5×10 pixels, no NMS is applied to the gradient magnitudes in order to keep as much edge and contour information as possible. Hence, the presence of FN rather than FP edge pixels helps to avoid object undersegmentation and merged detections. This effect is visualized with four examples in Fig. 5.14. In addition to the proposed LBP approach (2), gradients are calculated without noise reduction using the simple filter matrices $\mathbf{M}_x = (1\ -1)$ and $\mathbf{M}_y = (1\ -1)^T$ (3), Canny gradient with $\sigma^2 = 0.5$ (4), and morphological gradient [Lee87] with a structuring element *se* of size 3×3 pixels (5). While (3) and (4) are linear methods for gradient calculation, (2) and (5) are non-linear. For all four examples there is less noise in the gradient magnitude image when using LBP instead of the other approaches. Thus, the occurrence of undersegmentation for the examples *vehicle* and *person* in Fig. 5.14 (a) and (b) is less likely. In Fig. 5.14 (c) and (d), potential situations for merged detections are shown where gradient magnitudes of multiple moving objects and moving shadows grow together. As highlighted by red circles, LBP visually work best for object separation in this qualitative evaluation. The quantitative evaluation in context of the entire processing chain is presented in Chapter 7.

From Gradients to Objects

Gradient calculation is applied in order to emphasize the object's contour. Usually, the contour of a vehicle in top view appears as a bright rectangle in the gradient magnitude image as seen in Fig. 5.14. The gradient magnitudes have to be further processed for getting connected edge pixels. However, it cannot be assumed that each edge of the object contour is clearly visible since blurry edges can occur due to sunlight or shadow. Even if only three out of four edges of a vehicle are visible, the approach still has to be able to segment the object correctly. Furthermore, the method has to be robust against outlier edge pixels coming from curbs or road markings that cannot be removed by image stacking.

The entire process is visualized in Fig. 5.15. Right after gradient calculation with LBP, high gradient magnitudes are binarized using quantile based thresholding [Shi10]. This is an adaptive thresholding technique where the

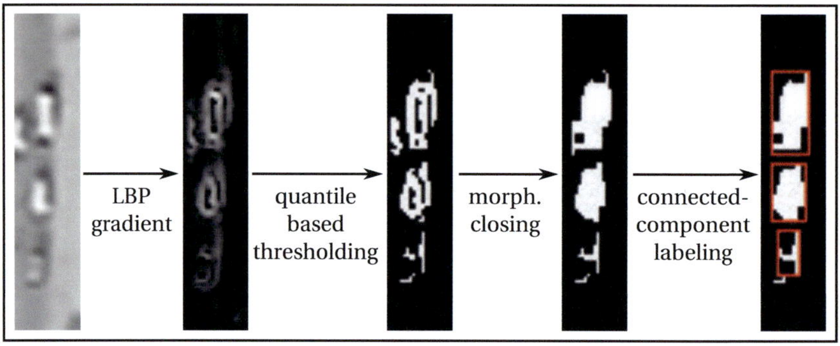

Figure 5.15: From gradients to objects.

threshold T_q is chosen based on the pixel gray-value distribution in the current motion ROI. All gray-values of the gradient magnitude image are collected in a histogram as depicted in Fig. 5.16. The quantile value q is between 0 and 1 and separates the histogram in a brighter and a darker gray-value part. A typical value for the quantile is 0.15. This means, that 15 % of the brightest pixels in the gradient magnitude image are kept in a binary image after thresholding. If the quantile is set too low, objects with weak contrast are missed, and if it is set too high, merged detections occur. Given the gradient magnitude image G, the thresholded binary image B at pixel position (x, y) is then calculated by

$$B(x,y) := \begin{cases} 1, & \text{if } G(x,y) \geq T_q \\ 0, & \text{if } G(x,y) < T_q. \end{cases} \tag{5.14}$$

This approach is based on the assumption that there must be an object inside the motion ROI even if the contrast is weak. The performance in this context is better compared to fixed value or hysteresis thresholding [Can86].

Since there can be small holes and gaps in the object contours, morphological closing [Dou92, Bey12] with a structuring element *se* of size 3 × 3 pixels is applied. Connected areas are determined with a standard connected-component labeling algorithm [Dil92]. These connected components are

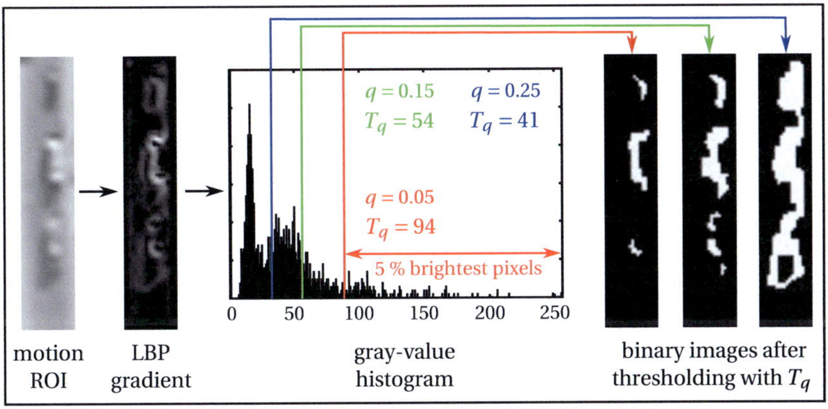

Figure 5.16: Calculation of quantile based thresholding.

represented by bounding boxes that are paraxial to the motion ROI in order to keep the motion direction. An alternative method is the detection of peaks in row/column gray-value histograms [Teu11c, Teu11d]. However, undersegmentation is likely to occur for blurred object edges. Finally, a size constraint is used to reject bounding boxes with an area less than 10 pixels. The resulting red boxes in Fig. 5.15 fully contain the two upper objects. The lowest object is partially detected due to weak contrast.

5.4.2 Object Segmentation using Relative Connectivity

While gradient based object segmentation is hardly using any assumptions about object shape and appearance, the local sliding window approach presented in Section 5.4.3 is automatically learning an appearance model from object and non-object training samples. The approach described in this section is somewhere in between. Human expert knowledge is used to model basic relations between object edges. The main assumption is that each object can be described by pairs of opposing edges with opposite orientations in both horizontal and vertical direction. This is the case for objects both brighter and darker than the background. However, inner structures

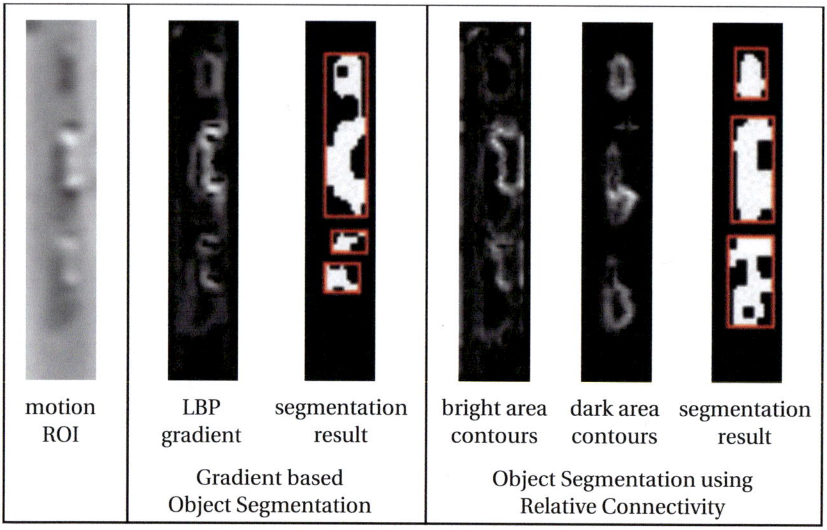

Figure 5.17: Comparison of gradient based object segmentation and object segmentation using relative connectivity. Bright and dark object regions are emphasized with relative connectivity and provide a more precise segmentation result compared to LBP gradient.

such as the windshield and the rear window of vehicles as well as other kinds of textures can lead to split detections. Relative connectivity [Yip94] is introduced to handle this problem. Figure 5.17 shows that contours of bright and dark areas are emphasized with this method and some merged and split detections can be handled well compared to the LBP gradient approach. In the follow-up, these contours are processed in a similar way as presented in the previous section.

Relative Connectivity

The Hough transform [Dud72] is a commonly used method for line segmentation due to its easy implementation and good performance. For a binary image containing edge pixels, the pixel positions are mapped to the parameter space of potential straight lines. This parameter space is called *Hough accumulator* and straight lines are detected by finding maxima in this accumulator. However, there are some demanding challenges:

1. Similarity: maxima in the Hough accumulator close to each other lead to similar straight lines.
2. Connectivity: collinear and contiguous points inside an image create maxima in Hough accumulator space, but may not be part of the same line segment.
3. Start/Endpoints: maxima in Hough accumulator represent straight lines of undefined length. If line segments are to be detected, they have to be extracted subsequently.

In his paper, Yip [Yip94] deals with the mentioned problems. He proposes to use a modified Hough transform, namely the *Line Patterns Hough transform (LPHT)*, to directly extract potential start and end points of line segments. Therefore, he uses the principle of relative connectivity of points along a line segment instead of straight lines. Relative connectivity is defined as *the relationship of a set of collinear and equidistant points with regard to contiguity* [Yip94]. Input image I is scanned pixel by pixel in all possible directions for points potentially belonging to a line segment. If pixel intensity $I(x,y)$ at position (x,y) exceeds a specific intensity threshold T_{rc}, the pixel is assumed to belong to a line. Using the mean gray-value μ_I and standard deviation σ_I of image I, this intensity threshold can be adaptively set to $T_{rc} := \mu_I + \sigma_I$. This leads to the binary belonging function f_b:

$$f_b(x,y) := \begin{cases} 1, & \text{if } I(x,y) \geq T_{rc} \\ 0, & \text{if } I(x,y) < T_{rc}. \end{cases} \tag{5.15}$$

For a set of collinear and equidistant points $P_i(x_i, y_i)$ with $i \in \{1, \ldots, n\}$ and $\forall i$: $f_b(x_i, y_i) = 1$, the relative displacement $(\Delta x, \Delta y)$ is given by

$$\Delta x = x_2 - x_1 \tag{5.16}$$

$$\Delta y = y_2 - y_1. \tag{5.17}$$

In order to be a start point, P_1 has to satisfy the constraint

$$f_b(x_1,y_1) = 1 \qquad \text{and} \qquad f_b(x_1 - \Delta x, y_1 - \Delta y) = 0. \tag{5.18}$$

The definition of P_n that may be an end point is by analogy

$$f_b(x_n,y_n) = 1 \qquad \text{and} \qquad f_b(x_n + \Delta x, y_n + \Delta y) = 0. \tag{5.19}$$

Here, n is the connectivity number, since

$$f_b(x_n + \Delta x, y_n + \Delta y) = f_b(x_1 + n \cdot \Delta x, y_1 + n \cdot \Delta y) = 0 \tag{5.20}$$

and

$$f_b(x_1 + i \cdot \Delta x, y_1 + i \cdot \Delta y) = 1 \qquad \forall i \in \{0,\ldots,n-1\}. \tag{5.21}$$

To store this found relative connectivity, n is added at start and end point position (x_1, y_1) and (x_n, y_n) to the LPHT accumulator image A_I which has same dimension as I. Initially, $A_I(x,y) = 0$ for all positions (x,y). Noise in A_I can be avoided by defining a minimum number of points T_m to describe a line and adding n to A_I only if $n \geq T_m$. A typical value is $T_m = 3$.

LPHT can be used for object segmentation in noisy and blurry images. Therefore, LPHT is not applied to edge pixels but directly to a natural image I such as the original image in Fig. 5.17. The estimated complexity for calculating relative connectivity with the original LPHT algorithm [Yip94] is $O(M \cdot N \cdot \log M \cdot \log N)$ for an input image of size $M \times N$. For only few edge pixels in an image satisfying f_b, this is not a problem. However, for a natural image, this can be very time-consuming. In order to reduce the complexity, the original algorithm for two-dimensional images can be modified to process one-dimensional arrays with a complexity of $O(N \cdot \log N)$ for array size N [Teu11e]. In this thesis, another modification is used to process two-dimensional natural images with a complexity of $O(M \cdot N \cdot \log(\max(M,N))$. Since objects are oriented along the direction of their motion, the object edges run parallel to the image borders. In order to detect opposing edge pairs with relative connectivity, it is sufficient to scan the image row by row and column by column instead of a full two-dimensional scan. Start and end points are detected in each row and column separately and stored in the

LPHT accumulator. Algorithm 1 describes horizontal row-by-row scanning and Fig. 5.18 visualizes the entire method. According to Yip [Yip94], $\frac{M-x_1}{T_m-1}$ is the size of the search space for an end point given a start point. The contours of bright and dark object areas are detected separately and combined afterwards to fill gaps and holes in the object texture. In contrast to gradient based object segmentation, opposing edge pairs get the same intensity value even if one edge is blurred.

Algorithm 1 Horizontal scanning to calculate relative connectivity.

```
/* let R be one row in the input image with R ∈ {0,...,N−1} */
for x_1 = 0 to M−1 do
  if I(x_1,R) ≥ T_rc then
    for x_2 = x_1 + 1 to x_1 + (M−x_1)/(T_m−1) do
      if I(x_2,R) ≥ T_rc then
        Δx = x_2 − x_1
        if I(x_1 − Δx, R) < T_rc then
          /* found start point */
          x_n = x_2
          n = 2
          ready = 0
          while ready = 0 do
            if I(x_n + Δx, R) ≥ T_rc then
              /* found another line point */
              n = n + 1
              x_n = x_n + Δx
            else
              /* found end point */
              ready = 1
            end if
          end while
          if n ≥ T_m then
            /* found enough line points */
            /* add start and end point to accumulator */
            A_I[x_1, R] = A_I[x_1, R] + n
            A_I[x_n, R] = A_I[x_n, R] + n
          end if
        end if
      end if
    end for
  end if
end for
```

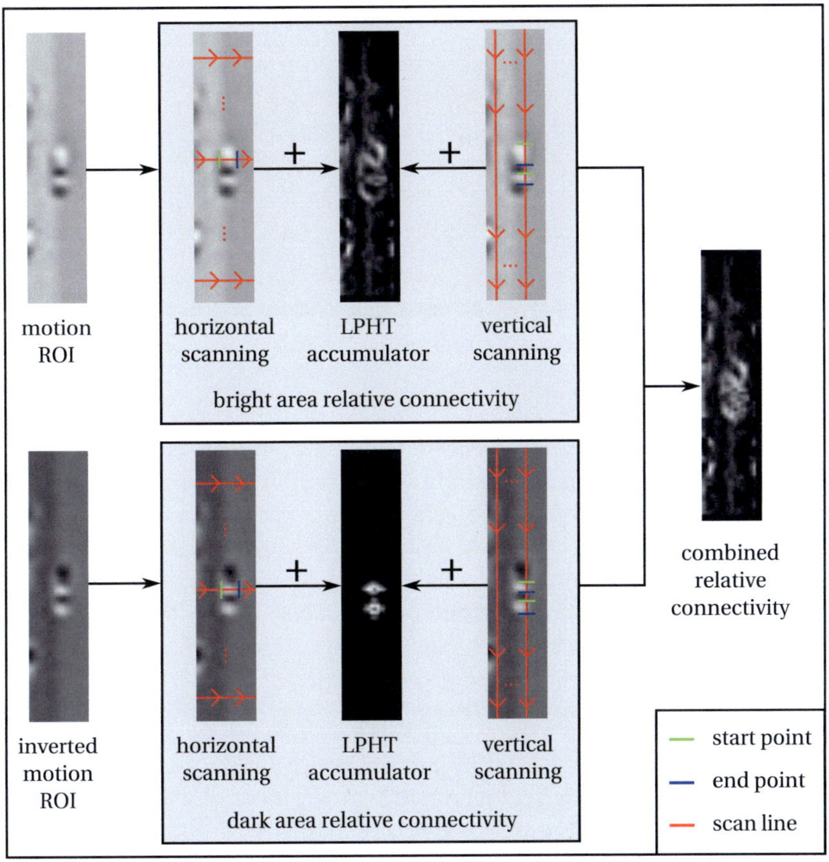

Figure 5.18: Proposed algorithm for calculating relative connectivity. The image is scanned separately in horizontal and vertical direction. Start and end points are detected along each scan line and stored in the LPHT accumulator image. By inverting the image, contours of bright and dark image regions can be extracted. They are fused to fill gaps and holes in the object texture.

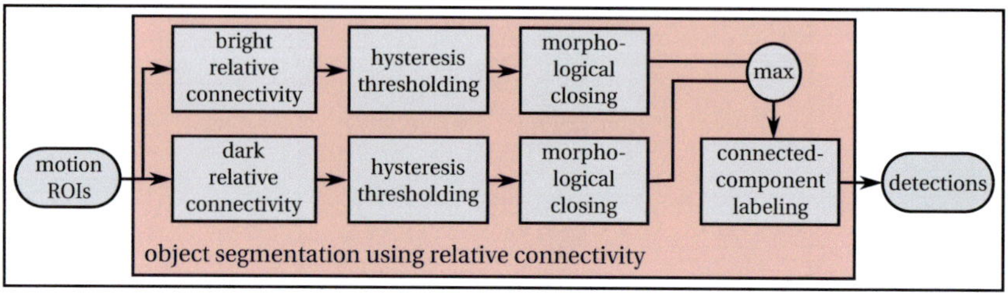

Figure 5.19: Concept of object segmentation using relative connectivity.

From Relative Connectivity to Objects

Similarly to gradient based object segmentation, the object contour is emphasized by calculating relative connectivity and further processing is necessary to segment individual objects. The concept is depicted in Fig. 5.19. Relative connectivity is calculated separately for bright and dark image areas. These partial results are fused using the *max*-operator right after separate hysteresis thresholding and morphological closing. Hence, the fused binary image B at pixel position (x,y) is calculated by

$$B(x,y) = \max(B_{BA}(x,y), B_{DA}(x,y)), \quad (5.22)$$

where B_{BA} is the thresholded binary image for bright and B_{DA} for dark image areas. Finally, individual objects are segmented using connected-component labeling. Hysteresis thresholding is the standard method to separate edge and background pixels in the Canny edge detection algorithm [Can86]. Two thresholds are defined: the lower threshold T_l and the upper threshold T_u. Given the LPHT accumulator image A_I, a pixel at position (x,y) is considered to be *strong*, if $A_I(x,y) \geq T_u$. Strong pixels are considered to belong to an edge or contour and, thus, are accepted for the thresholded binary image B. Positions of *weak* pixels with $A_I(x,y) < T_l$ are directly rejected. All other pixels are *candidates*. A candidate is accepted if it belongs to a set $\mathfrak{I}$ of connected pixels (x_i, y_i) with $A_I(x_i,y_i) \geq T_l$ and at least one pixel $(x_j, y_j) \in \mathfrak{I}$ with $A_I(x_j,y_j) \geq T_u$. In combination with relative connectivity, hysteresis thresholding achieves higher object detection rates

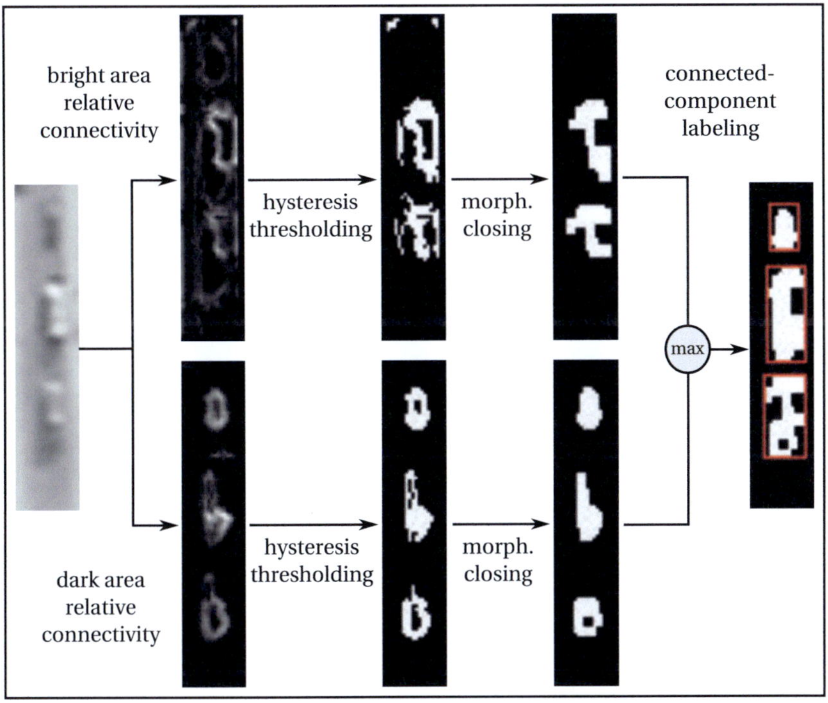

Figure 5.20: From relative connectivity to objects.

compared to quantile based thresholding. The entire process is depicted in Fig. 5.20. Apart from object segmentation in aerial VIS images, this approach appeared to be very effective for line and object segmentation in IR and SAR images [Teu11e] affected by strong speckle noise.

5.4.3 Object Detection using Local Sliding Window

Machine learning is introduced in this section by using a local sliding window approach. The concept is depicted in Fig. 5.21. Sliding window is a widely used method for object detection by scanning an image in a search

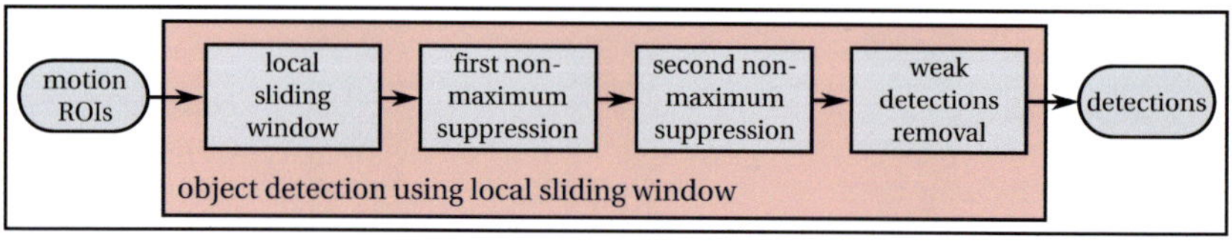

Figure 5.21: Concept of object detection using local sliding window.

for instances of a certain object class such as vehicle or person. Therefore, a search window is shifted in both horizontal and vertical direction across the image. In order to detect objects of different sizes, either the image or the window can be rescaled. At each window position, a classifier returns a decision value representing its certainty that the current window contains an object or not. Based on these decision values, the first NMS rejects all positions of windows with lower certainty compared to their neighbors. Each remaining local maximum stands for one object hypothesis represented by a bounding box with size and position of the current window. If there is sufficient overlap with another local maximum based on the IoU criterion, it is likely that these bounding boxes come from the same object. Then, a second NMS is applied to keep the one with highest certainty and reject the others. Finally, a decision threshold is used to reject weak local maxima. In the remainder of this section, the local sliding window is described, appropriate object descriptors and classifiers and presented and discussed, and finally, a novel classifier is introduced.

Local Sliding Window

The standard sliding window is a global approach where the entire image is scanned without any constraints. In this thesis, a local sliding window is applied only in image areas of detected independent motion. Hence, instead of the entire image, each extended motion ROI is scanned for objects. Further search space reduction can be achieved since the orientation of objects inside the motion cluster is assumed to be known. As the length of usual vehicles is larger than their width, the sliding window size is adapted to this condition and set to 16×32 pixels. The classifier is only trained for

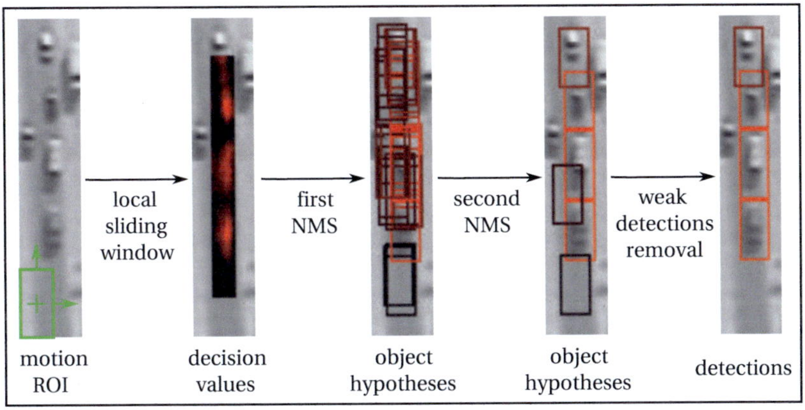

Figure 5.22: Example for object detection using local sliding window.

vehicles since other moving objects such as motorcycles, bicycles, or persons do not have a distinguishable appearance in the data used in this thesis. As already mentioned in Section 2.3.2, there are two main methods to scan for vehicles of different sizes in the image: while N different window sizes with N classifier models (one per window size) and no image rescaling are considered in the first method, one fixed window size with one classifier model and N different rescaled images are used in the second. Here, the second method is used that is inspired by the work of Dollár et al. [Dol09]. This means that one classifier model is trained and each motion ROI is scanned at different scales with a sliding window of fixed size.

This procedure is depicted in Fig. 5.22. The sliding window is visualized by a green rectangle that is oriented in motion direction. The decision values for one scale of the motion ROI are represented by red dots. Each dot is located at the center of one sliding window and as the window is shifted pixel by pixel in both horizontal and vertical direction, a dense decision function appears. Lighter red stands for higher certainty of the classifier.

The first NMS is applied in order to find local maxima in this decision function but usually many object hypotheses are left across all image scales. Red bounding boxes visualize these hypotheses and light red again represents high classifier certainty. Subsequently, a second NMS is used to keep the strongest hypothesis in a set of overlapping boxes. Therefore, a minimum overlap threshold value[1] T_{dov} has to be defined. The remaining local maxima are further reduced by rejecting all hypotheses with a weak classifier certainty using a decision threshold T_d. In this example, all moving vehicles are correctly detected. Vehicles that have not been detected are stationary.

Usually, about 50 different image scales are used for person detection in ground level images [Ben12]. This is due to the highly variable size of persons in the image depending on the distance to the camera. Since the distance between object and camera is nearly fixed in UAV data that is evaluated in this thesis, the number of different image scales can be significantly reduced. However, it has to be considered that the vehicle size can vary strongly: while the width of different vehicles is nearly constant, the length ranges between 4–5 meters for a standard car and 15–20 meters for buses or trucks. So, three different scales are introduced to the sliding window approach by keeping image width stable and varying image length as shown in Fig. 5.23. This is different compared to person detection where the ratio of width and length is fixed during image rescaling. By using only three different image scales, the search space for the sliding window is reduced. Not only can a lot of processing time be saved, but also the occurrence of additional FPs is avoided. The reason is that a vehicle model in top view and at low resolution of 16×32 pixels does not have the discriminative power of a person model in side view and at high resolution of 64×128 pixels. Since gradients are the most important information for modelling an object's shape, it is worth to examine their potential for a classifier model of high discriminative power. Therefore, the mean gradient magnitude images for persons [Dal05] and four different datasets of vehicle samples (see Fig. 7.4 and 7.5) are depicted in Fig. 5.24. While head, shoulders, torso, and legs provide good features for a model of high discriminative power, vehicles can be described only by their rectangular shape. Not even inner textures such as windshield or trunk are helpful since they vary strongly from vehicle to vehicle. The influence of such a weakly discriminative classifier model, image rescaling, and overlap threshold T_{dov} to the robustness of the sliding window approach is visualized

1 The abbreviation *dov* stands for detection overlap.

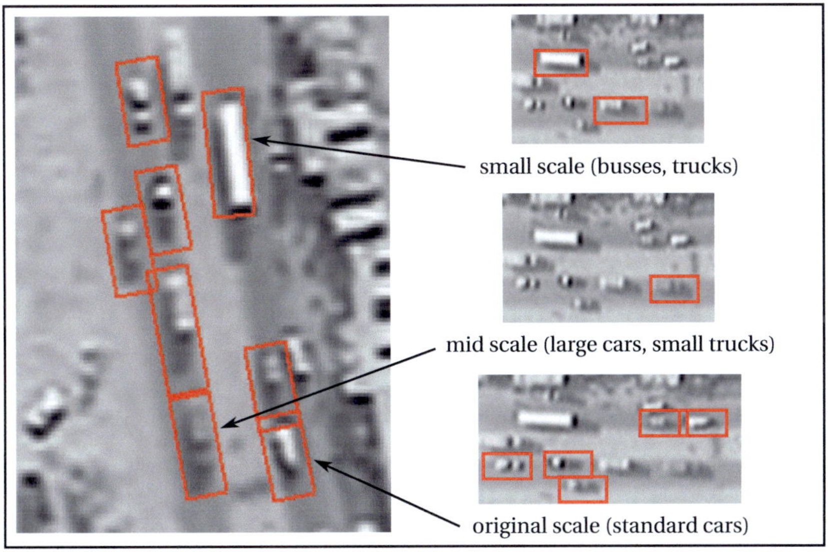

Figure 5.23: Image rescaling for detection of differently sized objects using local sliding window.

in Fig. 5.25. In this sequence, four vehicles drive close to each other in the same motion direction. In addition to the scale of the original image, one smaller and one larger scale are calculated with variable image width and fixed image length. Sliding window is applied first to the combination of smaller and original scale, and then to the combination of original and larger scale. For each combination, T_{dov} is set to both 0.2 and 0.3. Again, light red colored bounding boxes indicate higher classifier certainty. For each case, the detection result is different demonstrating the sensitivity of the approach with respect to these parameters. In each case, there is a false positive detection at the area between the vehicles. The reason is that the edges of two vehicles and the curb generate a rectangular shape similar to the appearance of a vehicle. Blurry edges, shadows, and inner textures of vehicles make vehicles look different compared to the samples in Fig. 5.24 that were used for classifier training. As a result, there is a higher

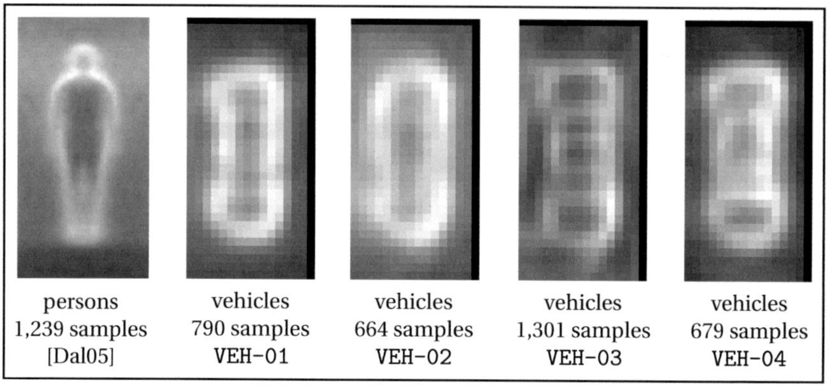

Figure 5.24: Comparison of average gradient magnitudes: persons in side view and at high resolution provide shape features for a classifier model of higher discriminative power than vehicles in top view and at low resolution.

certainty for the area between the vehicles than for the vehicles themselves. A similar effect was discovered by Türmer et al. [Tür13] where dormers or chimneys of buildings were misclassified as vehicles due to their rectangular shape. This problem is handled by using SFM and rejecting detections with significantly lower distance to the camera than the ground plane. In this thesis, only three image scale levels are introduced as presented in Fig. 5.23 in order to mitigate this problem. The effectiveness of this approach is demonstrated in Section 7.3.3 together with the optimization of T_{dov}. Retraining the classifier with vehicle samples from the used UAV videos would probably improve object detection performance since the specificity of the classifier is increased for this dataset, but at the same time generality and transferability are decreased this way.

Object Descriptors and Classifiers

The choice of the object descriptor and classifier is crucial for the performance of the sliding window approach. The trained classifier model should be able to separate objects and non-objects by a large margin in the feature space. Then, it is possible to find a value for decision threshold T_d that mini-

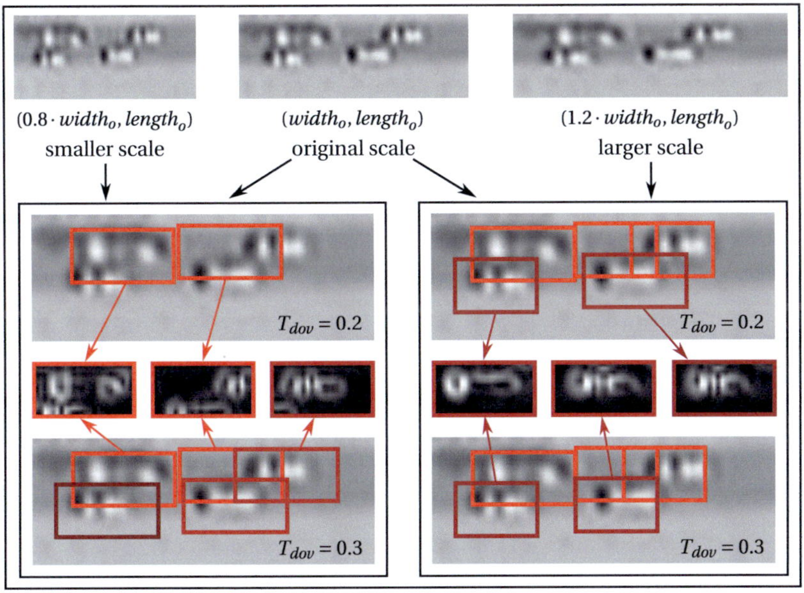

Figure 5.25: Influence of a weakly discriminative classifier model, image rescaling, and overlap threshold T_{dov} to the performance of the sliding window approach.

mizes the number of FPs and FNs while still being able to provide generality and transferability.

Only few descriptors are promising to model the appearance of small vehicles in top view. Color features cannot be used as color is not available in the considered UAV videos. Part based models such as DPM or ISM are not expected to perform well due to the small object size in the image. As seen in Fig. 5.24, no specific inner texture can be assumed for vehicles. Thus, the focus lies on contour and shape features. The following descriptors are taken from the literature for evaluation:

- MOMENTS [Teu13b]: This descriptor is a feature mix consisting of Hu moments, central moments, and Haralick features. The idea is to represent the object blob shape in the motion ROI by a few sophisticated features in a low dimensional feature space. The dimension of the descriptor is 178.

- Discrete Cosine Transform (DCT) [Eke05]: Since the environmental conditions, object motion, and shadows cause blurred edges that affect the object appearance, a local DCT based descriptor is applied to handle these effects. DCT is calculated in 8 × 8 pixel blocks and only the first 21 DCT coefficients are kept. Higher DCT coefficients represent high frequencies in the image that are assumed to be the result of image noise. The block stride is 4 pixels in order to have overlapping blocks. The final descriptor is set up by concatenation of the DCT coefficients of each block. The descriptor size is 441.

- Histogram of Oriented Gradients (HOG) [Dal05]: HOG is one of the most common descriptors to represent object shape and widely used in combination with an SVM classifier for object detection. In this thesis, HOGs are calculated in overlapping blocks of 8 × 8 pixels in size, with 4 pixels block stride, and 9 histogram bins per block. The descriptor dimension is 756.

- Integral Channel Features (ChnFtrs) [Dol09]: ChnFtrs describe object shape and have become very common features for object detection in recent years [Dol10, Ben12, Ben13, Dol14]. This is mainly due to easy implementation, short processing time, and good optimization opportunities. Gradient magnitudes are calculated and subdivided in several gradient orientation images (channels). As shown in Fig. 5.26 (a), seven channels are chosen here. While channel 0 contains all magnitudes, the other six channels contain only the magnitudes of specific gradient orientations. Local sums are calculated in randomly picked rectangular regions across all seven channels and concatenated to set up the descriptor. These local sums are called first-order features [Dol09] and visualized by green boxes in Fig. 5.26. Haar-like features are a subset of ChnFtrs and called second-order features. In this thesis, however, better results are achieved by using only first-order features. Usually, an AdaBoost classifier is chosen for both feature selection and classification. The first four features selected by the classifier are depicted in Fig. 5.26 (b). The vehicle's lateral areas seem to provide useful information for separation of objects and non-objects. The decision values for the sliding window examples in Fig. 5.22, 5.23, and 5.25 are calculated with ChnFtrs and AdaBoost classifier. The descriptor consists of 2,000 features.

- Multi-LBP [Hen12]: Multi-LBP is the only evaluated texture descriptor. LBP are calculated in four different kinds of quantization. 8×8 pixels are chosen for block size and 8 for block stride. Thus, blocks are non-overlapping as proposed by Heng et al. [Hen12]. Blocks of smaller size cause strong locality of the features leading to worse generality. In the original paper, the combination of Multi-LBP together with boosting achieves very good results for the low resolution Daimler-Chrysler VIS pedestrian classification dataset [Mun06]. The descriptor size is 8,192.

Besides the evaluation of established classifiers such as SVM, AdaBoost, and Random Forest, the modified version of a Random Naïve Bayes (RNB) classifier [Pri07] is analyzed. Originally, it was developed for person detection in ground-level long wave infrared (LWIR) video data where it outperformed the mentioned classifiers [Teu14b]. The motivation is to achieve high generality across different datasets and to be robust against slight appearance variations such as blurry edges or object shadow. If these issues are ignored, one consequence can be that not all features may still fit to the learned model. This can lead to poorer classification performance if the feature space is considered as a whole, which is the case for SVMs. Decision trees as used by classification meta-algorithms such as boosting [Fre97] or bagging [Bre01] provide better generality since features are considered separately. However, non-optimal depth values can lead to overfitting or underfitting, feature selection and splitting values may be biased, and there is oversensitivity to the training set, to irrelevant attributes, and to noise [Qui92].

The Naïve Bayes (NB) classifier can provide good classification performance and generality across different datasets even when the assumption of conditional independence of the used features is obviously violated by a wide margin [Dom97]. Actually, it can even be an advantage that NB considers features independently: even if few features do not fit to the model at all, the classifier decision may still be correct since these features will cause low

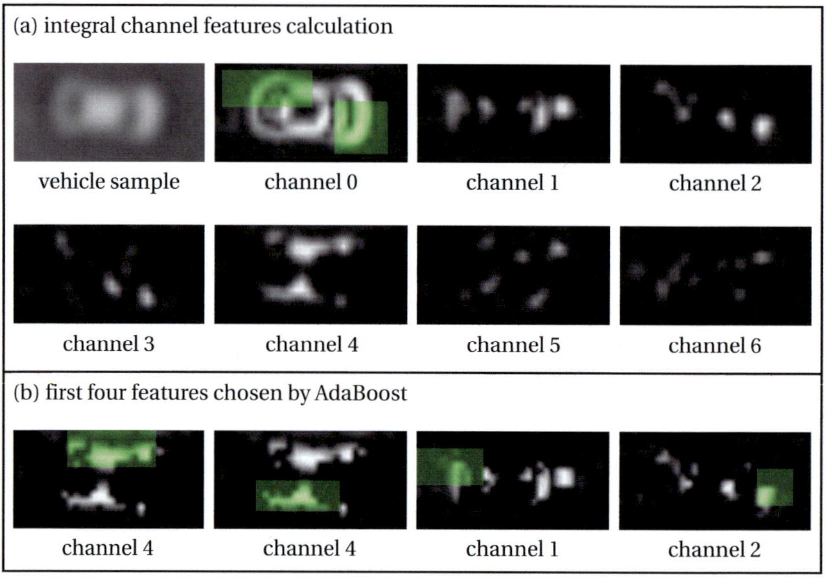

Figure 5.26: Calculation of Integral Channel Features (ChnFtrs) and the first four selected features by AdaBoost classifier.

likelihoods for both object and non-object and, thus, do not significantly affect the classification decision. Instead, the classifier will focus more on the features fitting to its model. Note that this happens on-line.

The NB classification decision is given by

$$\text{class}_{\text{NB}}(\mathbf{f}) = \arg\max_i \{P(c_i) \cdot \prod_{j=1}^{n} P(f_j \mid c_i)\}, \tag{5.23}$$

where $\mathbf{f} = (f_1, \ldots, f_n)^T$ is the feature vector, $P(c_i)$ is the prior probability for class c_i with $i \in \{0,1\}$ and $P(f_j \mid c_i)$ is the likelihood for feature f_j with $j \in \{1, \ldots, n\}$ given class c_i. The product $\prod$ of these likelihoods is based on the naïve assumption that the features f_j of a descriptor are conditionally independent. Many different likelihood models can be used depending on the distribution of the training samples for each feature. Since standard distributions such as Gaussian or Log-Gaussian do not fit well to the distributions of many of the evaluated features, best results are achieved by using normalized, smoothed class-conditional histograms $h_j^{(c_i)}$ as likelihood model for each feature f_j. Another promising option is to use multivariate Gaussians instead of histograms.

In order to weaken the violated assumption of conditional independence of the features, Independent Component Analysis (ICA) [Hyv01] can be applied to the feature vector prior to classification. Since the unsupervised training of ICA can lead to poorer class separability when using the transformed feature vectors, Bressan and Vitria [Bre02] propose to use Class-Conditional Independent Component Analysis (CC-ICA). This idea is adopted here leading to the formalization

$$\text{class}_{\text{NB}}(\mathbf{W}_i\mathbf{f}) = \underset{i}{\arg\max}\{P(c_i) \cdot \prod_{j=1}^{n} h_j^{(c_i)}(f_j^{(\mathbf{W}_i)})\}, \tag{5.24}$$

where $\mathbf{W}_i$ is the class-conditional unmixing matrix and $f_j^{(\mathbf{W}_i)}$ denotes the feature f_j transformed by $\mathbf{W}_i$. FastICA [Hyv01] is chosen to calculate $\mathbf{W}_i$.

When it comes to the idea of using NB as weak classifier for classification meta-algorithms, the classification performance compared to one single NB is not improved significantly by AdaBoost [Tin03] but by approaches similar to RF [Pri07, God10]. Thus, a RF framework is used with few adoptions from boosting as seen in Algorithm 2. For training of each weak classifier, standard RNB or RF meta-algorithms use random selection of features, bootstrap aggregation for selection of training samples, and majority voting for the final decision [Bre01]. The Out-Of-Bag (OOB) set of not selected training samples for each weak classifier can be used to reject the current classifier if it is too weak. These techniques are adopted here and further extended: CC-ICA is trained for each bootstrap and applied to each weak classifier. The overall decision is calculated by the sum of weighted posteriors instead of majority voting. The weight w_k for each classifer NB_k is calculated similarly to AdaBoost but by using the OOB set only instead of the entire training data. While majority voting would cause a discrete decision function, the posteriors P_k induce a continuous decision function.

Algorithm 2 Modified Random Naïve Bayes classifier

for $k = 1$ to K **do**
  Generate bootstrap $\mathcal{B}$ from training set $\mathcal{T}$
  Choose F features randomly
  Calculate $\mathbf{W}_i^{(k)}$ with CC-ICA using $\mathcal{B}$
  Train weak classifier NB_k using $\mathcal{B}$ after CC-ICA
  Calculate error e_k with OOB set $\mathcal{T} \setminus \mathcal{B}$
  Set classifier weight $w_k = \frac{1}{2} \cdot \ln \frac{(1-e_k)}{e_k}$
  if $e_k > T_a$ **then**
    Reject classifier NB_k
    $k = k - 1$
  end if
end for
return $\arg\max_i \{\sum_{k=1}^{K} w_k \cdot P_k(c_i \mid \mathbf{W}_i^{(k)} \mathbf{f})\}$

A typical parameter setup is $K = 1000$ weak classifiers, $F = 10$ features per weak classifier, $T_a = 0.6$ as acceptance threshold (see Algorithm 2), and $P(c_i) = 0.5$ for $i \in \{0,1\}$ as prior probability.

Several other descriptors, classifiers, and feature space reduction methods such as Sequential Forward Selection (SFS), PCA, Linear Discriminant Analysis (LDA), and ICA were evaluated with different kinds of data [Sau10, Teu10, Teu11d, Teu11c, Teu11b, Teu13b] but did not perform promising enough to be considered in this thesis.

5.5 Outlier and Duplicate Removal

Duplicate and outlier detections cause FPs that can decrease the performance of object detection and segmentation severely. Although duplicates and outliers represent different problems, they both occur due to the extension of the motion clusters before object detection and segmentation is applied. Motion clusters have to be extended, however, in order to handle split detections. In the following sections, effective methods are presented to remove duplicate and outlier detections.

5.5.1 Rejection of Duplicate Detections

Duplicate detections are defined as multiple detections for one object that cannot be associated to any other object. They emerge from detections in adjacent motion clusters which overlap with each other after they have been extended. As seen in Fig. 5.27, motion cluster extension is important to handle split detections. As the large vehicle does not have any inner structure, moving corners are detected and tracked only at the front and the rear. Thus, two separate motion clusters appear causing a split detection. Since object detection and segmentation is applied to each extended motion cluster individually, the vehicle in this overlap area is detected twice. After the detections of each motion cluster are collected and added to the detections of the entire image, duplicate detections are recognized as bounding boxes with similar orientation and strong overlap. Different removal strategies are used for object segmentation and object detection.

- Duplicate removal for *object segmentation* is implemented by fusing all detections sufficiently overlapping each other into one single detection. The bounding box of this fused detection is the union of all duplicates' bounding boxes. The reason for choosing this approach is the following: assumed that a moving object is not fully inside the overlap area of two motion clusters, there can be one correct and one partial detection for this object. There is no applicable criterion to robustly suppress the partial detection and keep the correct one. Hence, fusion by bounding box union is an appropriate removal method although it can facilitate merged detections.

- Duplicate removal for *object detection* is done by NMS. Partial detections do usually not occur in the object detection approach presented in Section 5.4.3 since the sliding window size is fixed. However, if they do occur, the decision value is expected to be lower than the one for the correct detection. Due to its robustness against merged detections, suppression of duplicates is more effective compared to fusion for object detection.

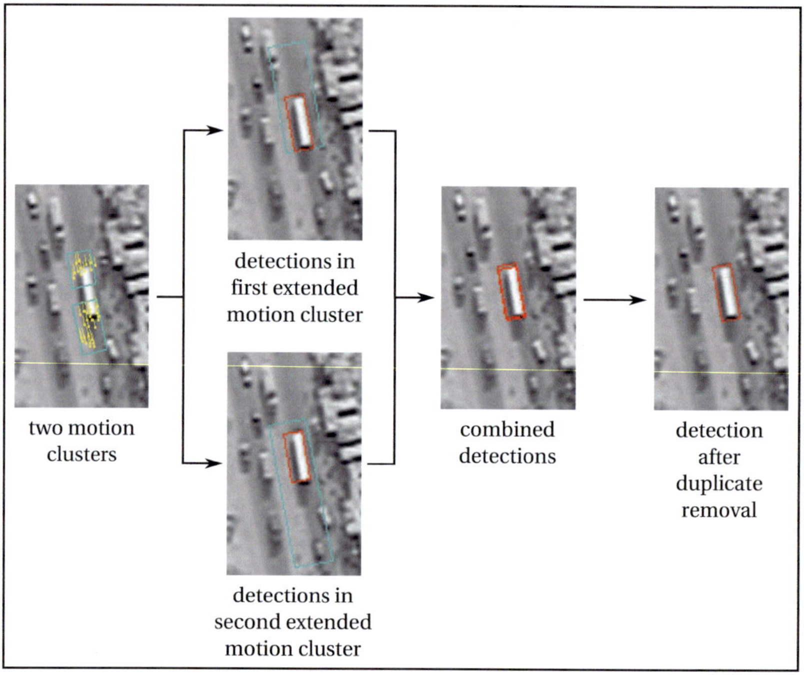

Figure 5.27: Example for emergence and removal of duplicate detections.

5.5.2 Rejection of Outlier Detections

Outliers are detections at image regions where no independent motion was detected. Emergence and rejection of outlier detections is visualized in Fig. 5.28. The motion cluster is extended in order to search for objects. In addition to moving objects, both object detection and segmentation can detect stationary objects such as parked vehicles at the roadside. Since this thesis focuses on moving objects only, detections at stationary objects are undesired and considered FPs. To eliminate them, the number of motion vectors inside the detection bounding box is checked. A detection is accepted, if minimum threshold T_{out} is exceeded. $T_{out} = 4$ is a usual value.

In Fig. 5.28 two out of the four objects detected by the local sliding window approach are obviously stationary since there are no motion vectors inside the detection bounding boxes. So, they are removed from the final detection result. On the other hand, gradient based object segmentation merges two nearby objects due to their prominent gradients and, hence, detects only three objects. While one FP detection at a parked car can be rejected using the motion vectors, the merged detection cannot be resolved. It is not counted as FP but the detection precision, which is the overlap of the GT and the detection bounding box, is decreased. However, image stacking can be used to handle such situations. As object detection implicitly segments objects due to the fixed size of the search window, it is expected that rejection of outlier detections is more effective for object detection, while object segmentation benefits from both image stacking and outlier removal.

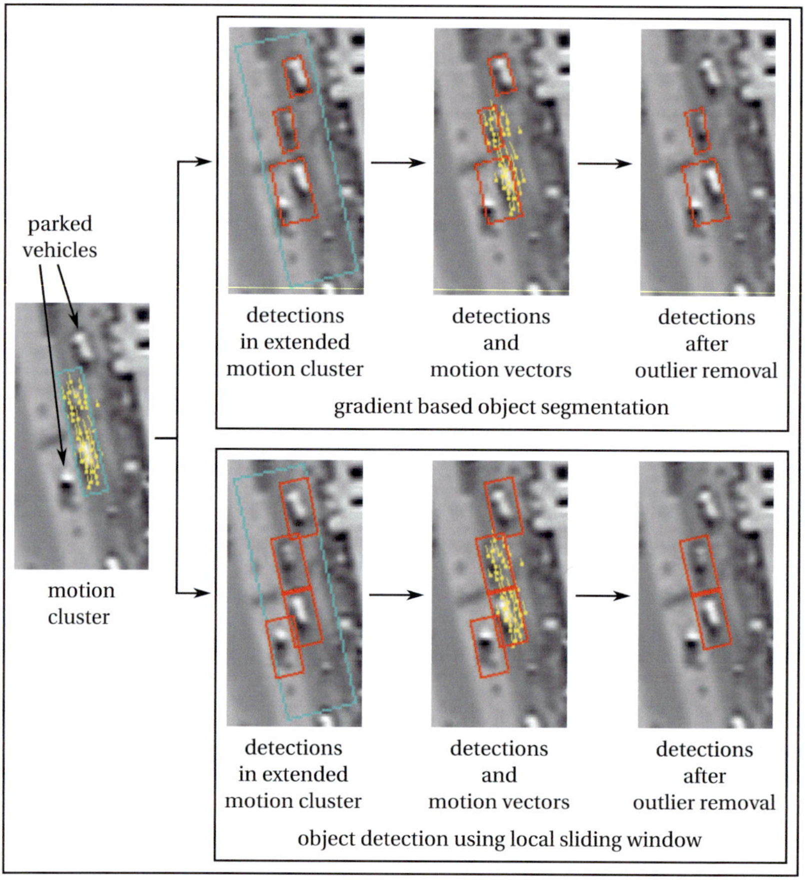

Figure 5.28: Example for emergence and removal of outlier detections. In this case, the outliers are coming from vehicles parked at the roadside.

6

Multiple Object Tracking

Multiple object tracking is a large field of research in radar signal processing [Bar88, Bla99] and computer vision [Yil06, Sme13]. In the context of this thesis, however, this topic is only briefly discussed. The intention is to demonstrate that (1) the performance of object detection and segmentation can be further improved by considering temporal information, and that (2) multiple object tracking can be implemented and processed efficiently when object detection is assumed to achieve a high detection rate with only few FPs and FNs. In contrast to existing TBD [Cao11a, Luo12, Sia12b] or DBT [Per06b, Rei10a, Sal13] methods, the fusion of detections and motion vectors is proposed here in order to handle split and merge situations both effectively and efficiently. This is the main contribution of the presented tracking approach. Actually, the benefit of multiple object tracking is lower when it is applied to the motion clusters directly since especially detections merged over several consecutive frames cannot be handled at all. The four object tracking components as presented in Section 2.4 are chosen as follows:

1. Object representation: since all object detection and segmentation approaches discussed in this thesis provide bounding boxes as detection results, bounding boxes are used as object representation.

2. Tracking features: position, size, orientation, and motion of the detections are chosen as tracking features.

3. Object detection: objects are detected and segmented with the methods presented in Chapter 5.

4. Object tracking algorithm: point tracking is applied using the Kalman filter. Therefore, the tracking features are organized as a vector that is one point in the tracking feature space.

The remainder of this chapter is based on two of the author's publications [Teu11a, Teu12a].

6.1 Concept

The concept of multiple object tracking in the context of the processing chain is visualized in Fig. 6.1. Main input is the detections provided by the object detection and segmentation module. They are associated to existing tracks or used to initialize new tracks. Motion vectors are associated to tracks, too, in order to support split and merge handling. Track management is responsible for the initialization and deletion of tracks. The Kalman filter is chosen as tracking algorithm and applied for track prediction and update using the existing tracks, the associated detections, and the camera motion. As the result, the multiple object tracking module outputs updated tracks.

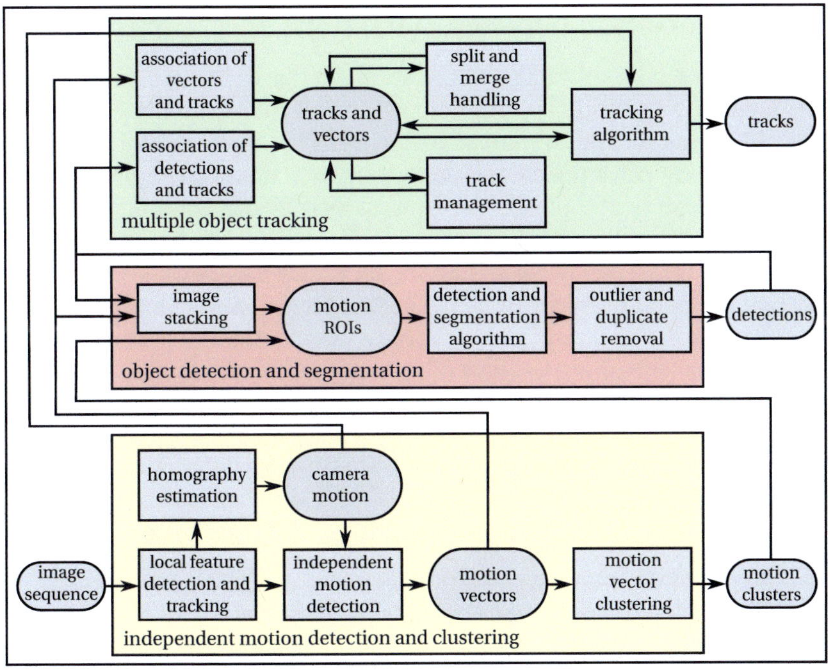

Figure 6.1: Concept of multiple object tracking.

6.2 The Association Problem

The association problem is probably the most important problem that has to be solved in multiple object tracking. Detections have to be associated to existing tracks in order to update and confirm the tracks. This is difficult in scenes with many tracks since there can be ambiguous associations and incorrect associations can lead to track fragmentation or even track loss. Complex association methods such as graph matching or MHT [Mag11] are not considered here since (1) objects are represented in a simple way by bounding boxes, (2) the number of objects tracked simultaneously is limited to about 30 in this thesis, and (3) processing time is limited.

6.2.1 Association between Detections and Tracks

The fundament for multiple object tracking in this thesis is the association of detections and tracks. Both detections and tracks are represented by bounding boxes. The overlap of these boxes based on the IoU criterion can be used to solve the association problem in an efficient way [Sia12a]. An association is accepted if the overlap area of the bounding boxes of detection and predicted track exceeds the minimum threshold[1] T_{tov}. Since large overlap is expected due to the high frame rate, a usual value is $T_{tov} = 0.5$. Acceptance and rejection can be represented by an overlap matrix $\mathbf{M}_{tov}$ for fast detection of split, merged, or missed associations. For m detections and n tracks with detection bounding boxes D_i for $i \in \{1,\dots,m\}$ and track bounding boxes T_j for $j \in \{1,\dots,n\}$, the overlap matrix is defined by

$$\mathbf{M}_{tov} = (m_{ij}), \quad \text{with } m_{ij} = \begin{cases} 1, & \text{if } \frac{|D_i \cap T_j|}{|D_i \cup T_j|} \geq T_{tov} \\ 0, & \text{else.} \end{cases} \tag{6.1}$$

This representation is also called *validation matrix* [Cha84] and can be interpreted as a kind of *validation gating* [Bar75]. Examples for initialization and interpretation of $\mathbf{M}_{tov}$ are given in Fig. 6.2. Bounding boxes of detections are depicted in red color, while tracks are visualized by green boxes. The first case shows an unambiguous association as each detection is associated to exactly one track. This is the desired case. In the second example, a merged detection occurs and is associated to both tracks. This critical case is detected in matrix $\mathbf{M}_{tov}$ since two 1s appear in one column. Analogously, there would be two 1s in one row in case of a split detection. Such situations are resolved by split and merge handling. A missed detection is visualized in the third example and recognized by one row in $\mathbf{M}_{tov}$ with only 0s. Furthermore, only 0s in one column represent a detection with no associated track. Missing detections or tracks are handled by track management.

Instead of bounding box overlap, the calculation of distance measures such as Euclidian distance or Mahalanobis distance is a common method in order to apply validation gating [Mag11].

1 The abbreviation *tov* stands for track overlap.

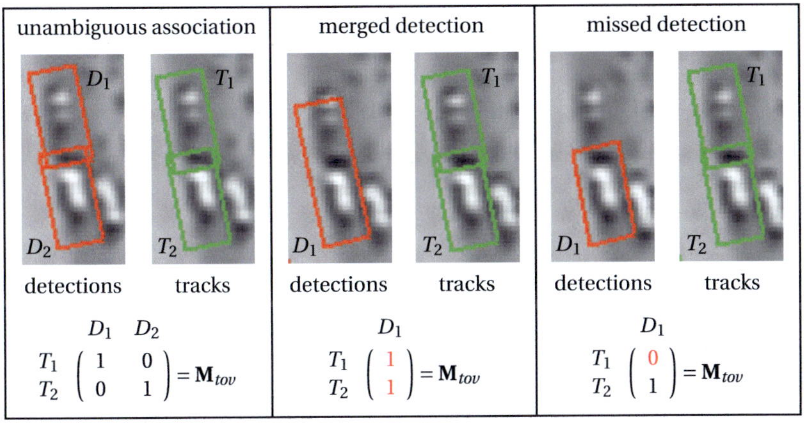

Figure 6.2: Association of detections and tracks using overlap matrix $\mathbf{M}_{tov}$.

6.2.2 Association between Motion Vectors and Tracks

As detections are the fundament for multiple object tracking, the association of motion vectors to tracks is optional. The idea is to use them as support for split and merge handling [Gri10]. Four criteria have to be fulfilled in order to associate a motion vector to a track:

1. The motion vector is not associated to another track.
2. The motion vector is located inside the bounding box of the predicted track.
3. The motion vector is not located inside the bounding box of another predicted track (overlap area). In this way, ambiguous associations are avoided.
4. The motion vector and the track have similar motion direction and velocity.

An example for motion vector association is given in Fig. 6.3. Motion vectors are depicted by yellow and green dots, detections by red bounding boxes,

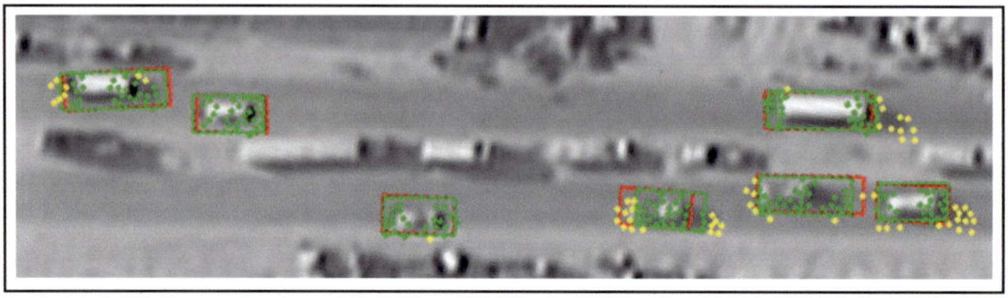

Figure 6.3: Association of motion vectors (dots) to tracks (green bounding boxes). Green dots represent associated motion vectors, while unassociated motion vectors are visualized in yellow color.

and tracks by green boxes. For the sake of clarity, motion vectors are visualized by dots instead of vectors. Green motion vectors are associated to the tracks in which they are located, while yellow vectors are unassociated.

For each associated motion vector, the related track's identifier (ID) as well as the position of the motion vector relative to the track's bounding box are stored. This information is needed for split and merge handling. Each track can list up to 20 associated motion vectors. Outlier vectors with respect to the related track's position or motion are removed from this list.

6.3 Split and Merge Handling

Splitting and merging in the context of multiple object tracking describe the situation when two detections associated to one track and one detection associated to two tracks, respectively. Without any further knowledge, the best fitting association would be accepted, while the unassociated detection is ignored and the unassociated track is kept alive by track prediction using motion information from previous time steps. In this section, however, the associated motion vectors are used to guide tracks through situations of split, merged, or missed detections. The basic assumption in order to make this approach work is that object detection and segmentation provide good detection performance with a high rate of correct detections and only few FPs and FNs. Then, short periods of split, merged, or missed detections

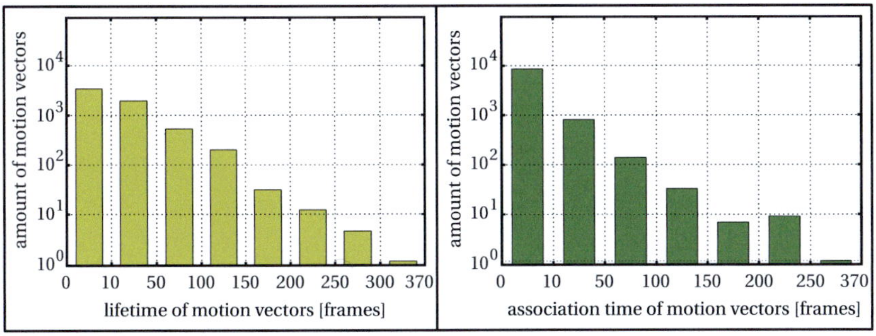

Figure 6.4: Lifetime (yellow color) and association time (green color) of 5,401 motion vectors in a sequence of 370 frames (see Fig. 6.3) visualized by histograms.

can be bridged by using detections reconstructed by the associated motion vectors. Hence, the average times of successful tracking (lifetime) and successful association (association time) of motion vectors have to be longer than potential detection gaps of about 3–10 consecutive frames.

5,401 motion vectors detected and tracked in a video sequence of 370 frames as seen in Fig. 6.3 are analyzed for their lifetime and association time in Fig. 6.4. The first bin of each of the two histograms contains the number of motion vectors with a lifetime (yellow color) or association time (green color) of 10 frames or less, the second bin represents a time period of 11 to 50 frames, and so on. For better visualization, the vertical axis scale is logarithmic. There are 221 features with a lifetime of at least 100 frames and the average lifetime of each motion vector is about 21.46 frames. Furthermore, 44 motion vectors were associated to a track for at least 100 frames. There are 20 object tracks in this sequence with a lifetime of at least 100 frames. Each of these long tracks has 15.57 associated motion vectors and 2.3 new and removed associations per frame on average. In summary, it can be said that associated motion vectors are applicable to handle split and merge situations.

With the recognition of a split, merged, or missing detection using matrix M_{tov}, it is assumed that detections in the current time step are not reliable. Inspired by Feature-Based Probabilistic Data Association (FBPDA) [Gri09],

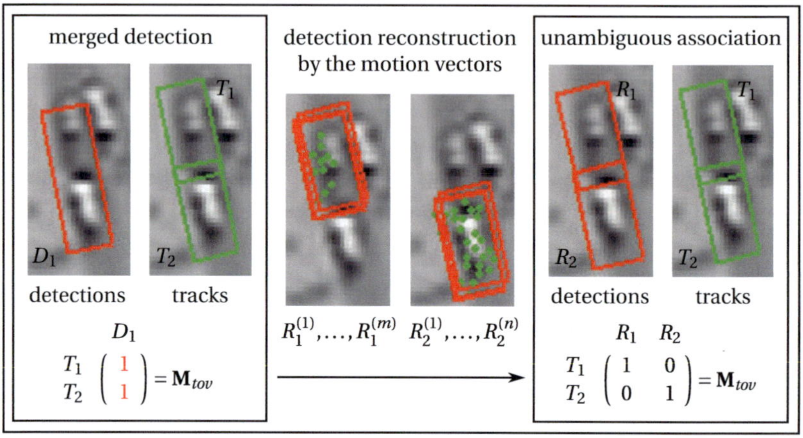

Figure 6.5: Example for reconstuction of detections R_1 and R_2 for a merged detection D_1 by using associated motion vectors (green dots).

the track's bounding box can be reconstructed, since for each associated motion vector both the relative position inside the track's bounding box and the size and the orientation of the box are available. This process is visualized for merged detection D_1 in Fig. 6.5. The sets of boxes $R_1^{(i)}$ with $i \in \{1,\ldots,m\}$ and $R_2^{(j)}$ with $j \in \{1,\ldots,n\}$ reconstructed by the associated motion vectors are used to generate new bounding boxes R_1 and R_2 by calculating the median position, size, and orientation of all $R_1^{(i)}$ and $R_2^{(j)}$, respectively. R_1 and R_2 are then considered as detections in the current time step. In contrast to simple track prediction based on previous motion information it is possible to consider changes in motion direction and velocity during split and merge situations. However, reconstruction of detections is limited to 10 consecutive frames in order to delete and reinitialize tracks that were initialized by split or merged detections. If there are no motion vectors available for an occluded object or a track involved in a split or merge situation, simple track prediction is applied. The effectiveness of this approach compared to split and merge handling without motion vectors is demonstrated in Section 7.3.6.

6.4 Track Management

Tracks are initialized and deleted by the track management. Since motion vectors can originate from parallax effects or outliers of the compensation for camera motion, they are not considered for track initialization or deletion. Instead, tracks can exist only if there are associated detections. Different thresholds for track lifetime are applied to verify whether a track is (1) still new and, thus, not reliable, (2) existing long enough to be considered as reliable, or (3) missing long enough to be deleted.

Multiple object tracking as presented here does not provide any approach for identification and reinitialization of previously lost track. In particular, this means that tracks of objects, which are stopping at an intersection or due to traffic jam, get lost. Methods for persistent tracking can be introduced to address this problem [Pel12, Pro14].

6.5 Tracking Algorithm

The bounding box parameters for object position (x,y), size (w,l), and orientation α are chosen for tracking. As the moving objects are tracked directly in the image, all parameters are considered in reference to the image coordinate system. This leads to the state vector $\mathbf{s} = (x, y, w, l, \alpha)$. Both camera and object motion are assumed to be linear and affected by Gaussian noise. In this case, the Kalman filter is an optimal state estimator with respect to the minimum mean square error on the state estimate [Mag11]. Its implementation is easy and the processing time is faster compared to other approaches such as particle filter. Thus, the Kalman filter is chosen as filter for point tracking of state vector $\mathbf{s}$.

The process of multiple object tracking is visualized as a flowchart in Fig. 6.6. Motion vectors and detections are given as input in each time step. The prediction step of the Kalman filter is applied to each existing track in order to determine a new state vector for the current time step based on information of the previous time step only. Subsequently, the detections are associated to the predicted tracks as described in Section 6.2.1. If there was no association possible for a detection, this detection is used to initialize a new track. Now all available motion vectors are associated to the

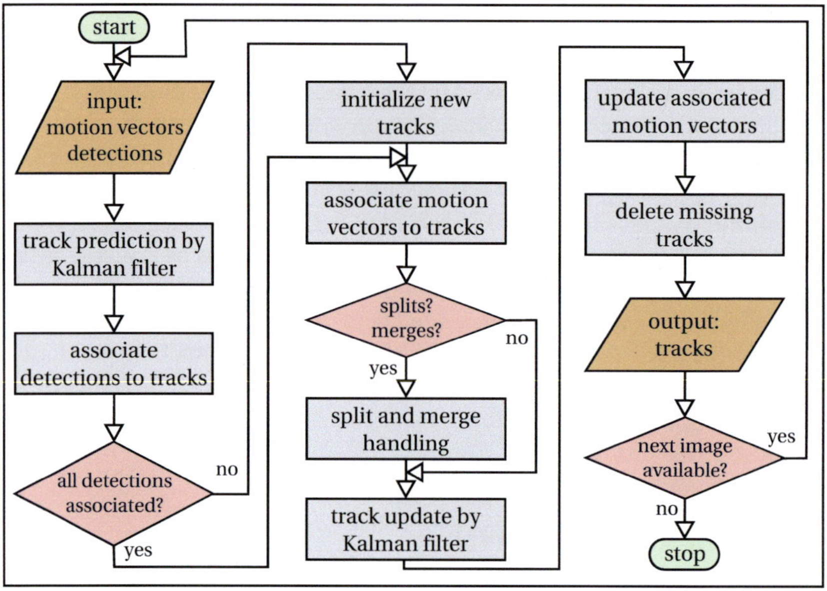

Figure 6.6: Flowchart of the multiple object tracking algorithm.

tracks either by using their ID for already associated vectors or by checking the four criteria introduced in Section 6.2.2. If split or merge situations occur according to the overlap matrix $\mathbf{M}_{tov}$, the involved detections are reconstructed by the motion vectors as presented in Section 6.3. Then, the update step of Kalman filtering improves the predicted tracks with the new information of the current time step given by the associated detections. Associated motion vectors are updated for their new relative position inside the associated track's bounding box. Tracks without any associated detection for a certain period of time are deleted. The final result of the multiple object tracking module is a set of updated and confirmed tracks.

7

Evaluation of the Proposed Methods

In this chapter, the approaches introduced in Chapters 4, 5, and 6, are evaluated individually and in the context of the entire processing chain. Existing algorithms taken from the literature are compared to the proposed methods in a qualitative and quantitative evaluation. In Section 7.1, the applied evaluation measures and methods are described. An introduction to the datasets is given in Section 7.2. Since each approach is dependent on several parameters, a systematic parameter optimization is employed and discussed in Section 7.3. The processing chain is evaluated module by module in Section 7.4. This is necessary to demonstrate the impact of each module on the overall performance. An evaluation and comparison of the processing times is provided in Section 7.5 and, finally, a summary is given in Section 7.6.

7.1 Evaluation Measures and Methods

In the literature, a large variety of different evaluation measures and methods exists to evaluate object detection and tracking [Mar02, Per06a, Ber08, Kas09, Jap11, Mil13, Sme13]. In this thesis, some of the most common ones

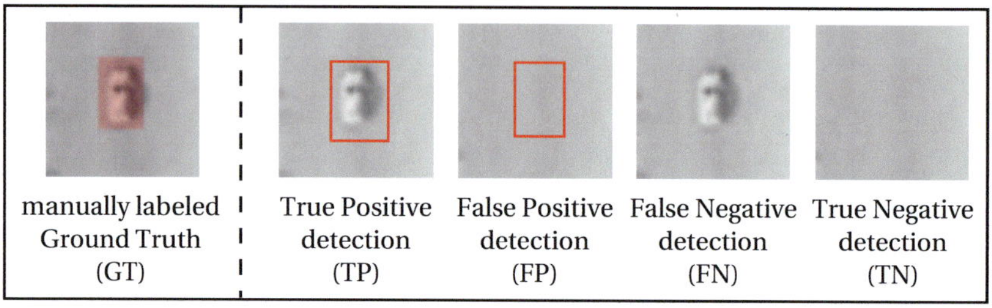

Figure 7.1: Visualization of ground truth as well as true positive, false positive, false negative, and true negative detections.

are employed to analyze the performance of the algorithms proposed in this thesis. In Fig. 7.1, the definition of *correct* and *incorrect* detection of an object is visualized. Usually, algorithms are compared against GT. In order to evaluate a moving object detection algorithm, all moving objects in a scene have to be labeled. Labeling is done manually or (semi-)automatically [Kim13] by tagging each object with a point or a bounding box. Bounding boxes are used in this thesis. Each object automatically detected by the algorithm is tagged analogously and bounding boxes coming from GT and detection algorithm are compared. A *True Positive (TP)* detection is a bounding box coming from the detection algorithm at the position of a GT object. This is a correct detection. There are two options for incorrect detections: FP, if no object is visible inside the algorithm's bounding box, and FN, if an object is visible but not detected. For some evaluations, *True Negative (TN)* detections are considered: no object is present and thus no object is detected. The aim of object detection algorithm development is to maximize the number of TP detections while minimizing the number of FP and FN detection at the same time.

7.1.1 Evaluation Measures for Object Detection

Since objects are represented by bounding boxes, the overlap of detection and GT bounding box based on the IoU criterion is an important measure to determine TPs, FPs, and FNs. For a given overlap threshold T_{ov}, detection D is TP, if

$$OV := \frac{|D_i \bigcap G_i|}{|D_i \bigcup G_i|} \geq T_{ov}, \tag{7.1}$$

where D_i and G_i is the i-th mapped pair of detection and GT. According to the PASCAL criterion [Eve10], Smeulders et al. [Sme13] propose to use $T_{ov} = 0.5$. For larger objects in an image covering several thousands of pixels, this is a suitable threshold. However, for small objects covering only 50–200 pixels even small deviations in size or position of the detection bounding box from the GT bounding box can induce a significantly lower overlap. These deviations can be caused by split, merged, and partial detections or object shadow. In order to demonstrate the impact of the overlap threshold T_{ov} to the performance evaluation, T_{ov} is varied between the values 0.1 and 0.3 in this chapter.

In addition to Fig. 7.1, the distribution of TPs, FPs, and FNs is demonstrated for different detections in Fig. 7.2. For this example, T_{ov} is set to 0.2. GT is visualized by filled red rectangles and OV represents the maximum overlap of detection and GT bounding box. The upper row shows examples for imprecise object detection due to the object shadow (2–6). While precise detection usually has an overlap of at least 0.7 (2), the merged detection of object and shadow immediately reduces the overlap to 0.5 or even 0.3 (3–4). Separate detections for object and shadow cause a FP (5) and the detection of the shadow only generates one FP and one FN due to the small overlap of detection and GT (6). In the lower row, the approach of counting TPs, FPs, and FNs for merged and split detections is depicted (8–12). Both vehicles are detected correctly even if the bounding boxes partially overlap each other (8). A missed vehicle causes a FN (9). In case of a merged detection (10), each GT object can have only one associated detection. The GT bounding box is associated to the detection with larger overlap while the other detection becomes a FN. Even a detection between two objects (11) can produce a TP if OV $\geq T_{ov}$. Finally, an example for split detection is shown (12). Since both detections have an overlap smaller than T_{ov}, two FPs and two FNs occur.

With this knowledge about TPs, TNs, FPs, and FNs, further evaluation measures can be defined. Most of these measures evaluate the detection

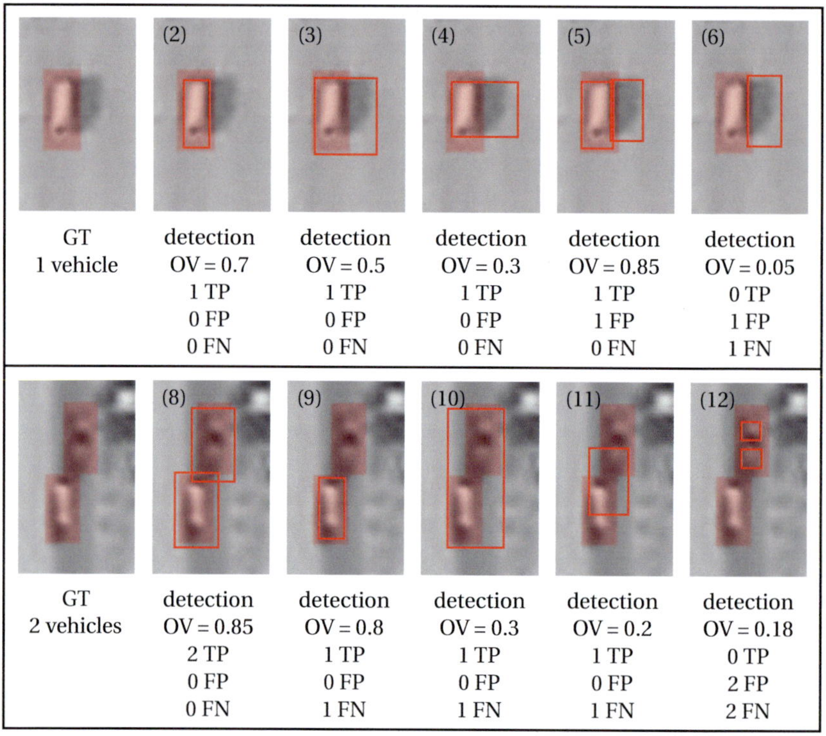

Figure 7.2: How to determine TPs, FPs, and FNs for the evaluation of object detection. In these examples, the overlap threshold is $T_{ov} = 0.2$.

accuracy which is the ratio between the correct detections and the detection errors. The True Positive Rate (TPR)

$$TPR := \frac{|TP|}{|TP| + |FN|} \tag{7.2}$$

and the False Positive Rate (FPR)

$$FPR := \frac{|FP|}{|FP| + |TN|} \tag{7.3}$$

can be used to evaluate the performance of a classifier, for example. Usually, a set of positive and negative samples is classified and with a fixed threshold for the classifier decision value, the TPR and the FPR can be calculated. The range of value is between 0 and 1 for both measures. By varying this threshold, many different pairs of values appear for TPR and FPR. They can be arranged in a Receiver Operating Characteristic (ROC) curve [Faw06, Jap11] where the TPR is plotted on the vertical and the FPR on the horizontal axis. Perfect classification is represented by the point $(0, 1)$ and a ROC curve getting close to this point indicates a well performing classifier. The Area Under the Curve (AUC) can be used as a compact representation of a ROC curve. It should be mentioned, that the number of TNs is known here since training and test set cover positive *and* negative samples.

In more realistic experiments, there is usually no knowledge about TNs. An object detector using a sliding window cannot produce TNs but aims at having a higher classifier decision value if the wanted object class is present and a low decision value otherwise. The most common measures to evaluate the performance of such an object detector are

$$precision := \frac{|TP|}{|TP| + |FP|} \tag{7.4}$$

and

$$recall := \frac{|TP|}{|TP| + |FN|}. \tag{7.5}$$

TPR and recall are identical. The

$$f\text{-}score := \frac{2 \cdot |TP|}{2 \cdot |TP| + |FP| + |FN|} \tag{7.6}$$

is the harmonic mean of precision and recall. In the literature, it is also known as f measure [Jap11]. The range of the value is between 0 and 1 for all three measures. Depending on the application, it can be more important to avoid either FPs or FNs. In such cases, either precision or recall is maximized. Maximizing the f-score achieves a good balance of both.

In addition to the detection accuracy, the CLEAR metrics [Ber08] also consider the *precision* of a detection system in a separate score [Kas09]. The accuracy aspect answers the question, whether an object was detected or not. Actually, all presented measures up to now consider the accuracy aspect only. This is the same for the Normalized Multiple Object Detection Accuracy (N-MODA) that is defined by

$$N\text{-}MODA := 1 - \frac{c_m(|FN|) + c_f(|FP|)}{|TP| + |FN|}, \tag{7.7}$$

where c_m and c_f are cost functions to individually weight FNs and FPs depending on the application. In this thesis, $c_m(x) = c_f(x) = x$ is used as value for the weighting functions. While MODA is originally defined for single frames, N-MODA is normalized to the entire sequence.

In contrast, the precision aspect evaluates the overlap of detection and GT bounding boxes. The Normalized Multiple Object Detection Precision (N-MODP) calculates the mean overlap of all TP detections over the entire sequence by

$$N\text{-}MODP := 1 - \frac{\sum_{i=1}^{|TP|} \frac{|D_i \cap G_i|}{|D_i \cup G_i|}}{|TP|} \tag{7.8}$$

where $i \in \{1, \ldots, |TP|\}$ denotes all mapped pairs of TP detection D_i and GT G_i.

There are several other evaluation measures for object detection [Mar02, Kas09], but only ROC curves, AUC, precision, recall, f-score, N-MODA, and N-MODP will be used for the experiments in this chapter.

7.1.2 Evaluation Measures for Object Tracking

Multiple object tracking adds temporal context to detections. Typical tracking mistakes such as ID switches or track interrupts need to be also included in the global evaluation measure along with the detection precision and accuracy. An extension of the CLEAR metrics for object tracking is given by the Multiple Object Tracking Accuracy (MOTA) and the Multiple Object Tracking Precision (MOTP). MOTA is defined by

$$MOTA := 1 - \frac{c_m(|FN|) + c_f(|FP|) + c_s(|ID|)}{|TP| + |FN|}, \tag{7.9}$$

where $|ID|$ is the number of ID switches in the sequence and c_s is the weighting function for ID switches. While Kasturi et al. [Kas09] propose to use $c_s(x) = \log_{10}(x)$, Bernardin and Stiefelhagen [Ber08] suggest $c_s(x) = x$. In this thesis, $c_s(x) = x$ is used as otherwise ID switches are hardly penalized compared to FPs and FNs. MOTP is calculated in a very similar way as N-MODP:

$$MOTP := 1 - \frac{\sum_{i=1}^{|TP|} \frac{|D_i \cap G_i|}{|D_i \cup G_i|}}{|TP|} \tag{7.10}$$

The only difference is that GT tracks and automatically acquired tracks are compared instead of detections. However, if a track candidate is considered to be a confirmed track starting from the first associated detection, then one has *N-MODP* = *MOTP*.

Further metrics used in this thesis are trajectory based measures [Wu06]. They are applied to evaluate tracking performance on entire trajectories instead of counting mistakes frame by frame [Mil13]. An object is considered to be mostly tracked (MT), if at least 80 % of its GT trajectory is found. It is mostly lost (MLT)[1], if is tracked correctly in less than 20 % of its presence. In all other cases, it is denoted as partially tracked (PT). Finally, each time a track's state changes from *tracked* to *not tracked*, the number of track fragmentations (FMs) is incremented to count how often the track is lost.

The presented measures are used to evaluate the performance of the multiple object tracking in Section 7.4. Further measures are described and discussed by Kasturi et al. [Kas09] and by Milan et al. [Mil13].

1 In the original paper [Li09b], the abbreviation ML is introduced for *mostly lost*. Since ML can be mistaken for machine learning or maximum likelihood, mostly lost is abbreviated by MLT in this thesis.

7.2 Datasets

Three videos are evaluated in the experiments as shown in Fig. 7.3. Two sequences, SEQ 1 and SEQ 2, coming from Luna UAV in top view and sequence EgTest01 of the VIVID dataset [Col05] in top and slight oblique view. Further sequences of the VIVID dataset are not used as the camera view is different compared to the Luna UAV videos and there is a large number of frame drops severely affecting independent motion detection. Since the Luna UAV videos do not provide color information, the EgTest01 sequence is converted to gray-values. The GT was generated manually by tagging all moving objects with bounding boxes. There are moving trucks, cars, motorcycles, bicycles, and persons appearing in the scenes. Furthermore, tracks of moving objects were annotated manually as well. In order to compare object segmentation and object detection approaches, only cars and trucks are considered for the evaluation. They are denoted by vehicles in the remainder of this section. The reason is that object segmentation focuses on edges only and can detect all kinds of moving objects, while object detection methods learn an appearance model of one specific object class and thus cannot detect objects of other classes. Vehicles for example have a different appearance compared to motorcycles and persons. It is possible to train separate object detectors for persons or motorcycles in addition to the vehicle detector, but since there is only little information available about the appearance of motorcycles and persons as seen in Fig. 2.4 and 3.2, object detection is prone to produce FPs. This would distort the evaluation. Instead, GT objects have been annotated for being either vehicle or non-vehicle. Any detection of a moving non-vehicle will not be included in the evaluation process. In this way, the detection of non-vehicles is not unintentionally penalized but simply ignored.

In SEQ 1, a busy urban street is shown. The sequence consists of 401 single images with a frame rate of 25 Hz. There are between 5 to 20 moving objects per image. With a GSD of about 0.345 m/pixel, a standard car covers an area of approximately 8×15 pixels in the image. In total, 4,785 moving objects in 42 tracks are labeled as GT of which 4,731 in 40 tracks are vehicles. Among the main challenges of this sequence are many vehicles closely driving one behind the other or overtaking each other.

SEQ 2 comprises 201 single images with a frame rate of 25 Hz and shows another busy urban street. The GSD is about 0.284 m/pixel and a normal car covers 10 × 20 pixels. There are many persons and motorcycles in this scene, so out of the 2,662 moving objects in 39 tracks only 1,373 GT objects in 18 tracks are vehicles. Partial occlusions by trees next to the street, large object shadows, and a large variance in different vehicle appearances represent some of the challenges of this scene.

The video EgTest01 is taken from the VIVID dataset and consists of 1,821 single images with a frame rate of 30 Hz. A runway is shown with six vehicles turning and driving one behind the other at low velocity. In total, there are 6,866 moving objects in 6 tracks. A standard vehicle covers about 20 × 40 pixels. So, the video is downscaled from 640 × 480 to 320 × 240 pixels in order to keep the object size stable compared to the Luna UAV sequences. This scenario is actually irrelevant for urban surveillance due to the low velocity and the runway environment without any buildings or trees. However, it is the only dataset which is publicly available and has been evaluated in the literature [Ers12, Sia12b, She13a]. In the original GT, only one object is labeled in order to perform single object tracking. So, the GT was extended manually to all six vehicles. In this scene, the GT bounding boxes are not rotated in the direction of object's motion but remain parallel to the image boundaries.

An overview of the most important statistics of the three sequences is given in Table 7.1.

Table 7.1: Statistics of the aerial video datasets.

video	frames	frame rate	ground truth			
			moving objects	object tracks	moving vehicles	vehicle tracks
SEQ 1	401	25 Hz	4,785	42	4,731	40
SEQ 2	201	25 Hz	2,662	39	1,373	18
EgTest01	1,821	30 Hz	6,866	6	6,866	6

For object detection using local sliding window, classifier models have to be trained before they can be applied. Therefore, negative samples of non-vehicles and positive samples of vehicles are necessary. The vehicles in four wide area aerial images are manually labeled in order to generate four training and test datasets. While the training data are used to train the classifier models, the classifier performance is evaluated with the test data. Each vehicle sample is cut out, rotated in horizontal position, and scaled to 16×32 pixels. Negative samples are generated in the same way at random positions in the background where no vehicles are visible. The four resulting datasets are denoted by VEH-01, VEH-02, VEH-03, and VEH-04 and some samples are depicted in Fig. 7.4 and 7.5. While the wide area aerial images considered for VEH-01 and VEH-02 were acquired by the same camera, different cameras were used for VEH-03 and VEH-04. The cameras used to capture the three videos SEQ 1, SEQ 2, and EgTest01 are different, too, but the camera angle is similar compared to the wide area aerial images. By using data that comes from different cameras at slightly different camera angles, generality and transferability of the trained classifier models is evaluated implicitly. Each classifier can be trained on one dataset and evaluated with the other three. In Table 7.2, the numbers of training and test samples for each image are presented. A similar amount of positive and negative samples is extracted for training in order to avoid biased learning or overfitting but a much larger set of negative samples is used for evaluation.

Table 7.2: Statistics of the wide area aerial images used for classifier training and evaluation.

image	training samples		test samples	
	non-vehicle	vehicle	non-vehicle	vehicle
VEH-01	780	790	20,000	790
VEH-02	680	664	20,000	664
VEH-03	–	–	20,000	1,301
VEH-04	–	–	20,000	679

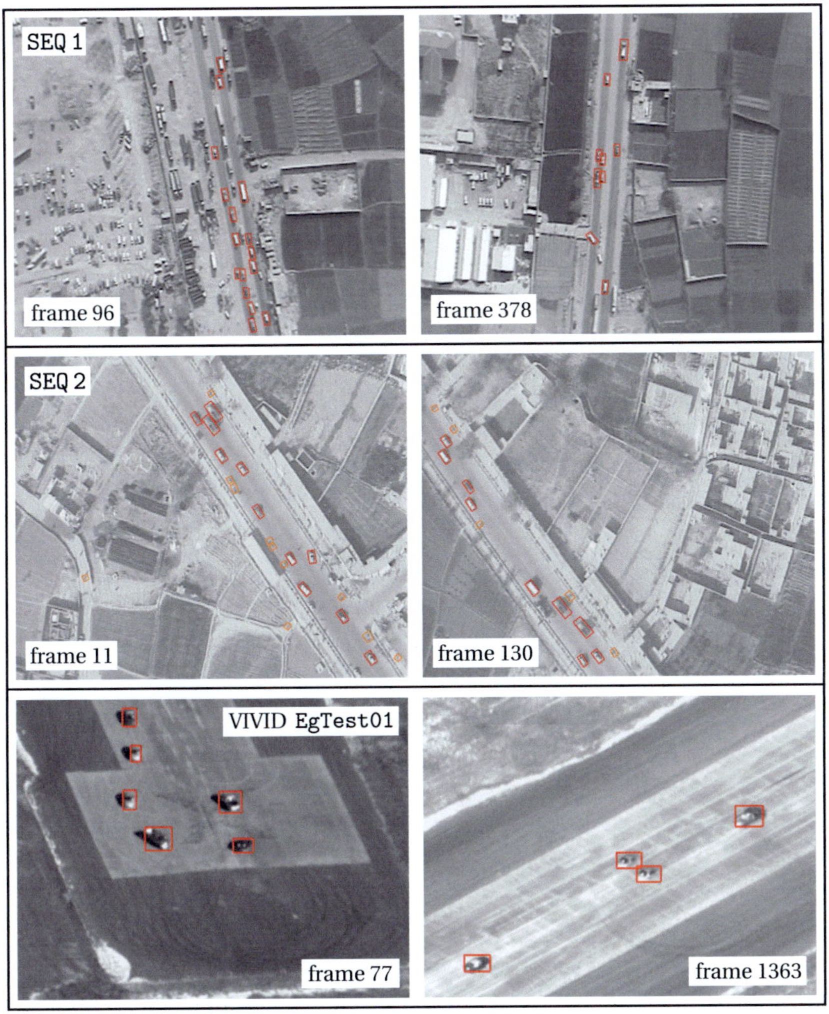

Figure 7.3: Aerial videos used for the experiments. GT objects are represented by bounding boxes. While the red color stands for vehicles, orange color indicates motorcycles, bicycles, or persons. The upper two sequences are coming from Luna UAV and the lower one from the VIVID dataset [Col05].

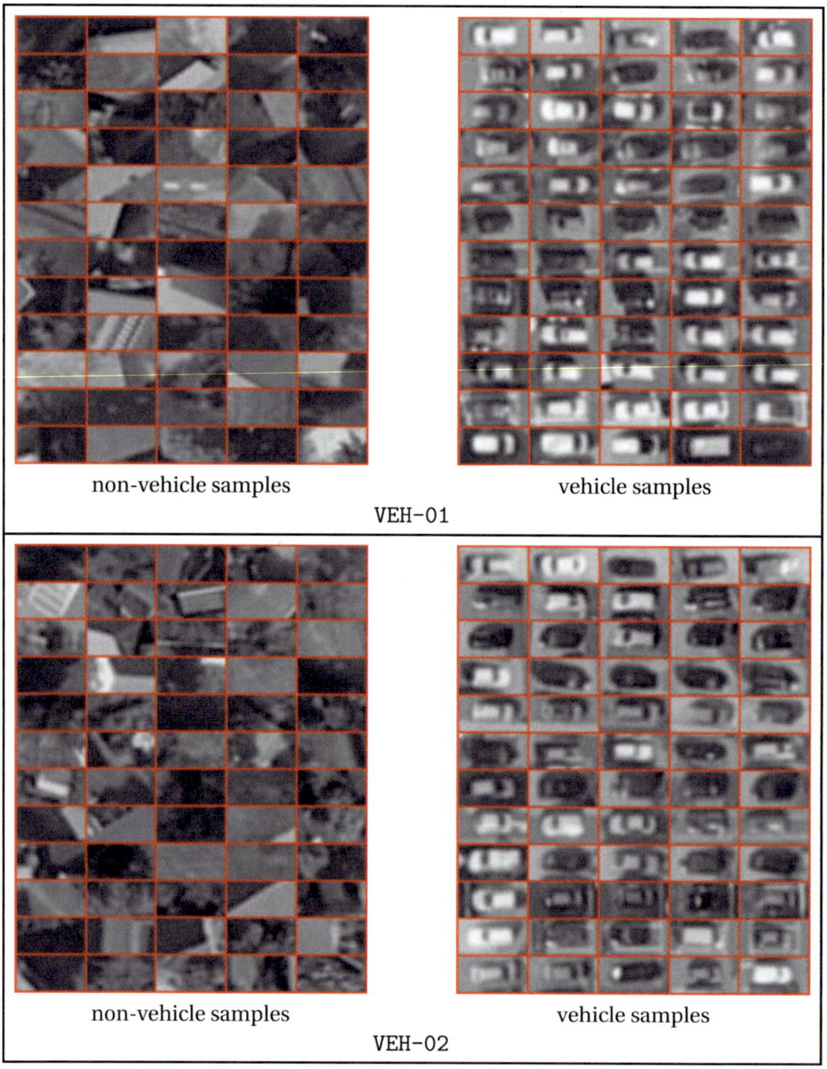

Figure 7.4: Samples of non-vehicles and vehicles are extracted from different wide area aerial images and used for classifier training and evaluation.

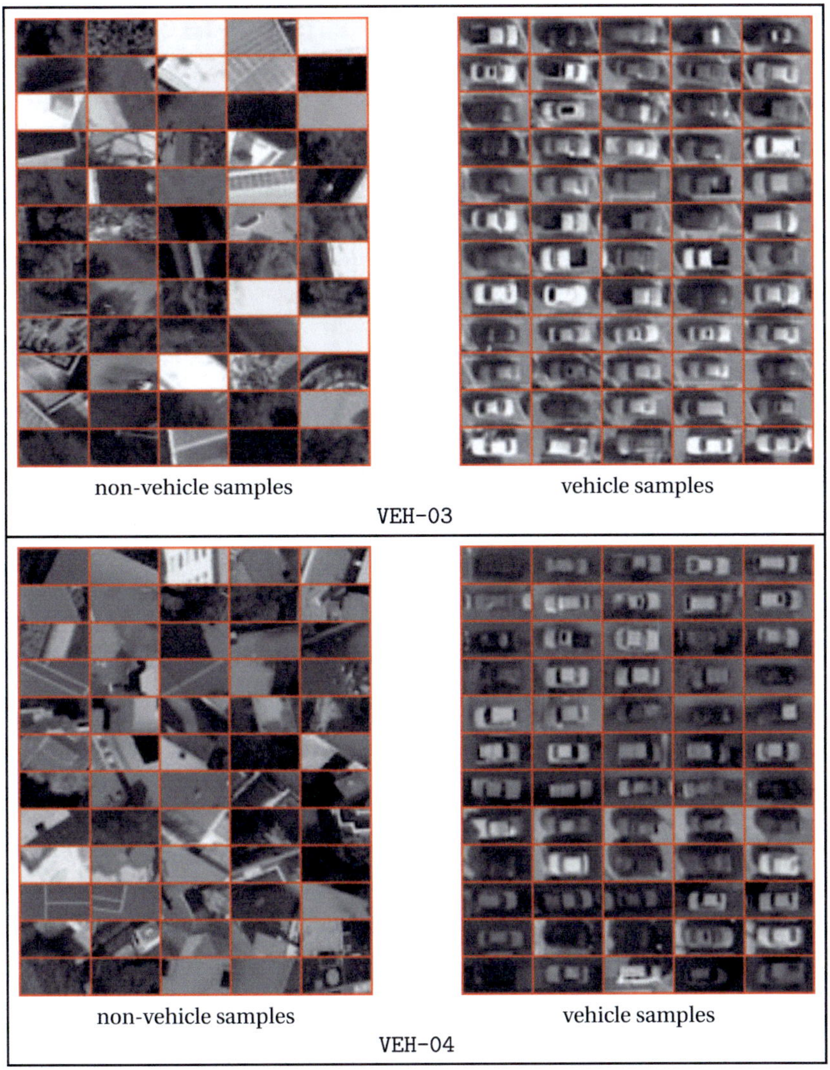

Figure 7.5: Samples of non-vehicles and vehicles are extracted from different wide area aerial images and used for classifier training and evaluation.

7.3 Parameter Estimation and Optimization

The performance of the algorithms presented in this thesis is influenced by few parameters. These parameters can be either continuous such as thresholds or the size of a considered ROI, or discrete such as the choice of a specific subroutine. The aim of this section is to determine parameter values that are maximizing the performance of the presented approaches. SEQ 1 is used for optimization and the determined values are applied in further experiments with all sequences in Section 7.4. Parameters are optimized in the context of the entire processing chain but presented here for each module individually. Maximization of the f-score for SEQ 1 is chosen as optimization criterion.

7.3.1 Gradient Based Object Segmentation

For this experiment, all modules of the processing chain are active except for *image stacking* and *multiple object tracking*. Two parameters are chosen for optimization: the choice of the approach for gradient calculation and the adaptive threshold T_q for quantile based thresholding of gradient magnitudes. These two parameters are expected to have the highest impact to the performance of this method. Four different methods to calculate gradients were introduced in Section 5.4.1: the novel LBP gradient, gradient calculation without noise suppression, Canny gradient, and morphological gradient. T_q is used to determine the gradient magnitudes accepted as edge pixels as seen in Fig. 5.16. For example, the 15 % largest gradient magnitudes are accepted for $q = 0.15$. The higher the value of quantile q, the more pixels are accepted.

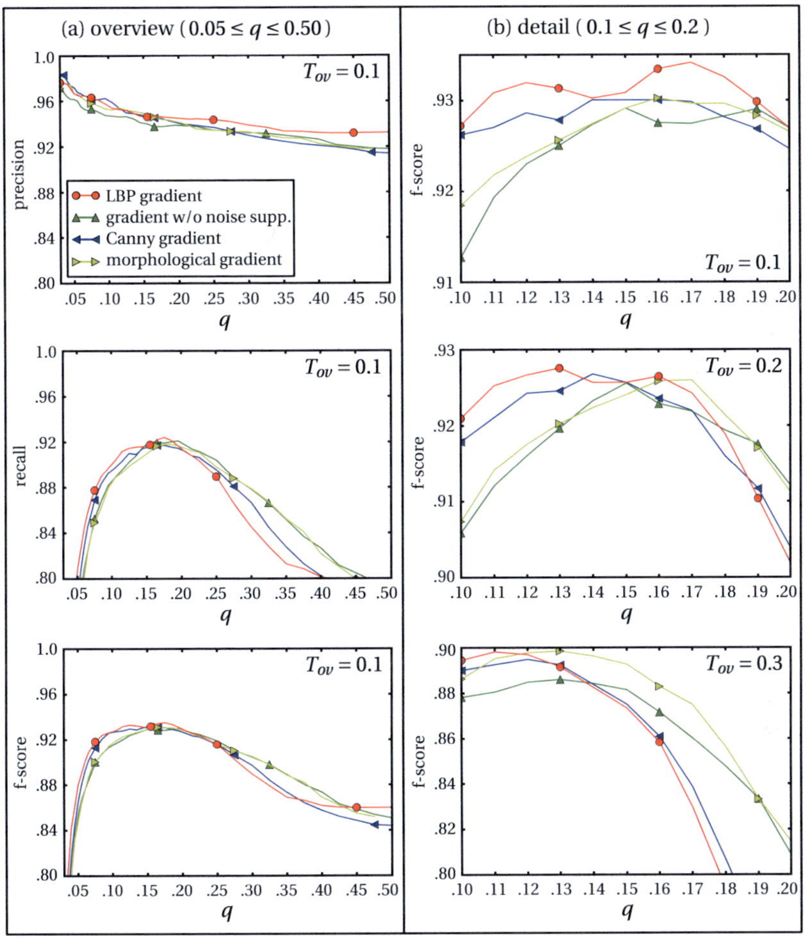

Figure 7.6: Parameter optimization for gradient based object segmentation.

In Fig. 7.6, the optimization results are visualized. Fig. 7.6 (a) gives an overview for a large parameter range of $0.05 \leq q \leq 0.5$. Precision, recall, and f-score are depicted for all five gradient calculation methods and fixed overlap threshold $T_{ov} = 0.1$. The decreasing precision shows that more and more FP detections appear with increasing q. This is expected as T_q decreases and more edge pixels are accepted. By contrast, recall has a clear maximum in the range $0.15 \le q \le 0.2$. FN detections occur for low q since only few edge pixels are accepted. The number of FNs decreases until the maximum is reached and increases again for $q > 0.2$. This happens because with decreasing T_q more and more merged detections appear which leads to more FNs. The best f-score is reached for the range $0.1 \le q \le 0.2$ and LBP gradient seems to be the best performing method. In order to confirm this assumption, a detailed visualization of this range is given in Fig. 7.6 (b). The three diagrams show the f-score for different overlap thresholds $T_{ov} \in \{0.1, 0.2, 0.3\}$. By averaging the performance of each method over the three values of T_{ov}, a more general and robust value for q can be determined. An example is given for the LBP gradient: for $T_{ov} = 0.1$, there are two maxima at $q = 0.12$ and $q = 0.17$. Although the maximum at 0.17 is higher, the mean f-score over all three values of T_{ov} is 0.918 for $q = 0.12$ and 0.895 for $q = 0.17$. The f-score difference of 0.023 may look small but it actually represents a difference of 25 FPs and FNs in the entire sequence `SEQ 1`.

With the optimized values for q, all four approaches for gradient calculation are compared with respect to the evaluation measures presented in Section 7.1.1. This comparison is done for each of the three videos and visualized in Table 7.3. The best performance for each evaluation measure is highlighted in red color. The most important measures f-score, N-MODA, and N-MODP are additionally underlined. In each sequence, the LBP gradient approach achieves the best results in both accuracy and precision although the performance difference is small compared to the other approaches and may not be statistically significant. Nevertheless, for further experiments in this section, LBP gradient with $q = 0.12$ is chosen for gradient based object segmentation. The f-score shows that sequence `EgTest01` is well processed with only 181 mistakes but 6,811 correct detections. `SEQ 1` and `SEQ 2` are more challenging as they represent realistic urban traffic scenarios. N-MODP is significantly lower for all approaches in `EgTest01` as the GT bounding boxes are not oriented in motion direction and, thus, less overlap between detection and GT is achieved.

Table 7.3: Comparison of the gradient calculation approaches for each of the three videos after parameter optimization.

video	evaluation measure	LBP gradient ($q = 0.12$)	gradient w/o noise supp. ($q = 0.15$)	Canny gradient ($q = 0.14$)	morph. gradient ($q = 0.16$)
SEQ 1	TP	4,322	4,349	4,322	4,332
	FP	223	282	242	252
	FN	409	382	409	421
	precision	0.953	0.939	0.947	0.945
	recall	0.914	0.919	0.914	0.916
	f-score	0.932	0.929	0.930	0.930
	N-MODA	0.866	0.859	0.862	0.862
	N-MODP	0.621	0.606	0.594	0.598
SEQ 2	TP	1,265	1,259	1,252	1,248
	FP	190	197	178	188
	FN	108	114	121	125
	precision	0.869	0.865	0.876	0.869
	recall	0.921	0.917	0.912	0.909
	f-score	0.895	0.890	0.893	0.889
	N-MODA	0.783	0.773	0.781	0.772
	N-MODP	0.573	0.552	0.544	0.540
EgTest01	TP	6,811	6,807	6,804	6,802
	FP	126	139	112	118
	FN	55	59	62	64
	precision	0.982	0.980	0.983	0.983
	recall	0.992	0.991	0.991	0.991
	f-score	0.987	0.986	0.987	0.987
	N-MODA	0.974	0.971	0.974	0.973
	N-MODP	0.515	0.493	0.483	0.491

7.3.2 Object Segmentation using Relative Connectivity

The processing chain modules *image stacking* and *multiple object tracking* are deactivated for this experiment, too. Three parameters are optimized: threshold T_{rc} for determining start and end points as well as the two hysteresis thresholds T_u and T_l. T_{rc} is an adaptive threshold using the gray-value mean μ and standard deviation σ of the considered image by $T_{rc} = \mu + a \cdot \sigma$. Actually, the parameter a is optimized in order to find a good weighting factor of the standard deviation. In hysteresis thresholding, the upper threshold T_u is usually given as a multiple of the lower threshold T_l by $T_u = b \cdot T_l$. In the follow-up, b and T_l are optimized jointly.

In Fig. 7.7, the optimization result is visualized. Figure 7.7 (a) shows the f-score for parameter a with fixed hysteresis thresholds $T_l = 50$ and $b = 2.5$. Reasonable performance is achieved even for $a = 0.0$ since μ is already a good initialization value for T_{rc}. The maximum, however, is reached between $1.0 \leq a \leq 1.5$ and a is set to 1.2. In Fig. 7.7 (b), the joint optimization of T_l and b is depicted. T_l is plotted against the f-score for five different values of b. The best f-score is achieved for $T_l = 40$ and $b = 2.0$.

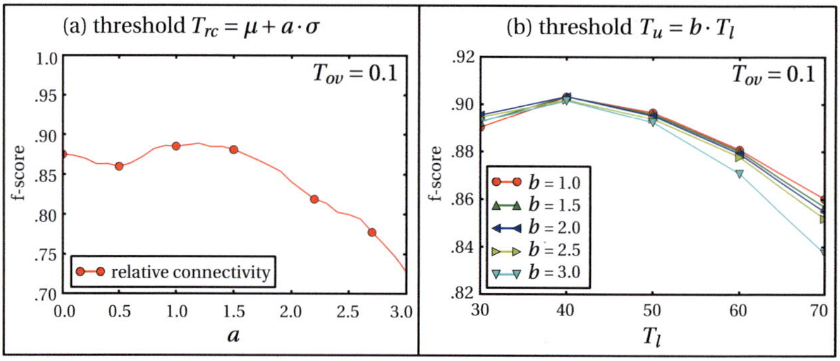

Figure 7.7: Parameter optimization for object segmentation using relative connectivity.

7.3.3 Object Detection using Local Sliding Window

Again, the processing chain modules *image stacking* and *multiple object tracking* are deactivated in this subsection. In the first experiment, the most promising descriptor/classifier combinations are determined. Therefore, the five descriptors presented in Section 5.4.3 are applied in combination with different classifiers and evaluated for their AUC values. Six classifiers are used for the evaluation: (1) SVM with RBF kernel and 3-fold cross validation, (2) Gentle AdaBoost with 1,000 decision trees of depth 2, (3) RF with 1,000 decision trees, and the proposed RNB classifier (4) without ICA, (5) with ICA, and (6) with CC-ICA. Classifier training is fully supervised using the classification evaluation datasets `VEH-01`, `VEH-02`, `VEH-03`, and `VEH-04`. For each classifier, two separate models are trained with `VEH-01` and `VEH-02`, and evaluated with the remaining three datasets. So, for each combination of descriptor and classifier there are six test cases with one ROC curve as result per test case. In order to achieve a compact representation of the results, AUC mean and standard deviation are calculated as seen in Table 7.4. Performance differences can be significant even in the fourth decimal place of the AUC values. This is demonstrated by using the *two-matched-samples* t-test [Jap11] that is a method to prove the statistical significance of the performance difference of two competing classifiers. Hill and Lewicki [Hil07] provide a detailed description of the t-test. The parameters of the t-test are chosen so that the null hypothesis, which indicates that the results of two classifiers are coming from the same distribution and, thus, the performance difference is not statistically significant, can be rejected with a probability of at least 0.95.

In Table 7.4, the t-test is applied to the AUC means of each row, which means constant classifier and variable descriptor, and each column, which means constant descriptor and variable classifier. For most t-tests, the descriptors MOMENTS and DCT are outperformed significantly by HOG, ChnFtrs, and Multi-LBP nearly independent of the classifier. Thus, MOMENTS and DCT are not considered for further experiments anymore. For the remaining three descriptors, the AUC means of CC-ICA + RNB are consistently higher compared to RNB, ICA + RNB, and RF. These performance differences are statistically significant for HOG and ChnFtrs descriptor. This shows that the proposed CC-ICA + RNB classifier is able to outperform other bagging based approaches in terms of AUC. Furthermore, the results confirm the conclusions of Bressan and Vitria [Bre02], Fan and Poh [Fan07], and Teutsch et al. [Teu14b] that CC-ICA can improve NB classifier performance.

Table 7.4: Comparison of AUC mean and standard deviation for 5 descriptors and 6 classifiers. Two models were trained for each classifier with `VEH-01` and `VEH-02`, and evaluated with the other three classification datasets. The highest AUC value for each descriptor is highlighted in red color.

classifier	descriptor				
	MOMENTS	DCT	HOG	ChnFtrs	Multi-LBP
SVM	0.9878 ±0.0109	0.9369 ±0.0574	0.9993 ±0.0004	0.9908 ±0.0041	0.9981 ±0.0014
AdaBoost	0.9795 ±0.0198	0.9841 ±0.0171	0.9991 ±0.0004	0.9967 ±0.0033	0.9983 ±0.0014
RF	0.9490 ±0.0483	0.9552 ±0.0480	0.9983 ±0.0004	0.9858 ±0.0136	0.9960 ±0.0034
RNB	0.9456 ±0.0496	0.9468 ±0.0595	0.9991 ±0.0003	0.9805 ±0.0195	0.9971 ±0.0008
ICA + RNB	0.9699 ±0.0304	0.9405 ±0.0653	0.9991 ±0.0003	0.9698 ±0.0311	0.9970 ±0.0008
CC-ICA + RNB	0.9745 ±0.0263	0.9347 ±0.0753	0.9993 ±0.0002	0.9897 ±0.0109	0.9973 ±0.0012

In the second experiment, the sliding window thresholds T_d and T_{dov} are optimized jointly using precision-recall-curves. Each classifier has a different decision function and a comparison between classifiers is difficult as range and scale of the decision values usually do not fit. Variation of the decision threshold T_d and plotting the resulting values for precision and recall to common graphs as seen in Fig. 7.8 is a way to overcome this problem. The first five graphs show five different promising combinations of descriptors and classifiers. For each combination, best performance is achieved for sliding window overlap threshold $T_{dov} = 0.1$. In the sixth graph, the five combinations of descriptors and classifiers are compared to each other. ChnFtrs clearly outperform the other descriptors and further combinations such as HOG + RNB or Multi-LBP + SVM did not affect this result. RF and RNB achieve similar results but AdaBoost achieves by far the best values for precision and recall.

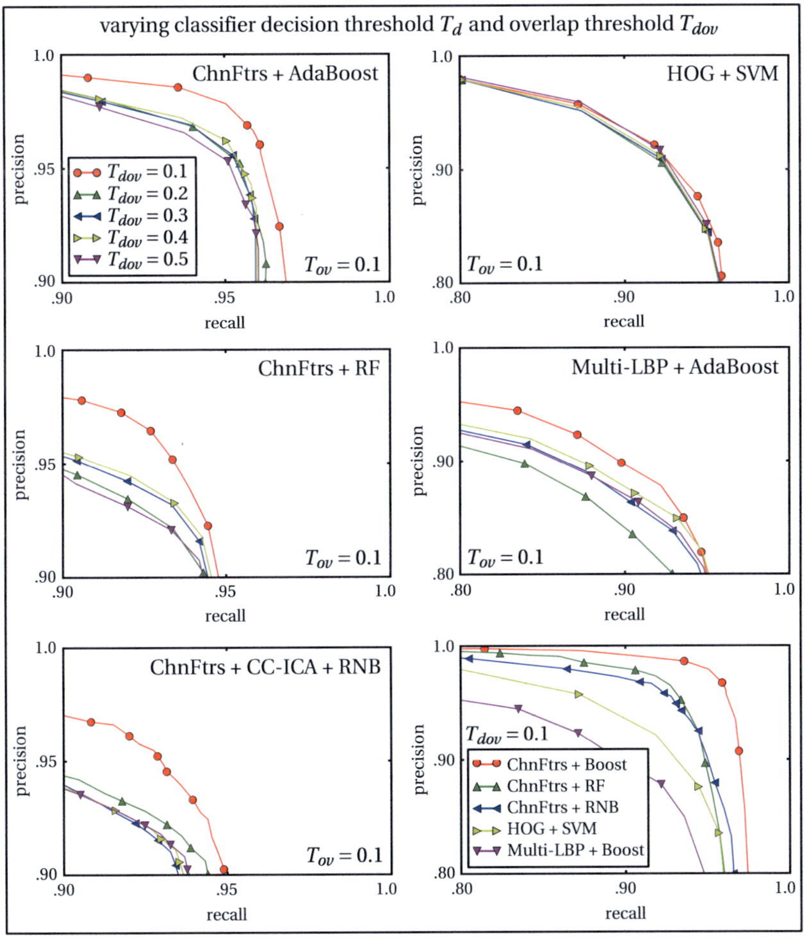

Figure 7.8: Parameter optimization for local sliding window.

It is particularly noticeable that the descriptors HOG, ChnFtrs, and Multi-LBP achieve similar performance in Table 7.4, but obviously different performance in Fig. 7.8, where ChnFtrs clearly outperform HOG and Multi-LBP. There are two explanations: (1) According to Benenson et al. [Ben12], the automatic feature selection of AdaBoost contributes the most compared to hand designed descriptors such as HOG and Multi-LBP: while all HOG and Multi-LBP blocks are located at fixed positions with fixed size and uniformly distributed weights, the AdaBoost classifier chooses features with largest discriminative power without such limitations. These features can be located between blocks and do not have fixed size. (2) Large AUC values only prove the existence of a decision threshold T_d that provides good class separability for each individual test dataset. However, in order to achieve good object detection performance, it is important that the intra-class variance is minimized while the inter-class variance is maximized at the same time. Then, a value for T_d can be determined that provides good generality and transferability. Some examples for decision functions of different descriptor/classifier combinations are visualized in Fig. 7.9. While HOG and Multi-LBP generate ambiguous local decision value maxima indicating a lower discriminative power than ChnFtrs, the margin of CC-ICA + RNB is much smaller compared to AdaBoost and RF. The performance difference between AdaBoost and RF can be a result of the different feature selection strategies: greedy feature selection for AdaBoost and random feature selection for RF.

In the third and final experiment, the impact of the amount of different image scales on object detection is analyzed. As already mentioned in Section 5.4.3, the classifier model for vehicles in top view does not have high discriminative power and, thus, the amount of FPs can increase faster than the decrease of FNs when using many image scales. This is demonstrated in Table 7.5. For both HOG + SVM and ChnFtrs + AdaBoost, three different cases of image rescaling are evaluated. Case 1 is the baseline approach as it is inspired by image rescaling for person detection: eleven different scale factors s_i are used to rescale the original motion ROI of width w_0 and length l_0. For the i-th rescaled motion ROI, width $w_i = s_i \cdot w_0$ and length $l_i = s_i \cdot l_0$ are rescaled jointly. In case 2, width $w_i = w_0$ is constant while only length $l_i = s_i \cdot l_0$ is rescaled by eleven scale factors s_i. Finally, case 3 is the proposed approach of Section 5.4.3 and similar to case 2 but with

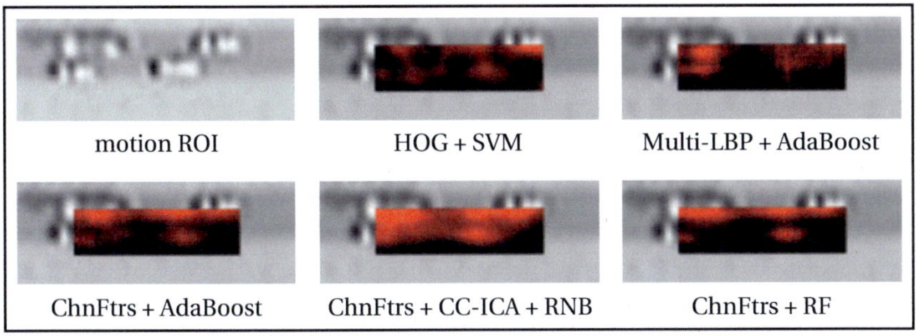

Figure 7.9: Decision values of different descriptor/classifier combinations in the sliding window approach. Each dot represents the center of one sliding window and light red indicates a high classifier decision value.

three scale factors instead of eleven. Rescaling the length of the motion ROI only is outperforming the baseline approach, but even larger improvement is achieved by using only three different scales. This is visible for both HOG + SVM and ChnFtrs + AdaBoost. The application of more scale levels reduces the amount of FNs but increases the amount of FPs much more at the same time since more object shadows or other rectangular non-vehicle appearances are detected.

In summary, the chosen parameters for the local sliding window approach are ChnFtrs as features, AdaBoost as classifier, $T_{dov} = 0.1$ for the window overlap threshold, and three levels of image rescaling in length direction of the motion ROI.

7.3.4 Image Stacking

Although image stacking is the first algorithm of the module *object detection and segmentation*, it is an optional preprocessing step for the subsequent detection and segmentation algorithms. So, the parameters of these algorithms have to be optimized first in order to determine if image stacking is really able to improve the optimal detection and segmentation results. All processing chain modules are active except for *multiple object tracking*. Gradient based object segmentation is used as detection and segmentation

Table 7.5: Evaluation of different image rescaling approaches for object detection using local sliding window. While 11 scale levels are applied in order to rescale the motion ROI width and length jointly in case 1, width is constant and length is rescaled by 11 and 3 levels for case 2 and 3, respectively. The best values for each descriptor/classifier are highlighted in red color.

evaluation measure	HOG + SVM rescale case 1	HOG + SVM rescale case 2	HOG + SVM rescale case 3	ChnFtrs + AdaBoost rescale case 1	ChnFtrs + AdaBoost rescale case 2	ChnFtrs + AdaBoost rescale case 3
TP	4,486	4,473	4,125	4,501	4,487	4,463
FP	889	780	190	357	283	83
FN	245	258	606	230	244	268
precision	0.835	0.852	0.956	0.972	0.941	0.982
recall	0.948	0.945	0.872	0.951	0.948	0.943
f-score	0.888	0.896	0.912	0.939	0.945	0.962

algorithm in this subsection since image stacking is removing background gradients and, thus, larger improvement is expected compared to model based approaches such as relative connectivity or local sliding window. Four parameters are selected for optimization: minimum stack height H_{min} and stack area A are continuous parameters while *stack initialization* and *stack arrangement* are discrete parameters. The height of a stack has to exceed H_{min} before the motion cluster is replaced by the stack for object detection and segmentation. If H_{min} is not exceeded, the motion cluster is used instead. A is the spatial extent of a stacked area in the image. With a larger size, it is more likely that extended motion clusters are inside the stack area and can be replaced by stacks. Two approaches for stack initialization are presented in Section 5.3.1: initialization by k-means clustering of moving corners and initialization by detections. Finally, two different methods are introduced for stack arrangement in Section 5.3.3: accumulation image and

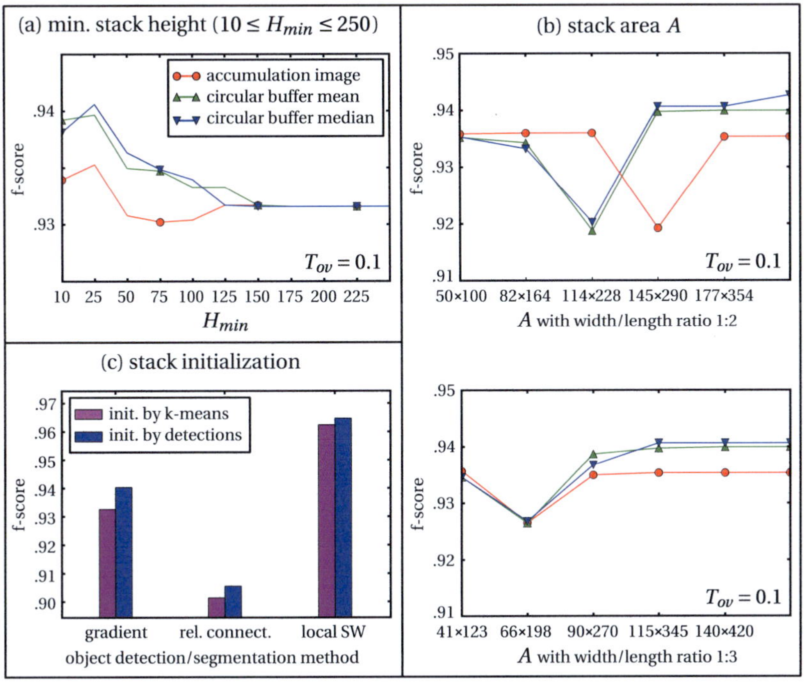

Figure 7.10: Parameter optimization for image stacking.

circular buffer. The stack image of a circular buffer can be calculated by pixelwise mean or median. Both approaches are analyzed.

The optimization results are visualized in Fig. 7.10. In Fig. 7.10 (a), the f-score of H_{min} for all three stack arrangement methods is depicted. $10 \leq H_{min} \leq 250$ is the chosen range clearly demonstrating that $H_{min} = 25$ is the best value for each method. Figure 7.10 (b) shows the optimization for stack area A. The f-score of the three stack arrangement approaches is plotted against the stack area size in pixels. With $1:2$ and $1:3$, two different ratios of width to length of A are evaluated. The variance of the f-score is smaller for ratio $1:3$ compared to $1:2$, so $1:3$ is further considered. 115×345 pixels is the best value for the stack area since there is no improvement of the

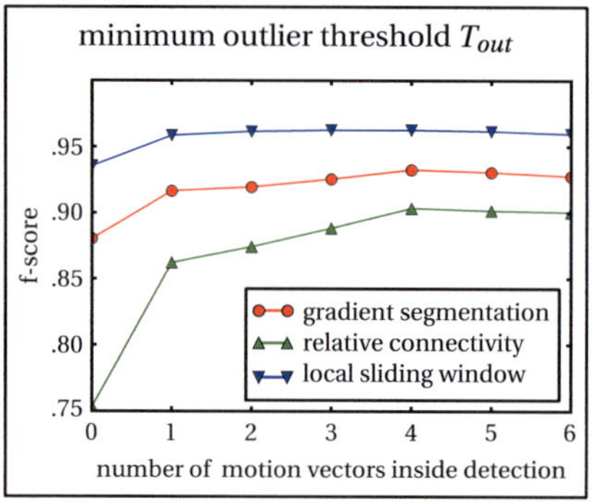

Figure 7.11: Parameter optimization for outlier removal.

f-score anymore for larger values. In all evaluations, the accumulation image achieves a worse maximum f-score than the circular buffer. Eventually, the circular buffer with pixelwise median image is chosen since it performs slightly better compared to the pixelwise mean image. Stack initialization is evaluated for gradient based object segmentation, segmentation using relative connectivity, and object detection using local sliding window in Fig. 7.10 (c). For all three detection and segmentation algorithms, k-means clustering performs worse compared to initialization by detections, so the latter one is chosen in order to initialize stacks.

7.3.5 Duplicate and Outlier Removal

The processing chain modules *image stacking* and *multiple object tracking* of the processing chain are deactivated again for this experiment. As there are no parameters for duplicate removal, just the minimum threshold T_{out} for outlier removal is optimized. The detection of a moving object is accepted only if the minimum number of motion vectors that are located inside the detection bounding box is not lower than T_{out}. Otherwise, the detection is considered to belong to the stationary background. The optimization result is visualized in Fig. 7.11. The f-score is plotted against the minimum number of motion vectors inside the detection. For each object

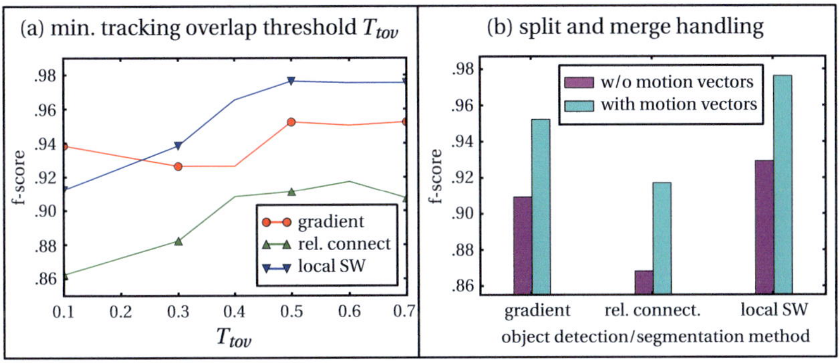

Figure 7.12: Parameter optimization for multiple object tracking.

detection and segmentation approach the maximum f-score is achieved for $T_{out} = 4$. Thus, this value is chosen for all further experiments.

7.3.6 Multiple Object Tracking

With deactivated processing chain module *image stacking*, two parameters of multiple object tracking are evaluated: the minimum overlap threshold T_{tov} and split and merge handling with and without support by associated motion vectors. The results are visualized in Fig. 7.12. T_{tov} is used to solve the association problem. A detection is associated to a track only, if the overlap of the detection bounding box and the track bounding box exceeds T_{tov}. The tracking performance is represented by the f-score in this experiment. Object detection using local sliding window and gradient based object segmentation reach a maximum at $T_{tov} = 0.5$, while object segmentation using relative connectivity achieves the highest f-score for $T_{tov} = 0.6$. Split and merge handling can be supported by motion vectors that are associated to existing tracks as described in Section 6.3. On the contrary, it is also possible to handle split and merge situations without motion vectors by track prediction using the Kalman filter instead. The performance increases significantly, if motion vectors are used as support. This is demonstrated for each of the object detection and segmentation approaches in Fig. 7.12 (b). In the follow-up, the value $T_{tov} = 0.5$ and split and merge handling supported by motion vectors are chosen.

7.4 Experiments and Evaluation

With optimized parameters, the methods proposed in this thesis are compared to approaches taken from the literature. The same measures are used for evaluation as presented in Section 7.1. Object detection and segmentation, image stacking, and multiple object tracking are evaluated individually.

7.4.1 Object Detection and Segmentation

In addition to the three proposed methods, three object segmentation approaches from the literature were implemented and integrated into the processing chain. This means that independent motion detection as well as outlier and duplicate removal are applied just as presented in Section 5. The concepts for all three algorithms are depicted in Fig. 7.13. Similar to the proposed methods, the primary idea is to find regions brighter or darker than the background assuming that they come from objects on the street. While one method is based on contour extraction [Che12c], the two other algorithms perform blob extraction [Mat02, Zhe13]. The parameters of each method are optimized in a similar way as in Section 7.3. The first solution introduced by Zheng et al. [Zhe13] uses the morphological operation *black and white tophat transform* [Dou92] to detect dark and bright image regions. Knowing about the GSD, the size of the structuring element can be chosen depending on the size of a standard vehicle in the image. The influence of background textures such as road markings is reduced by applying morphological closing and opening prior to the tophat transform. Objects are segmented by Otsu thresholding and connected-component labeling. The second method is based on blob detection using MSER [Mat02]. Connected regions brighter or darker than the background are the result of this algorithm. By applying size and eccentricity constraints, FP detections in the background are reduced. Finally, Cheng et al. [Che12c] apply clustering of Canny edge pixels and Harris corners. Morphological closing and connected-component labeling are used to segment objects. Further developments include color classification with a DBN to detect object pixels in areas of motion and edges. This part is skipped here since there is no color in the videos considered in this thesis.

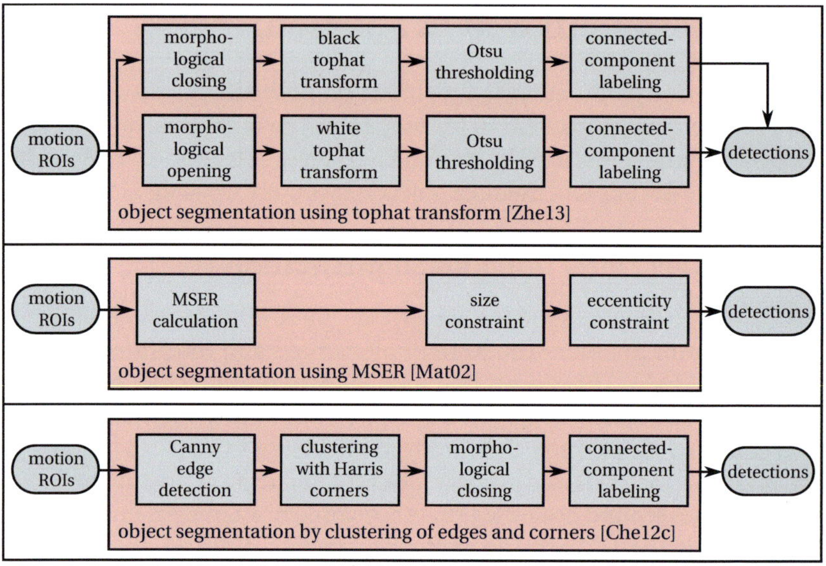

Figure 7.13: Concepts of the implemented algorithms from the literature. They are used for comparison with the methods proposed in this thesis.

A quick overview of the f-score of all object detection and segmentation methods and all three videos is visualized as bar diagram in Fig. 7.14. This overview creates the impression that the local sliding window provides the best overall performance and that most object detection and segmentation methods work well for video `EgTest01`. When analyzing the detailed quantitative evaluation as shown in Table 7.6 and 7.7, this impression gets stronger. Again, for each video the best result for each measure is highlighted in red color and the most important measures f-score, N-MODA, and N-MODP are underlined. Together with motion vector clustering as baseline algorithm and the three proposed methods for object detection and segmentation, seven approaches are compared in total for each of the three videos. In `SEQ 1`, all object detection and segmentation methods significantly improve the baseline approach except for MSER. The local sliding window clearly

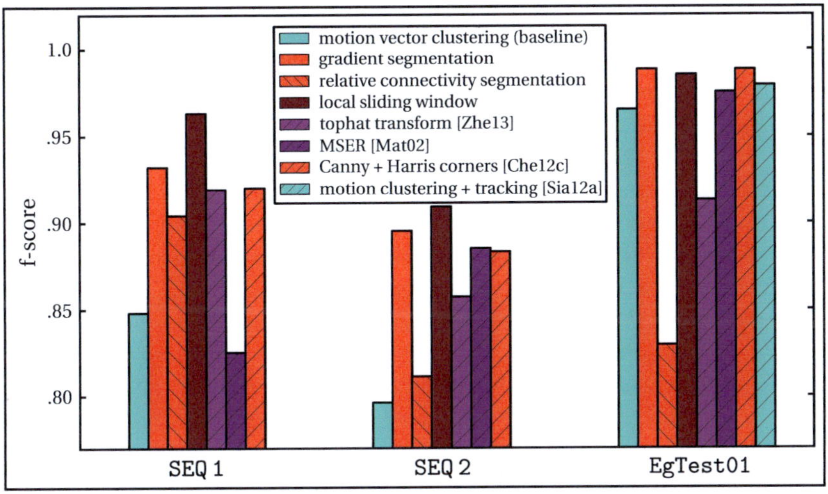

Figure 7.14: Evaluation of the f-score as quick overview of the performance of object detection and segmentation for the three videos SEQ 1, SEQ 2, and EgTest01. Most considered algorithms work well for video EgTest01. The local sliding window (dark red color) provides the best overall performance.

outperforms all other methods with respect to all evaluation measures. The second best approach is gradient based object segmentation with 281 more FPs and FNs as well as 0.075 less N-MODP. As N-MODP describes the mean overlap of GT bounding box and detection for all TPs, this means that about 7.5 % less overlap was achieved in average. However, these two approaches clearly outperform the algorithms taken from the literature. Object segmentation using relative connectivity is the second worst among the object detection and segmentation methods.

In SEQ 2, nearly all evaluation measures for each approach decrease. Large and strong object shadows and some partial occlusions by trees cause imprecise segmentation or even FPs. The baseline algorithm reaches the highest amount of TPs together with the largest number of FPs. All evaluated methods improve the baseline approach. The performance difference between the different object detection and segmentation algorithms is similar to

SEQ 1 with the exception that MSER achieves much better results in comparison. The local sliding window performs best followed by gradient based object segmentation with 59 more FPs and FNs.

Although many authors evaluate their methods with the video EgTest01 from the VIVID dataset [Xia08, Yao08, Yu09, Che12d, Mun12], they use the original GT where only one object is labeled and has to be tracked over the entire sequence. Some authors extended the GT to all visible moving objects in order to evaluate object detection and segmentation. Of these, two methods are added to the quantitative evaluation of the EgTest01 scene. Siam et al. [Sia12a] use motion vector clustering and tracking in a similar way as presented in this thesis. Shen et al. [She13b] detect spatiotemporal saliency for moving object segmentation. The numbers for precision, recall, and f-score presented in Table 7.7 are directly taken from their papers. EgTest01 differs from the other two videos with respect to camera angle and environment. The camera angle is between top and oblique view. There is no disturbing background in the video and only six vehicles are driving in a row with a quite large distance between each other compared to SEQ 1 and SEQ 2. So, object detection and segmentation is easier here. This can be seen in Fig. 7.14, Table 7.6, and Table 7.7 since by far the best values for f-score and N-MODA are reached. N-MODP is generally lower as the GT bounding boxes are not oriented in motion direction and, thus, there is less overlap between GT and detections. The baseline approach already achieves high performance and detects 6,844 out of 6,866 correctly. The large number of 487 FPs occurs due to the turning vehicles in the beginning of the video where front and back of the vehicles seem to move in different directions. These FPs can be reduced to 73 by the local sliding window, but due to the variation of the camera angle the trained classifier model does not fit to the vehicle appearance anymore and 140 FNs occur. Gradient based object segmentation is able to reduce the number of FPs to 128 while only 54 FNs appear. Similar performance is achieved by the approach of Cheng et al. which is based on Canny edge detection. Altogether, gradient based approaches perform best in this video followed by the local sliding window.

The qualitative evaluation is depicted in Fig. 7.15 and 7.16. Four image sections are chosen from SEQ 1 and SEQ 2 where missed, merged, and split detections are likely to occur. Six object detection and segmentation approaches are applied and the results are visualized with red bounding boxes.

Cyan bounding boxes represent motion vector clustering and are plotted to each example image in order to demonstrate how object detection and segmentation improves the baseline approach. While the first example in Fig. 7.15 (a) can be solved well by most methods, more and more FNs and FPs appear for each method except for the local sliding window. The last example in Fig. 7.15 (d) is the most challenging. Three vehicles move very close to each other and their shadows are overlapping. Only the local sliding window is able to detect each object although only the shadow of the leftmost object is detected. This is a typical problem of the sliding window approach that occurs when the shadow has the same size as the object but stronger contrast. Then, both object and shadow are detected and the NMS decides for the shadow while suppressing the object. Instead, gradient based approaches merge object and shadow and produce one large bounding box as seen in Fig. 7.15 and 7.16. Cyan boxes where no object was detected by the local sliding window come from moving motorcycles, bicycles, or persons which are considered to be irrelevant for vehicle detection.

Overall, it can be said that the local sliding window performs best for top view videos followed by the gradient based methods. Especially in complex urban scenarios with many objects overtaking each other the sliding window clearly outperforms the other approaches. This is not only due to the trained vehicle appearance model but also due to the fixed size of the sliding window and the reduced search space. However, the performance of the sliding window decreases with a changing camera view. This is expected since only top view samples were used to train the classifier. Re-training the classifier with vehicle samples similar to the ones in `EgTest01` may improve the results but this was not tested. As gradient based approaches do not use any shape or appearance model, they are more robust against changes in camera angle. Relative connectivity and algorithms based on blob extraction achieve the worst performance. They are prone to produce FPs due to blurry object edges. Although relative connectivity is well applicable for object segmentation in SAR imagery [Teu11e], it seems to be inappropriate for VIS images. So, for the next experiments, only the local sliding window and the gradient based object segmentation are considered.

Table 7.6: Quantitative evaluation for the three proposed object detection and segmentation methods. See Table 7.7 for the second part.

video	evaluation measure	motion vector clustering (baseline)	gradient segmentation	rel. connect. segmentation	local sliding window
SEQ 1	TP	4,070	4,322	4,267	4,463
	FP	807	223	453	83
	FN	661	409	464	268
	precision	0.835	0.952	0.904	0.982
	recall	0.860	0.913	0.902	0.943
	f-score	0.847	0.931	0.903	0.962
	N-MODA	0.689	0.866	0.806	0.925
	N-MODP	0.481	0.621	0.585	0.696
SEQ 2	TP	1,289	1,265	1,216	1,181
	FP	579	190	414	47
	FN	84	108	157	192
	precision	0.690	0.869	0.746	0.961
	recall	0.939	0.921	0.886	0.860
	f-score	0.795	0.894	0.810	0.908
	N-MODA	0.517	0.782	0.584	0.825
	N-MODP	0.514	0.573	0.545	0.593
EgTest01	TP	6,844	6,812	6,142	6,726
	FP	487	128	1,836	73
	FN	22	54	724	140
	precision	0.934	0.982	0.770	0.989
	recall	0.997	0.992	0.895	0.980
	f-score	0.964	0.987	0.828	0.984
	N-MODA	0.925	0.973	0.627	0.968
	N-MODP	0.448	0.549	0.493	0.526

Table 7.7: Quantitative evaluation for further object detection and segmentation methods taken from the literature. See Table 7.6 for the first part.

Zheng et al. [Zhe13]	Matas et al. [Mat02]	Cheng et al. [Che12c]	Siam et al. [Sia12a]	Shen et al. [She13b]	evaluation measure	video
4,253	3,395	4,141	–	–	TP	SEQ 1
286	113	136	–	–	FP	
478	1,336	590	–	–	FN	
0.937	0.968	0.968	–	–	precision	
0.899	0.718	0.875	–	–	recall	
0.918	0.824	0.919	–	–	f-score	
0.838	0.693	0.846	–	–	N-MODA	
0.530	0.482	0.526	–	–	N-MODP	
1,276	1,200	1,207	–	–	TP	SEQ 2
334	142	157	–	–	FP	
97	173	166	–	–	FN	
0.793	0.894	0.885	–	–	precision	
0.929	0.874	0.879	–	–	recall	
0.856	0.884	0.882	–	–	f-score	
0.686	0.770	0.765	–	–	N-MODA	
0.590	0.473	0.499	–	–	N-MODP	
6,782	6,703	6,785	–	–	TP	EgTest01
1,231	195	100	–	–	FP	
84	163	81	–	–	FN	
0.846	0.972	0.985	0.996	0.735	precision	
0.988	0.976	0.988	0.961	0.725	recall	
0.912	0.974	0.987	0.978	0.730	f-score	
0.808	0.947	0.973	–	–	N-MODA	
0.489	0.497	0.527	–	–	N-MODP	

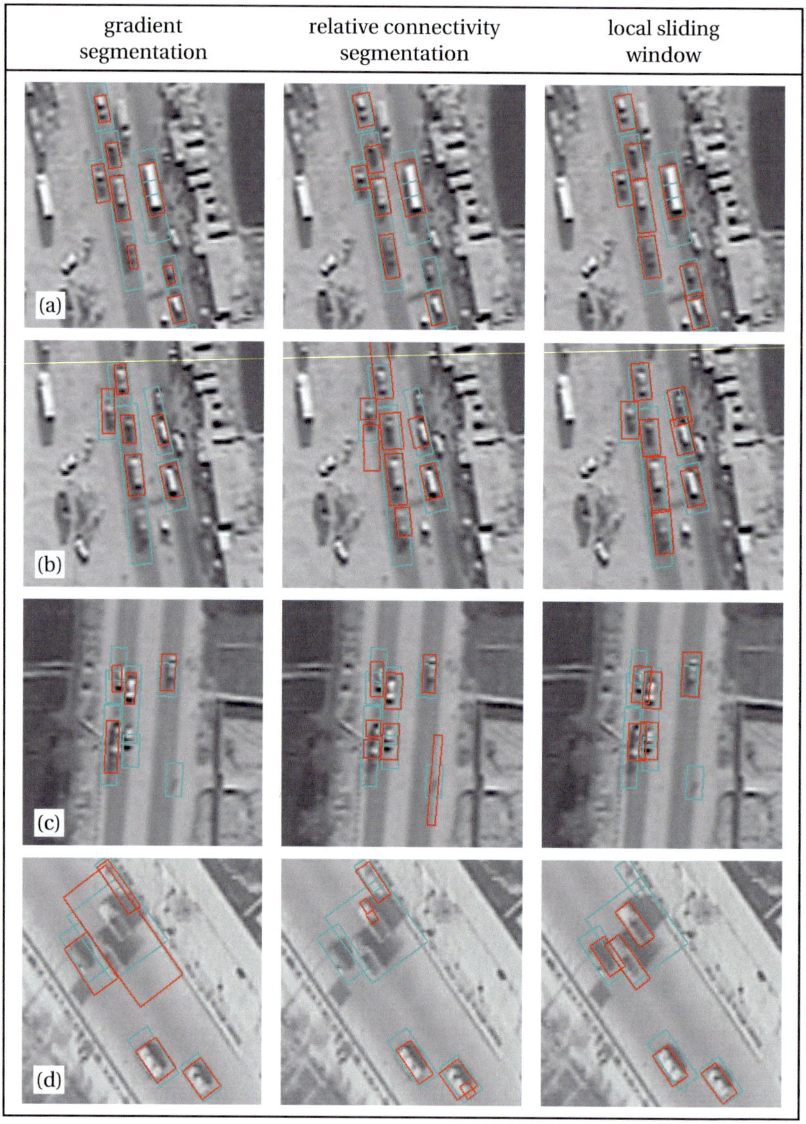

Figure 7.15: Qualitative evaluation for the three proposed object detection and segmentation methods. See Fig. 7.16 for the second part.

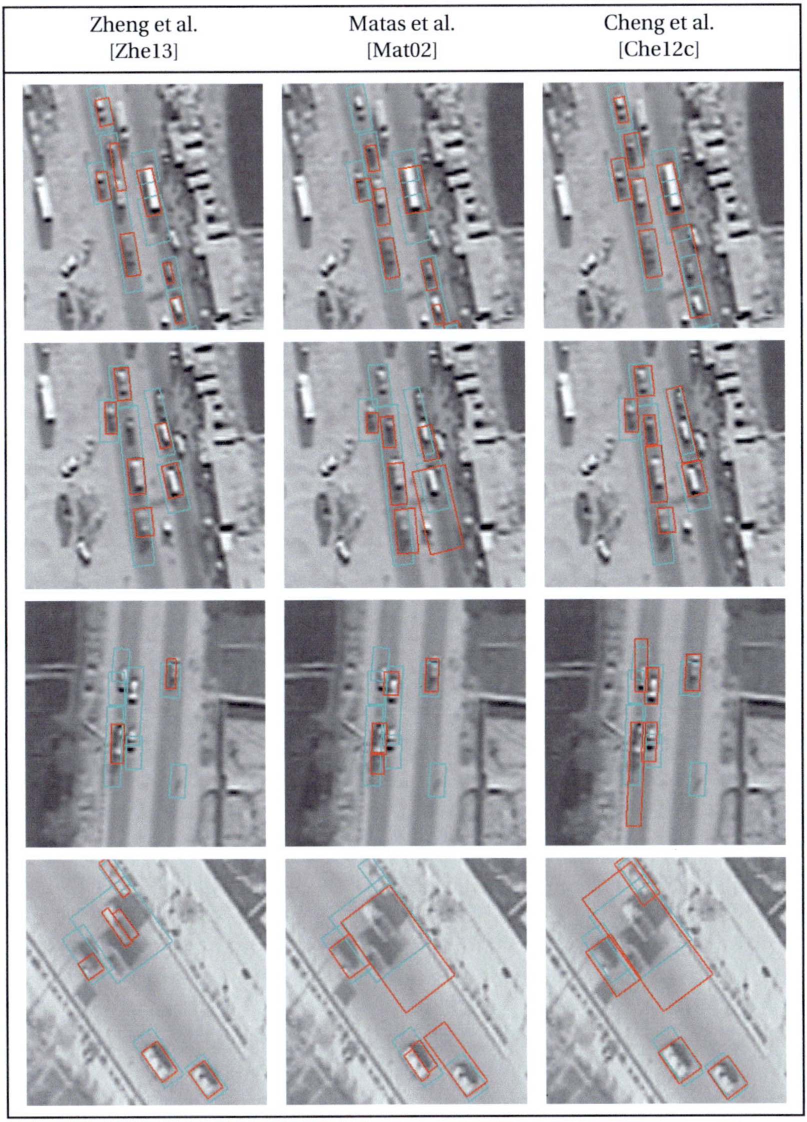

Figure 7.16: Qualitative evaluation for further object detection and segmentation methods taken from the literature. See Fig. 7.15 for the first part.

7.4.2 Image Stacking

In this experiment, the two proposed object detection and segmentation approaches *gradient based object segmentation* and *local sliding window* are evaluated with and without image stacking for each of the three aerial videos. The aim is to determine the situations in which the application of image stacking is beneficial and to measure the potential improvement. The quantitative evaluation is presented in Table 7.8. In `SEQ 1`, image stacking reduces the number of FPs and FNs by 76 for the gradient approach and by 14 for the local sliding window, respectively. A similar result is achieved for `SEQ 2`, where the number of FPs and FNs is decreased by 29 and 19. The improvement of the f-score is between 0.002 and 0.011. In general, there is stronger enhancement of gradient based object segmentation by image stacking compared to the local sliding window. The reason is that outlier removal is able to cover most situations where stacking can improve the local sliding window: due to the fixed size of the sliding window, usually no undersegmentation occurs in case of merged detections. Instead, objects are either missed or FP detections appear. These FP detections are reduced by both image stacking and outlier removal. At the same time, undersegmentation as occurring regularly in gradient based segmentation cannot be handled well by outlier removal but only by image stacking.

However, image stacking does not improve the results for the `EgTest01` video. The number of FPs and FNs is reduced by only 15 for gradient based segmentation. In this video, there are no merged detections, no partial occlusions, and only few disturbing street textures. At the same time, the performance of the local sliding window is even decreased. Image stacking works well as long as the object appearance is stable. If this is not the case, the object gets blurred or deformed in the image stack. As mentioned earlier in Section 7.4.1, the camera angle and, thus, the vehicle appearance are varying in `EgTest01`. This is difficult to handle for the classifier that was only trained with top view samples. It is even more challenging, when the turning vehicles at the beginning of the scene get deformed during image stacking as demonstrated by two examples in Fig. 7.17. The impaired appearance reduces the certainty of the classifier and more FNs occur.

The qualitative evaluation is done separately for gradient based object segmentation in Fig. 7.18 and local sliding window in Fig. 7.19. Four image

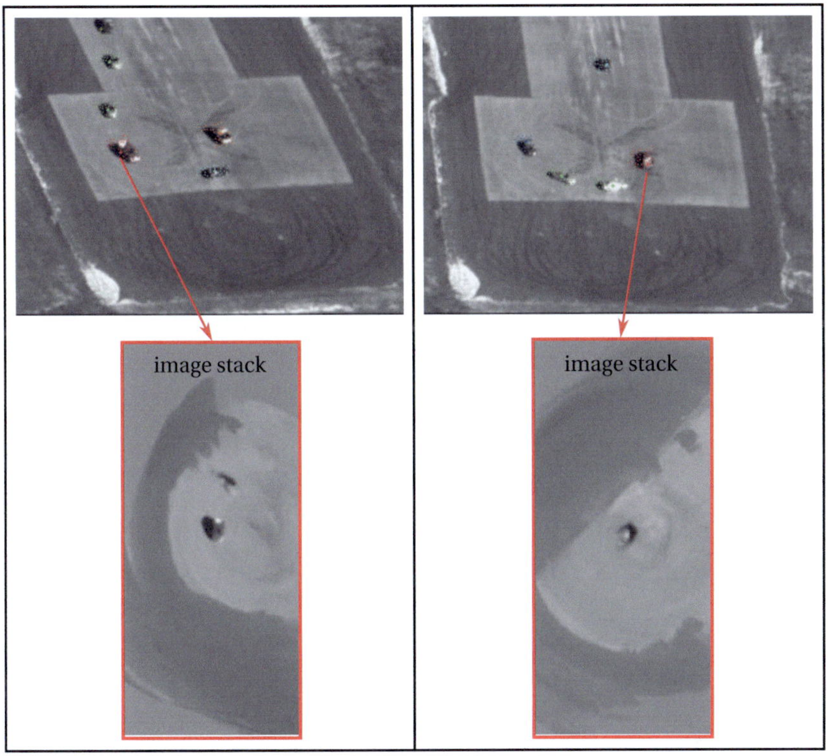

Figure 7.17: Image stacking as proposed does not work for turning vehicles and changing camera angle. The stacked object is blurred and its shape is deformed. This causes more FNs for the local sliding window in `EgTest01`.

sections are chosen for each of the two methods. GT is visualized in the left column, while the approach without and with image stacking are depicted in the center and right column. Orange GT bounding boxes represent moving motorcycles, bicycles, or persons that are not considered for evaluation. The red arrows point at the improvement by image stacking. In Fig. 7.18 (a) and (b), typical merge situations are shown where two objects drive close to each other and cause undersegmentation. They can be separated by image stacking since each object has its own stack without disturbing background. The right truck in Fig. 7.18 (c) is partially occluded by a tree, while there is disturbing street texture in Fig. 7.18 (d). Object segmentation is still possible but imprecise. Image stacking compensates for the occlusion and the street texture leading to more precise segmentation results. In Fig. 7.19, merged detections (a), FPs (b), and FNs (c) occur for the sliding window approach. In these cases, image stacking helps since the classifier certainty is higher inside the stacks with exactly one sharp object per stack and either no background at all or only blurred objects that achieve lower classifier certainty. The partial occlusion in Fig. 7.19 (d) is successfully handled with image stacking although only the shadow is detected for the left truck.

In summary, image stacking improves both gradient based object segmentation and the local sliding window. There is less benefit for the sliding window since both image stacking and outlier removal handle similar problems and, thus, complement each other.

Table 7.8: Quantitative evaluation for image stacking.

video	evaluation measure	gradient segmentation	gradient segmentation + stacking	local sliding window	local sliding window + stacking
SEQ 1	TP	4,322	4,389	4,463	4,461
	FP	223	214	83	67
	FN	409	342	268	270
	precision	0.952	0.954	0.982	0.985
	recall	0.913	0.928	0.943	0.943
	f-score	0.931	0.940	0.962	0.964
	N-MODA	0.866	0.882	0.925	0.928
	N-MODP	0.621	0.632	0.696	0.694
SEQ 2	TP	1,265	1,274	1,181	1,196
	FP	190	170	47	43
	FN	108	99	192	177
	precision	0.869	0.882	0.961	0.965
	recall	0.921	0.928	0.860	0.871
	f-score	0.894	0.905	0.908	0.916
	N-MODA	0.782	0.804	0.825	0.839
	N-MODP	0.573	0.575	0.593	0.593
EgTest01	TP	6,812	6,807	6,726	6,677
	FP	128	108	73	69
	FN	54	59	140	189
	precision	0.982	0.984	0.989	0.990
	recall	0.992	0.991	0.980	0.972
	f-score	0.987	0.988	0.984	0.981
	N-MODA	0.973	0.976	0.968	0.962
	N-MODP	0.527	0.544	0.526	0.518

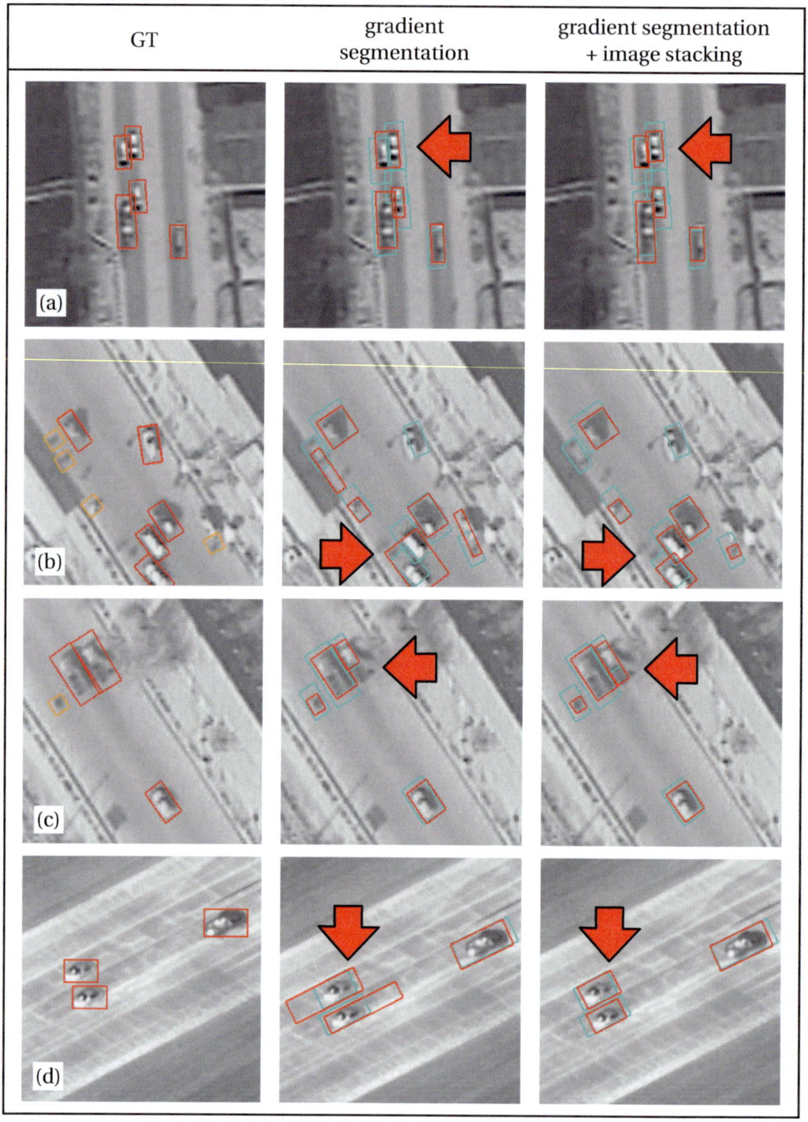

Figure 7.18: Qualitative evaluation for image stacking with gradient based object segmentation. The red arrows point at the improvement.

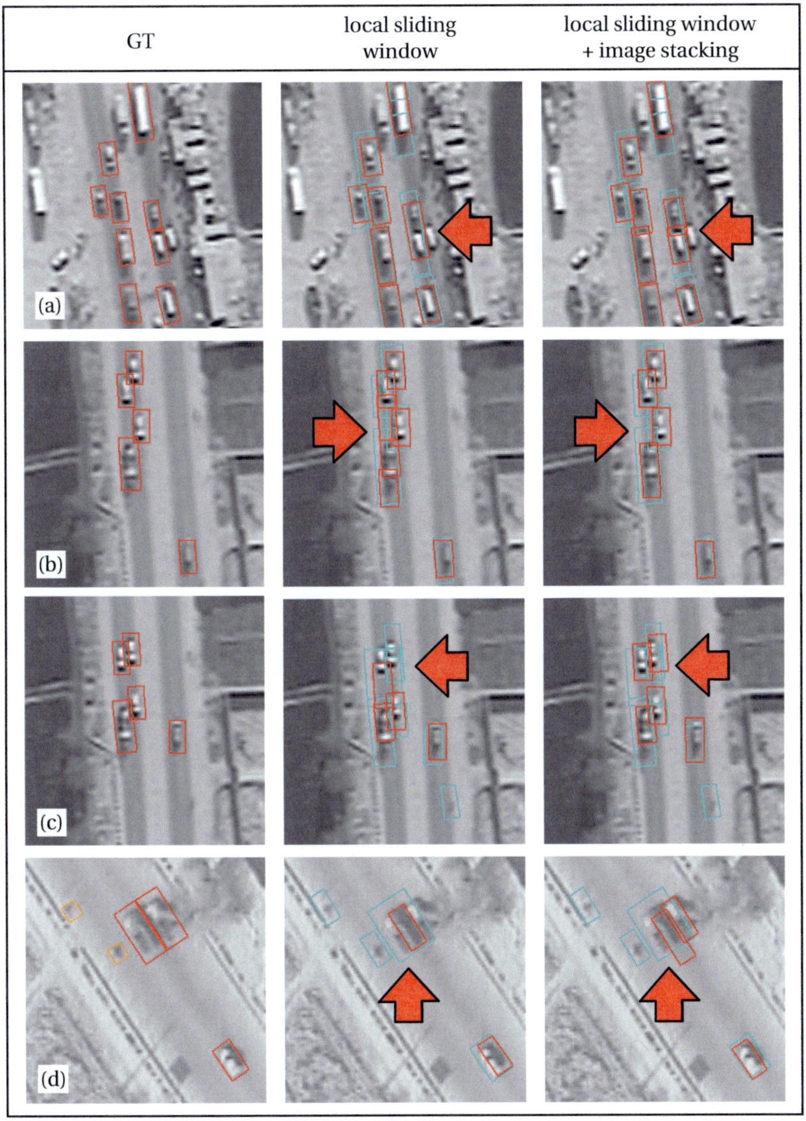

Figure 7.19: Qualitative evaluation for image stacking with local sliding window. The red arrows point at the improvement.

7.4.3 Multiple Object Tracking

Multiple object tracking is evaluated in this section. The quantitative results are shown in Table 7.9 and 7.10. Motion clustering + tracking is the baseline approach. In Table 7.9, gradient based object segmentation + image stacking and object detection by local sliding window + image stacking are applied with and without multiple object tracking and compared with each other. Therefore, the tracking evaluation measures presented in Section 7.1.2 are used. In SEQ 1, tracking improves the performance of all approaches by reducing the amount of FNs by about 50 %. The reason is that merged and missed detections can be reconstructed by the associated motion vectors. Thus, the f-score is improved significantly. The local sliding window approach performs best and achieves 36 mostly tracked, 4 partially tracked, and no mostly lost tracks. There are 41 track fragmentations which is the best value among the three compared methods.

In SEQ 2, the results show that tracking performance strongly depends on detection performance. Actually, tracking increases the amount of both FPs and FNs for motion clustering and gradient based object segmentation. This is due to the weak detection and segmentation performance as seen in Fig. 7.20 (b): since there are more merged detections than TP detections occurring for several consecutive frames, the track believes that the merged detection is correct. Then, TP detections are mistaken for split detections and the merged detection is reconstructed. In this case, the fixed size of the local sliding window approach avoids this problem and tracking improves the detection performance. Motion clustering + tracking achieves the largest number of MT tracks. The problem, however, is that at the same time the amount of ID switches is large and leads to a weak MOTA compared to the object detection and segmentation methods. Overall, the local sliding window approach achieves the best tracking performance.

The quantitative results for the VIVID sequence EgTest01 are shown in Table 7.10. Multiple object tracking is evaluated for motion clustering, gradient based object segmentation, and the local sliding window approach. No image stacking is applied to the local sliding window as it significantly decreases the detection performance due to strong variations in camera angle as demonstrated in the previous section. The f-score is improved for each approach with a maximum of 0.991 for gradient based object segmentation

+ image stacking. Four out of the six tracks are MT, while two are PT. This is the same for all approaches since tracks are prone to get lost in the area of image boundaries. The reason is that the oriented detection bounding boxes are rejected as soon as they are partially located outside of the image and FNs occur. In contrast, GT bounding boxes remain longer in the image as they are smaller and paraxial to the image boundaries.

In addition, two methods taken from the literature are compared: Siam et al. [Sia12b] propose tracking of motion clusters similar to the baseline approach, Shen et al. [She13a] improve their approach for moving object detection based on spatiotemporal saliency [She13b] by tracking of salient image regions. Precision, recall, and f-score are taken directly from their papers. In summary, gradient based object detection + image stacking + tracking achieves the best performance in this video.

The qualitative evaluation is depicted in Fig. 7.20. For each of the two object detection and segmentation methods, three frames are taken from both sequences SEQ 1 and SEQ 2 and a small image section is shown for each frame. Detections are represented by red bounding boxes and tracks are visualized by green boxes. The red arrows point at tracks where missing detections, merged detections, or FPs occur. While tracking is successfully handling merged and missed detections for gradient based object segmentation in frame 51 and frame 104 of example (a), it is not possible to separate the two undersegmented objects in example (b) and more FNs occur than without tracking. Furthermore, tracking improves the local sliding window approach by handling merged detections as in frame 35 and FP as in frame 46 of example (c). However, the large shadows in SEQ 2 are regularly mistaken for objects in frame 10, 73, and 81 of example (d). This causes the additional amount of FPs as seen in Table 7.9.

Table 7.9: Quantitative evaluation for multiple object tracking (only SEQ 1 and SEQ 2).

video	evaluation measure	motion clustering + tracking	gradient segmentation + stacking	gradient seg. + stacking + tracking	local sliding window (SW) + stacking	local SW + stacking + tracking
SEQ 1	TP	4,427	4,389	4,588	4,461	4,582
	FP	1040	214	238	67	72
	FN	304	342	143	270	149
	precision	0.810	0.954	0.951	0.985	0.985
	recall	0.936	0.928	0.970	0.943	0.969
	f-score	0.868	0.940	0.960	0.964	0.976
	MOTA	0.688	–	0.916	–	0.950
	MOTP	0.541	–	0.642	–	0.715
	MT	33	–	36	–	36
	PT	4	–	2	–	4
	MLT	3	–	2	–	0
	FM	49	–	42	–	41
SEQ 2	TP	1,281	1,274	1,263	1,196	1,258
	FP	900	170	184	43	81
	FN	92	99	110	177	115
	precision	0.587	0.882	0.873	0.965	0.939
	recall	0.933	0.928	0.920	0.871	0.916
	f-score	0.721	0.905	0.896	0.916	0.928
	MOTA	0.240	–	0.774	–	0.845
	MOTP	0.513	–	0.570	–	0.624
	MT	15	–	12	–	13
	PT	3	–	6	–	4
	MLT	0	–	0	–	1
	FM	31	–	52	–	28

Table 7.10: Quantitative evaluation for multiple object tracking (`EgTest01`).

video	evaluation measure	motion clustering + tracking	gradient seg. + stacking + tracking	local sliding window + tracking	Siam et al. [Sia12b]	Shen et al. [She13a]
`EgTest01`	TP	6,866	6,813	6,821	–	–
	FP	320	73	87	–	–
	FN	0	53	45	–	–
	precision	0.955	0.989	0.987	0.991	0.770
	recall	1.000	0.992	0.993	0.971	0.790
	f-score	0.977	0.991	0.990	0.980	0.780
	MOTA	0.951	0.981	0.980	–	–
	MOTP	0.446	0.536	0.508	–	–
	MT	4	4	4	–	–
	PT	2	2	2	–	–
	MLT	0	0	0	–	–
	FM	9	13	13	–	–

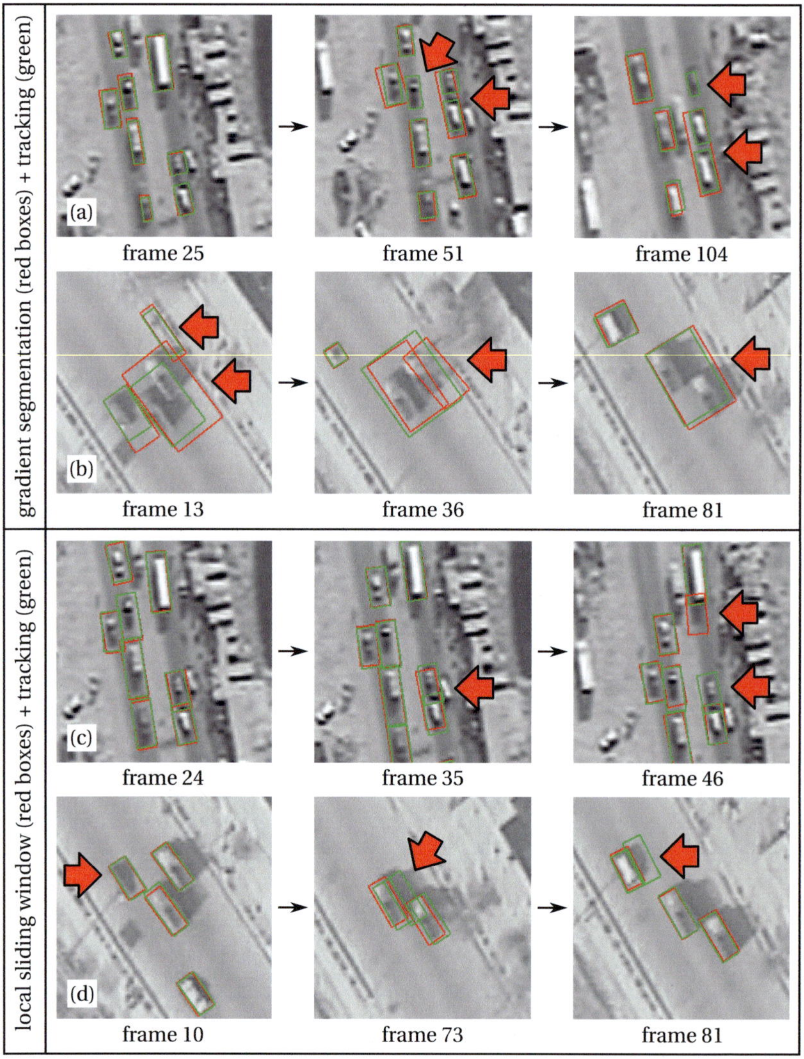

Figure 7.20: Qualitative evaluation for multiple object tracking. The red arrows point at the improvement in (a) and (c) or drawback in (b) and (d).

7.5 Processing Time and Optimization

In addition to high object detection and tracking accuracy and precision, the proposed methods should be able to run in real-time. For a frame rate of 25 Hz, there is one image acquired every 40 ms and the entire processing chain consisting of independent motion detection, moving object detection and segmentation, and multiple object tracked has to be finished before the next image is acquired in order to meet real-time requirements. The proposed methods' runtimes are presented in Table 7.11. The runtime for each method is calculated for 125 consecutive frame of SEQ 1. In order to avoid the influence of initialization time, the first 25 frames are not considered for runtime calculation. The processing times per frame as presented in Table 7.11 are average times of the remaining 100 frames. There are about 15 moving objects per frame. Except for independent motion detection and clustering, the proposed methods are not optimized at all.

The processing times for image stacking vary severely dependent on the choice of the stack arrangement: while stack initialization and association of motion vectors to stacks, and replacement of motion clusters by stacks take less than 20 ms altogether, stack update claims between 60 % of the processing time, if the accumulation image is used, and even 98 %, if the stack is arranged as a circular buffer. Optimization can be achieved by fast, approximated, or incremental calculation of the median pixel values in the circular buffer [Tib08, Cad12].

Object segmentation is calculated in around 20 ms while object detection takes about 700 ms. 95 % of the time for object detection is needed to calculate the descriptors and classifier decision values. However, the sliding window approach using ChnFtrs + AdaBoost is already significantly faster compared to HOG + SVM or other descriptors and classifiers. There is still high potential for runtime optimization of the proposed object detection and segmentation methods. Parallel processing of the motion ROIs on multiple CPU cores can be the first step and is easy to implement. Then, the combination of independent motion detection and clustering, gradient based object segmentation, and multiple object tracking can be processed in real-time. In the literature, several approaches are proposed in order to optimize the sliding window approach such as fast pre-scanning to detect promising

Table 7.11: Evaluation of the proposed methods' processing time.

method	processing time
independent motion detection and clustering (~22,000 motion vectors per image)	24.2 ms
image stacking (~18 stacks per image)	48.0 – 870.0 ms
gradient based object segmentation (~14 detections per image)	20.8 ms
object segmentation using relative connectivity (~14 detections per image)	18.9 ms
object detection using local sliding window (~15 detections per image)	700.0 ms
duplicate and outlier removal	1.5 ms
multiple object tracking (~15 tracks per image)	2.4 ms

hypotheses [Che14, Zit14], scale space approximation [Ben12, Dol14], probabilistic search space reduction [Gua12], or speeding up the AdaBoost classification process [Ben12]. Assumed that a frame rate of 100 Hz [Ben12] can be achieved for the local sliding window, the runtime of object detection can be reduced to 10 ms. Then, in combination with independent motion detection and clustering and multiple object tracking, the overall runtime is 38.5 ms and real-time processing is achieved. However, further optimization of independent motion detection and clustering or local sliding window is still possible.

7.6 Summary

Finally, it is worth to discuss, which combination of methods should be used to implement the processing chain. The TBD algorithm is a good choice for independent motion detection and clustering as long as the video frame rate is higher than 10 Hz. Best performance for object detection and segmentation in the Luna UAV videos is achieved by the proposed local sliding window approach with ChnFtrs and AdaBoost classifier. If a large variation of the camera angle is expected such as in the VIVID dataset, gradient based object segmentation can be a better choice as no assumptions are made about object appearance and, thus, the amount of FNs can be reduced compared to the local sliding window. Image stacking slightly improves the results but severely increases the processing time. Learning individual object appearance models for regression tracking [Pro14] can be a better choice instead. Duplicate and outlier removal is a very important processing step as it significantly reduces the amount of FP detections. Multiple object tracking is able to further reduce the amount of FPs and FNs by introducing track prediction for missing detections as well as split and merge handling. By implementing the optimization approaches presented in the previous subsection, it is possible to achieve real-time processing.

A quick overview of the f-score of the proposed methods in the context of the entire processing chain is given in Fig. 7.21. Motion vector clustering as presented in Chapter 4 is the baseline approach. The f-score is clearly improved by the introduction of gradient based object segmentation as seen in Fig. 7.21 (a) and object detection using the local sliding window as visualized in Fig. 7.21 (b). Image stacking and multiple object tracking can further improve the performance.

Some examples for object detection and tracking are shown in Fig. 7.22. Two frames are taken from each video. Green bounding boxes represent object tracks. Here, the local sliding window approach is used with duplicate and outlier removal but without image stacking. The related GT for the chosen frames is depicted in Fig. 7.3.

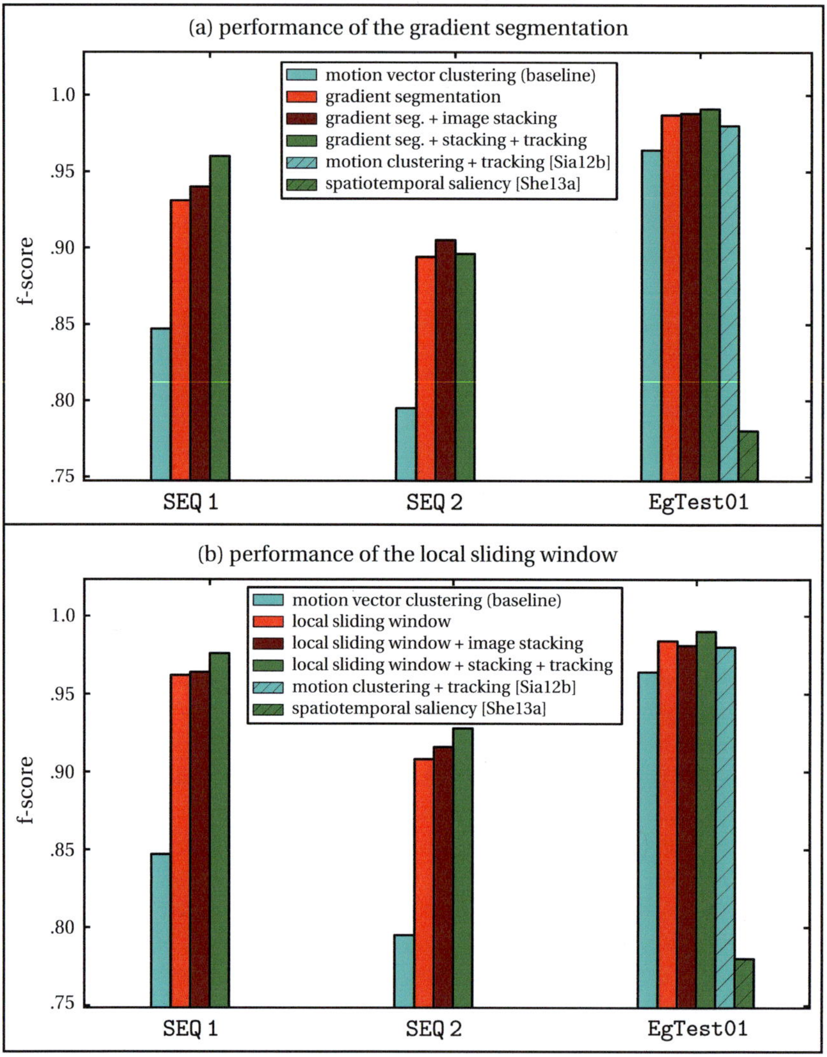

Figure 7.21: Evaluation of the entire processing chain. The f-score of independent motion detection (IMD) and clustering is clearly improved by the introduction of object segmentation (a) and object detection (b).

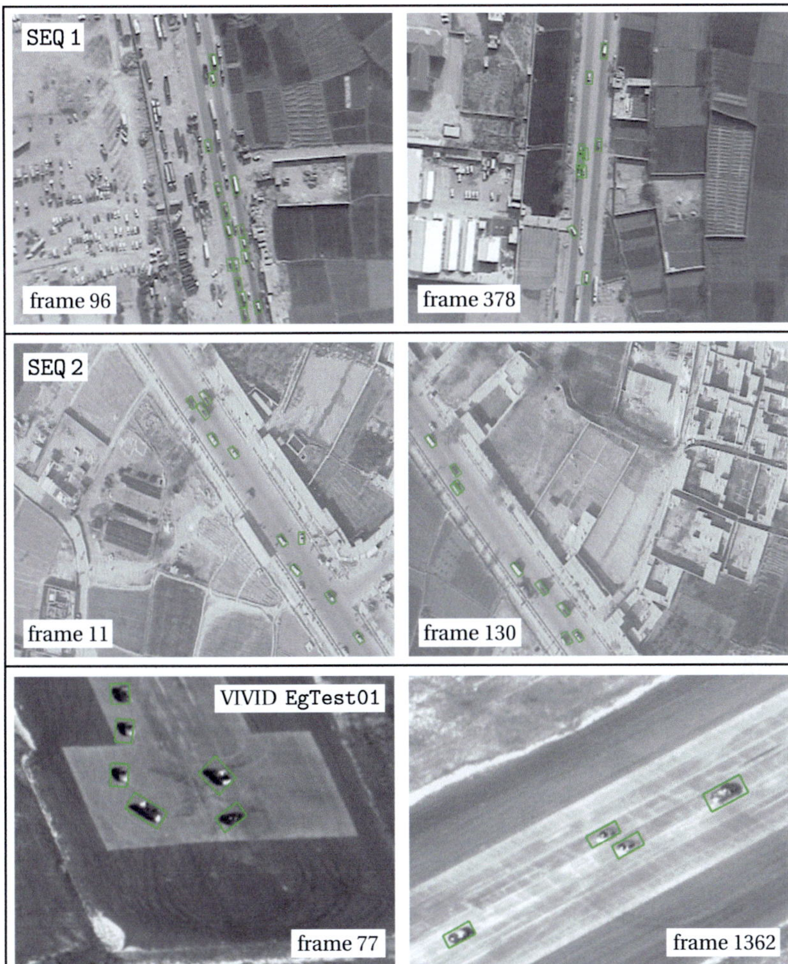

Figure 7.22: Some examples for the local sliding window approach taken from SEQ 1, SEQ 2, and VIVID EgTest01. Related GT is depicted in Fig. 7.3.

8 Conclusions and Outlook

8.1 Conclusions

In this thesis, approaches are presented to improve the performance and robustness of object detection in remote video surveillance with moving cameras. The focus lies on moving vehicle detection in aerial VIS videos acquired by UAVs or airplanes. Compensation for camera motion is achieved by image registration using local corner features and homography estimation. Then, motion is detected that is independent of the camera motion. In contrast to many other existing approaches, a TBD algorithm is applied for independent motion detection and clustering instead of difference images. For the analyzed aerial videos with high frame rate of 15–30 Hz, TBD achieves higher detection rates and robustness due to consideration of temporal context. In scenes with dense traffic, the segmentation of individual objects inside motion clusters is challenging as partial detections of large objects such as trucks or merged detections of multiple objects with similar motion can occur. Most contributions in this thesis are made in order to handle such effects and, thus, improve object detection and segmentation.

Image stacking is a preprocessing step that incorporates temporal information at a level between independent motion detection and object detection to remove the stationary background from the motion clusters. This way, short occlusions or street texture disturbing the detection and segmentation process can be removed.

Due to the large distance between camera and objects, the objects appear small in the image with a usual size of 10×20 pixels per object. Three novel or modified algorithms are presented for detection and segmentation of such small objects. The first one implements clustering of edge pixels that are determined with a novel approach for noise resistant gradient calculation based on LBP. The second approach uses clustering of relative connectivity that can be interpreted as a simple hand designed object model. Finally, the third one is a modification of the sliding window approach. Significant search space reduction is achieved and therefore the robustness for object detection is improved. In top view videos, the sliding window clearly outperforms the other two methods while clustering of edge pixels performs best in case of a variable camera angle. One important conclusion for the sliding window approach is that learning a highly discriminative classifier model in order to separate objects and non-objects is difficult. The shape of a person in lateral view is for example much more unique than the shape of a vehicle in top view. Especially across different datasets, the shape of a vehicle can only be represented by a rectangle with variable length. Integral channel features in combination with AdaBoost classifier appeared to be the best choice for object description and classification. Even the introduction of a novel modified RNB classifier did not provide improvement in terms of generality and transferability.

Multiple object tracking is introduced in order to utilize temporal information and reach higher robustness and stability for object detection. By fusion of object motion and detection results, effective split and merge handling is achieved. Detection accuracy and precision is improved consistently.

In summary, the standard TBD algorithm taken as baseline is improved significantly by the proposed methods. Furthermore, existing approaches for object detection and segmentation taken from the literature are outperformed with respect to detection accuracy and precision. This is demonstrated in a quantitative and qualitative evaluation for three different videos.

8.2 Outlook

Although the proposed methods achieve good results with respect to object detection accuracy, there is still high potential for enhancement. Especially shadow handling, multiple object tracking, and processing time are among the most promising topics in order to improve the current processing chain.

Explicit handling of object shadows is not considered at all in this thesis. As a result, object detection precision given by overlap of GT and detection bounding boxes is only between 50 and 70 % in the evaluated videos. In some cases, even the shadow is detected instead of the related object or detections jump between the object and its shadow. This problem is to some extend ignored for the calculation of object detection accuracy as the overlap threshold for accepting a detection as TP is set to 10 % only. This is justified because objects are not detected by chance but just imprecisely due to their shadows. Shadow removal for gray-value images [Fin06] can improve both detection accuracy and precision significantly but is difficult to apply as shadows and many dark objects have similar appearance. Shadow estimation for bright objects can serve as a basis to learn a shadow model directly from the images. Meta information such as camera angle, camera position, daytime, and weather can help to improve this shadow model.

The multiple object tracking algorithm presented in this thesis can also be further improved. There is effective split and merge handling but objects get lost as soon as they stop at intersections, traffic lights, or in traffic jam. This can be handled by the implementation of persistent tracking [Pel12, Pro14] where an appearance model is learned for each tracked object in order to re-identify it as soon as it starts moving again. Further improvement can be achieved by the introduction of MHT: multiple detection hypotheses together with their classifier decision values can be passed to the tracking module to choose the detection best fitting to the track in terms of position, size, or appearance. Especially detections jumping between object and its shadow can cause the initialization of FP tracks which can be avoided by applying NMS to overlapping tracks.

All proposed methods are suitable for real-time processing. The entire processing chain, however, is not running in real-time, yet. There are mainly two bottlenecks: image registration and the local sliding window approach.

While image registration can be speeded up by transferring processing steps such as the detection of corner features to the GPU, several effective methods exist for the optimization of the sliding window [Dol10, Ben12].

Finally, there are some more visionary ideas. The generality and transferability of object detection using the sliding window approach could be enhanced with respect to variations of camera angle or object's orientation as seen in the VIVID sequence `EgTest01`. One option is generating a model with more discriminative power. This could be achieved by applying super-resolution to each moving object in order to make inner object structures visible such as windows, engine cover lid, or trunklid. Furthermore, the information flow between the single modules of the processing chain is unidirectional so far. Information feedback offers high potential to improve both detection accuracy and processing time: (1) tracks can serve as priors for object detection. (2) Tracks or detections can be used as priors for independent motion detection in order to speed up image registration: the detection of a large number of moving corner features is time-consuming but crucial for independent motion detection as there must be a sufficient number of features for each motion cluster. In contrast, image registration only needs few features located uniformly distributed at the stationary background. So, image regions could be determined where independent motion is not expected and, hence, few features are detected. (3) Reinforcement learning can be applied to adjust the parameters of processing chain modules by evaluating the results of subsequent modules. For example, tracks that get lost regularly can induce a lower decision value threshold for the classifier used in object detection.

Bibliography

[Ach12] ACHANTA, Radhakrishna; SHAJI, Appu; SMITH, Kevin; LUCCHI, Aurelien; FUA, Pascal and SÜSSTRUNK, Sabine: SLIC Superpixels Compared to State-of-the-art Superpixel Methods. *IEEE Transactions on Pattern Analysis and Machine Intelligence* (2012), vol. 34(11):pp. 2274–2282

[Aho06] AHONEN, Timo; HADID, Abdenour and PIETIKÄINEN, Matti: Face Description with Local Binary Patterns: Application to Face Recognition. *IEEE Transactions on Pattern Analysis and Machine Intelligence* (2006), vol. 28(12):pp. 2037–2041

[Ali06] ALI, Saad and SHAH, Mubarak: COCOA – Tracking in Aerial Imagery, in: *Airborne Intelligence, Surveillance, Reconnaissance (ISR) Systems and Applications*, vol. 6209 of *Proceedings of SPIE (2006)*

[Ali07] ALI, Saad; REILLY, Vladimir and SHAH, Mubarak: Motion and Appearance Contexts for Tracking and Re-Acquiring Targets in Aerial Videos, in: *Proceedings of the 2007 IEEE International Conference on Computer Vision and Pattern Recognition (CVPR)*

[Arb06] ARBELAEZ, Pablo: Boundary Extraction in Natural Images Using Ultrametric Contour Maps, in: *Proceedings of the 2006 IEEE International Conference on Computer Vision and Pattern Recognition Workshops (CVPRW)*

[Arb11] ARBELAEZ, Pablo; MAIRE, Michael; FOWLKES, Charless and MALIK, Jitendra: Contour Detection and Hierarchical Image Segmentation. *IEEE Transactions on Pattern Analysis and Machine Intelligence* (2011), vol. 33(5):pp. 898–916

[Arn10] ARNOLD, Thomas; BIASIO, Martin De; FRITZ, Andreas and LEITNER, Raimund: UAV-based multispectral environmental monitoring, in: *Proceedings of 2010 IEEE Sensors*

[Arn13] ARNOLD, Thomas; BIASIO, Martin De; FRITZ, Andreas and LEITNER, Raimund: UAV-based measurement of vegetation indices for environmental monitoring, in: *Proceedings of the 2013 International Conference on Sensing Technology (ICST)*

[AT01] ARREGUIN-TOFT, Ivan: How the Weak Win Wars: A Theory of Asymmetric Conflict. *International Security* (2001), vol. 26(1):pp. 93–128

[Aza07] AZAD, Pedram; GOCKEL, Tilo and DILLMANN, Rüdiger: *Computer Vision: Principles and Practice*, Elektor (2007)

[Bab11] BABENKO, Boris; YANG, Ming-Hsuan and BELONGIE, Serge: Visual Tracking with Online Multiple Instance Learning. *IEEE Transactions on Pattern Analysis and Machine Intelligence* (2011), vol. 33(8):pp. 1619–1632

[Bar75] BAR-SHALOM, Yaakov and TSE, Edison: Tracking in a Cluttered Environment with Probabilistic Data Association. *Automatica* (1975), vol. 11(5):pp. 451–460

[Bar88] BAR-SHALOM, Yaakov and FORTMANN, Thomas E.: *Tracking and Data Association*, Elsevier Science Publishing (1988)

[Bay06] BAY, Herbert; TUYTELAARS, Tinne and VAN GOOL, Luc: SURF: Speeded Up Robust Features, in: Aleš Leonardis; Horst Bischof and Axel Pinz (Editors) *Computer Vision – ECCV 2006 (Part I)*, vol. 3951 of *Lecture Notes in Computer Science (LNCS)*, Springer (2006), pp. 404–417

[Ben12] BENENSON, Rodrigo; MATHIAS, Markus; TIMOFTE, Radu and VAN GOOL, Luc: Pedestrian detection at 100 frames per second, in: *Proceedings of the 2012 IEEE International Conference on Computer Vision and Pattern Recognition (CVPR)*

[Ben13] BENENSON, Rodrigo; MATHIAS, Markus; TUYTELAARS, Tinne and VAN GOOL, Luc: Seeking the strongest rigid detector, in: *Proceedings of the 2013 IEEE Conference on Computer Vision and Pattern Recognition (CVPR)*

[Ber08] BERNARDIN, Keni and STIEFELHAGEN, Rainer: Evaluating Multiple Object Tracking Performance: The CLEAR MOT Metrics. *EURASIP Journal on Image and Video Processing* (2008), vol. 2008

[Bey12] BEYERER, Jürgen; PUENTE LEÓN, Fernando and FRESE, Christian: *Automatische Sichtprüfung*, Springer (2012)

[Bla99] BLACKMAN, Samuel S. and POPOLI, Robert: *Design and Analysis of Modern Tracking Systems*, Artech House Inc (1999)

[Bla10] BLANCO, Jose Luis; GONZALEZ, Javier and FERNANDEZ-MADRIGAL, Juan Antonito: An Experimental Comparison of Image Feature Detectors and Descriptors applied to Grid Map Matching, Tech. Rep., Department of System Engineering and Automation, University of Málaga, Spain (2010)

[Boe08] BOERS, Yvo; EHLERS, Frank; KOCH, Wolfgang; LUGINBUHL, Tod; STONE, Lawrence D. and STREIT, Roy L.: Track before Detect Algorithms. *EURASIP Journal on Advances in Signal Processing* (2008)

[Bou08] BOUWMANS, Thierry; BAF, Fida El and VACHON, Bertrand: Background Modeling using Mixture of Gaussians for Foreground Detection - A Survey. *Recent Patents on Computer Science* (2008), vol. 1(3):pp. 219–237

[Bou11] BOUWMANS, Thierry: Recent Advanced Statistical Background Modeling for ForegroundDetection - A Systematic Survey. *Recent Patents on Computer Science* (2011), vol. 4(3):pp. 147–176

[Boy01] Boykov, Yuri; Veksler, Olga and Zabih, Ramin: Fast approximate energy minimization via graph cuts. *IEEE Transactions on Pattern Analysis and Machine Intelligence* (2001), vol. 23(11):pp. 1222–1239

[Bra00] Bradski, G.: The OpenCV Library. *Dr. Dobb's Journal of Software Tools* (2000)

[Bre01] Breiman, Leo: Random forests. *Machine Learning* (2001), vol. 45(1):pp. 5–32

[Bre02] Bressan, Marco and Vitrià, Jordi: Improving Naive Bayes using Class-Conditional ICA, in: Francisco J. Garijo; José C. Riquelme and Miguel Toro (Editors) *Advances in Artificial Intelligence – IBERAMIA 2002,* vol. 2527 of *Lecture Notes in Computer Science (LNCS),* Springer (2002), pp. 1–10

[Bro05] Broncelet, Charles: Image Noise Models, in: Alan C. Bovik (Editor) *Handbook of Image and Video Processing,* Academic Press, 2 edn. (2005)

[Bru11] Brusch, Stephan; Lehner, Susanne; Fritz, Thomas; Soccorsi, Matteo; Soloviev, Alexander and van Schie, Bart: Ship Surveillance With TerraSAR-X. *IEEE Transactions on Geoscience and Remote Sensing* (2011), vol. 49(3):pp. 1092–1103

[Bug08] Bugeau, Aurélie and Pérez, Patrick: Track and Cut: Simultaneous Tracking and Segmentation of Multiple Objects with Graph Cuts. *EURASIP Journal on Image and Video Processing* (2008), vol. 2008(3):pp. 603–619

[Cad12] Cadenas, Jose Oswaldo; Megson, Graham M.; Sherratt, R. Simon and Huerta, Pablo: Fast median calculation method. *Electronics Letters* (2012), vol. 48(10):pp. 558–560

[Can86] Canny, John: A Computational Approach to Edge Detection. *IEEE Transactions on Pattern Analysis and Machine Intelligence* (1986), vol. 8(6):pp. 679–698

[Cao11a] CAO, Xianbin; LAN, Jinhe; YAN, Pingkun and LI, Xuelong: KLT Feature Based Vehicle Detection and Tracking in Airborne Videos, in: *Proceedings of the 2011 International Conference on Image and Graphics (ICIG)*

[Cao11b] CAO, Xianbin; WU, Changxia; LAN, Jinhe; YAN, Pingkun and LI, Xuelong: Vehicle Detection and Motion Analysis in Low-Altitude Airborne Video Under Urban Environment. *IEEE Transactions on Circuits and Systems for Video Technology* (2011), vol. 21(10):pp. 1522–1533

[Cen99] CENSI, Alberto; FUSIELLO, Andrea and ROBERTO, Vito: Image stabilization by features tracking, in: *Proceedings of the 1999 IEEE International Conference on Image Analysis and Processing (ICIAP)*

[Cha84] CHANG, Kuo-Chu and BAR-SHALOM, Yaakov: Joint probabilistic data association for multitarget tracking with possibly unresolved measurements and maneuvers. *IEEE Transactions on Automatic Control* (1984), vol. 29(7):pp. 585–594

[Cha11] CHALLA, Subhash; MORELANDE, Mark R.; MUSICKI, Darko and EVANS, Robin J.: *Fundamentals of Object Tracking*, Cambridge University Press (2011)

[Che08] CHEN, Jia; YUAN, Lu; TANG, Chi-Keung and QUAN, Long: Robust Dual Motion Deblurring, in: *Proceedings of the 2008 IEEE International Conference on Computer Vision and Pattern Recognition (CVPR)*

[Che12b] CHEN, Shengyong: Kalman Filter for Robot Vision: A Survey. *IEEE Transactions on Industrial Electronics* (2012), vol. 59(11):pp. 4409–4420

[Che12c] CHENG, Hsu-Yung; WENG, Chih-Chia and CHEN, Yi-Ying: Vehicle Detection in Aerial Surveillance Using Dynamic Bayesian Networks. *IEEE Transactions on Image Processing* (2012), vol. 21(4):pp. 2152–2159

[Che12d] CHERAGHI, Seyed Ali and SHEIKH, Usman Ullah: Moving Object Detection Using Image Registration for a Moving Camera Platform, in: *Proceedings of the 2012 IEEE International Conference on Control System, Computing and Engineering (ICCSCE)*

[Che14] CHENG, Ming-Ming; ZHANG, Ziming; LIN, Wen-Yan and TORR, Philip: BING: Binarized Normed Gradients for Objectness Estimation at 300fps, in: *Proceedings of the 2014 IEEE Conference on Computer Vision and Pattern Recognition (CVPR)*

[Chu09] CHUNG, Kuo-Liang; LIN, Yi-Ru and HUANG, Yong-Huai: Efficient Shadow Detection of Color Aerial Images Based on Successive Thresholding Scheme. *IEEE Transactions on Geoscience and Remote Sensing* (2009), vol. 47(2):pp. 671–682

[Col01] COLLINS, Robert T.; LIPTON, Alan J.; FUJIYOSHI, Hironobu and KANADE, Takeo: Algorithms for cooperative multisensor surveillance. *Proceedings of the IEEE* (2001), vol. 89(10):pp. 1456–1477

[Col05] COLLINS, Robert T.; ZHOU, Xuhui and TEH, Seng Keat: An Open Source Tracking Testbed and Evaluation Web Site, in: *Proceedings of the 2005 IEEE International Workshop on Performance Evaluation of Tracking and Surveillance (PETS)*

[Com02] COMANICIU, Dorin and MEER, Peter: Mean Shift: A Robust Approach Towards Feature Space Analysis. *IEEE Transactions on Pattern Analysis and Machine Intelligence* (2002), vol. 24(5):pp. 603–619

[Dal05] DALAL, Navneet and TRIGGS, Bill: Histograms of Oriented Gradients for Human Detection, in: *Proceedings of the 2005 IEEE International Conference on Computer Vision and Pattern Recognition (CVPR)*, pp. 886–893

[Dav08] DAVEY, Samuel J.; RUTTEN, Mark G. and CHEUNG, Brian: A Comparison of Detection Performance for Several Track-Before-Detect Algorithms, in: *Proceedings of the 2008 International Conference on Information Fusion (FUSION)*, pp. 493–500

[Dil92] DILLENCOURT, Michael B.; SAMET, Hanan and TAMMINEN, Markku: A general approach to connected-component labeling for arbitrary image representations. *Journal of the ACM* (1992), vol. 39(2):pp. 253–280

[Dol09] DOLLÁR, Piotr; TU, Zhuowen; PERONA, Pietro and BELONGIE, Serge: Integral Channel Features, in: *Proceedings of the 2009 British Machine Vision Conference (BMVC)*

[Dol10] DOLLÁR, Piotr; BELONGIE, Serge and PERONA, Pietro: The Fastest Pedestrian Detector in the West, in: *Proceedings of the 2010 British Machine Vision Conference (BMVC)*

[Dol12] DOLLÁR, Piotr; WOJEK, Christian; SCHIELE, Bernt and PERONA, Pietro: Pedestrian Detection: An Evaluation of the State of the Art. *IEEE Transactions on Pattern Analysis and Machine Intelligence* (2012), vol. 34(4):pp. 743–761

[Dol14] DOLLÁR, Piotr; APPEL, Ron; BELONGIE, Serge and PERONA, Pietro: Fast Feature Pyramids for Object Detection. *IEEE Transactions on Pattern Analysis and Machine Intelligence* (2014), vol. 36(8):pp. 1532–1545

[Dom97] DOMINGOS, Pedro and PAZZANI, Michael: On the Optimality of the Simple Bayesian Classifier under Zero-One Loss. *Machine Learning* (1997), vol. 29:pp. 103–130

[Dou92] DOUGHERTY, Edward R.: *An Introduction to Morphological Image Processing*, SPIE - International Society for Optical Engineering (1992)

[Dou10] DOUTERLOIGNE, Koen; GAUTAMA, Sidharta and PHILIPS, Wilfried: On the Accuracy of 3D Landscapes from UAV Image Data, in: *Proceedings of the 2010 IEEE International Geoscience and Remote Sensing Symposium (IGARSS)*

[dS01] DE SÁ, J. P. Marques: *Pattern Recognition: Concepts, Methods, and Applications*, Springer (2001)

[Dud72] DUDA, Richard O. and HART, Peter E.: Use of the Hough transformation to detect lines and curves in pictures. *Communications of the ACM* (1972), vol. 15(1):pp. 11–15

[Eke05] EKENEL, Hazim Kemal and STIEFELHAGEN, Rainer: Local appearance based face recognition using discrete cosine transform, in: *Proceedings of the 2005 European Signal Processing Conference (EUSIPCO)*

[Enz09] ENZWEILER, Markus and GAVRILA, Dariu M.: Monocular Pedestrian Detection: Survey and Experiments. *IEEE Transactions on Pattern Analysis and Machine Intelligence* (2009), vol. 31(12):pp. 2179–2195

[Ers12] ERSOY, Ilker; PALANIAPPAN, Kannappan and SEETHARAMAN, Guna: Visual tracking with robust target localization, in: *Proceedings of the 2012 IEEE International Conference on Image Processing (ICIP)*, pp. 1365–1368

[Eve10] EVERINGHAM, Mark; VAN GOOL, Luc; WILLIAMS, Christopher K. I.; WINN, John and ZISSERMAN, Andrew: The Pascal Visual Object Classes (VOC) Challenge. *International Journal of Computer Vision* (2010), vol. 88(2):pp. 303–338

[Eve11] EVERITT, Brian S.; LANDAU, Sabine; LEESE, Morven and STAHL, Daniel: *Cluster Analysis*, Wiley, 5 edn. (2011)

[Eze14] EZEQUIEL, Carlos Alphonso F.; CUA, Matthew; LIBATIQUE, Nathaniel C.; TANGONAN, Gregory L.; ALAMPAY, Raphael; LABUGUEN, Rollyn T.; FAVILA, Chrisandro M.; HONRADO, Jaime Luis E.; CAÑOS, Vinni; DEVANEY, Charles; LORETO, Alan B.; BACUSMO, Jose and PALMA, Benny: UAV Aerial Imaging Applications for Post-Disaster Assessment, Environmental Management and Infrastructure Development, in: *Proceedings of the 2014 International Conference on Unmanned Aircraft Systems (ICUAS)*

[Fan07] FAN, Liwei and POH, Kim Leng: A Comparative Study of PCA, ICA and Class-Conditional ICA for Naïve Bayes Classifier, in: Francisco

Sandoval; Alberto Prieto; Joan Cabestany and Manuel Graña (Editors) *Computational and Ambient Intelligence*, vol. 4507 of *Lecture Notes in Computer Science (LNCS)*, Springer (2007), pp. 16–22

[Far04] FARSIU, Sina; ROBINSON, M. Dirk; ELAD, Michael and MILANFAR, Peyman: Fast and Robust Multiframe Super Resolution. *IEEE Transactions on Image Processing* (2004), vol. 13(10):pp. 1327–1344

[Faw06] FAWCETT, Tom: An introduction to ROC analysis. *Pattern Recognition Letters* (2006), vol. 27:pp. 861–874

[Fel10] FELZENSZWALB, Pedro F.; GIRSHICK, Ross B.; MCALLESTER, David and RAMANAN, Deva: Object Detection with Discriminatively Trained Part Based Models. *IEEE Transactions on Pattern Analysis and Machine Intelligence* (2010), vol. 32(9):pp. 1627–1645

[Fer08] FERRARI, Vittorio; MARÍN-JIMÉNEZ, Manuel and ZISSERMAN, Andrew: Progressive search space reduction for human pose estimation, in: *Proceedings of the 2008 IEEE International Conference on Computer Vision and Pattern Recognition (CVPR)*

[Fin06] FINLAYSON, Graham D.; HORDLEY, Steven D.; LU, Cheng and DREW, Mark S.: On the Removal of Shadows from Images. *IEEE Transactions on Pattern Analysis and Machine Intelligence* (2006), vol. 28(1):pp. 59–68

[Fis81] FISCHLER, Martin A. and BOLLES, Robert C.: Random sample consensus: a paradigm for model fitting with applications to image analysis and automated cartography. *Communications of the ACM* (1981), vol. 24(6):pp. 381–395

[För87] FÖRSTNER, Wolfgang and GÜLCH, Eberhard: A Fast Operator for Detection and Precise Location of Distict Point, Corners and Centres of Circular Features, in: *Proceedings of the 1987 ISPRS Conference on Fast Processing of Photogrammetric Data*, pp. 281–305

[For03] FORSYTH, David A. and PONCE, Jean: *Computer Vision: A Modern Approach*, Prentice Hall (2003)

[Fra05] Franke, Uwe; Rabe, Clemens; Badino, Hernán and Gehrig, Stefan: 6D-Vision: Fusion of Stereo and Motion for Robust Environment Perception, in: Walter G. Kropatsch; Robert Sablatnig and Allan Hanbury (Editors) *Pattern Recognition*, vol. 3663 of *Lecture Notes in Computer Science (LNCS)*, Springer (2005), pp. 216–223

[Fre97] Freund, Yoav and Schapire, Robert E.: A decision-theoretic generalization of on-line learning and an application to boosting. *Journal of Computer and System Sciences* (1997), vol. 55(1):pp. 119–139

[Fre07] Frey, Brendan J. and Dueck, Delbert: Clustering by passing messages between data points. *Science* (2007), vol. 315(5814):pp. 972–976

[Fuc09] Fuchs, Christian: Social Networking Sites and the Surveillance Society, Tech. Rep., University of Salzburg, Austria (2009)

[Gar07] Garcia, Mary Lynn: *Design and Evaluation of Physical Protection Systems*, Butterworth-Heinemann (2007)

[Gas11] Gaszczak, Anna; Breckon, Toby P. and Han, Jiwan: Real-time people and vehicle detection from UAV imagery, in: *Intelligent Robots and Computer Vision XXVIII: Algorithms and Techniques*, vol. 7878 of *Proceedings of SPIE (2011)*

[Ger10] Gerónimo, David; López, Antonio M.; Sappa, Angel D. and Graf, Thorsten: Survey of Pedestrian Detection for Advanced Driver Assistance Systems. *IEEE Transactions on Pattern Analysis and Machine Intelligence* (2010), vol. 32(7):pp. 1239–1258

[Gle11] Gleason, Joshua; Nefian, Ara V.; Bouyssounousse, Xavier; Fong, Terry and Bebis, George: Vehicle Detection from Aerial Imagery, in: *Proceedings of the 2011 IEEE International Conference on Robotics and Automation (ICRA)*

[God10] Godec, Martin; Leistner, Christian; Saffari, Amir and Bischof, Horst: On-line Random Naïve Bayes for Tracking, in: *Proceedings of the 2010 International Conference on Pattern Recognition (ICPR)*

[Gon08] GONZALEZ, Rafael C. and WOODS, Richard E.: *Digital Image Processing*, Pearson / Prentice Hall (2008)

[Gon14] GONG, Shaogang; CRISTANI, Marco; YAN, Shuicheng and LOY, Chen Change (Editors): *Person Re-Identification*, Springer (2014)

[Gra05] GRABNER, Helmut; BELEZNAI, Csaba and BISCHOF, Horst: Improving AdaBoost detection rate by wobble and mean shift, in: *Proceedings of the 2005 Computer Vision Winter Workshop (CVWW)*

[Gra08] GRABNER, Michael: *Visual Tracking through Online Learning of Discriminative Representations*, Dissertation, Graz University of Technology, Austria (2008)

[Gri09] GRINBERG, Michael; OHR, Florian and BEYERER, Jürgen: Feature-Based Probabilistic Data Association (FBPDA) for Visual Multi-Target Detection and Tracking under Occlusions and Split and Merge Effects, in: *Proceedings of the 2009 IEEE International Conference on Intelligent Transportation Systems (ITSC)*

[Gri10] GRINBERG, Michael; OHR, Florian; WILLERSINN, Dieter and BEYERER, Jürgen: Feature-based Probabilistic Data Association and Tracking, in: *Proceedings of the 2010 International Workshop on Intelligent Transportation (WIT)*

[Gri13] GRINBERG, Michael; OHR, Florian and BEYERER, Jürgen: What is a good evaluation measure for semantic segmentation?, in: *Proceedings of the 2013 British Machine Vision Conference (BMVC)*

[Gua12] GUALDI, Giovanni; PRATI, Andrea and CUCCHIARA, Rita: Multistage Particle Windows for Fast and Accurate Object Detection. *IEEE Transactions on Pattern Analysis and Machine Intelligence* (2012), vol. 34(8):pp. 1589–1604

[Guo05] GUO, Yanlin; HSU, Steve; SHAN, Ying; SAWHNEY, Harpreet and KUMAR, Rakesh: Vehicle Fingerprinting for Reacquisition & Tracking in Videos, in: *Proceedings of the 2005 IEEE International Conference on Computer Vision and Pattern Recognition (CVPR)*

[Guo10] GUO, Zhenhua; ZHANG, Lei and ZHANG, David: A Completed Modeling of Local Binary Pattern Operator for Texture Classification. *IEEE Transactions on Image Processing* (2010), vol. 19(6):pp. 1657–1663

[Guo13] GUO, Ruiqi; DAI, Qieyun and HOIEM, Derek: Paired Regions for Shadow Detection and Removal. *IEEE Transactions on Pattern Analysis and Machine Intelligence* (2013), vol. 35(12):pp. 2956–2967

[Had04] HADID, Abdenour; PIETIKÄINEN, Matti and AHONEN, Timo: A discriminative feature space for detecting and recognizing faces, in: *Proceedings of the 2004 IEEE International Conference on Computer Vision and Pattern Recognition (CVPR)*

[Hal06] HALL, Daniela: A System for Object Class Detection, in: Henrik I. Christensen and Hans-Hellmut Nagel (Editors) *Cognitive Vision Systems*, vol. 3948 of *Lecture Notes in Computer Science (LNCS)*, Springer (2006), pp. 73–85

[Hal08] HALL, David L. and LLINAS, James: Multisensor Data Fusion, in: Martin E. Liggins; David L. Hall and James Llinas (Editors) *Handbook of Multisensor Data Fusion: Theory and Practice*, CRC Press (2008)

[Har75] HARTIGAN, John A.: *Clustering algorithms*, Wiley (1975)

[Har88] HARRIS, Chris and STEPHENS, Mike: A combined corner and edge detector, in: *In Proceedings of the 1988 Fourth Alvey Vision Conference*, pp. 147–151

[Har04] HARTLEY, Richard and ZISSERMAN, Andrew: *Multiple-View Geometry in Computer Vision*, Cambridge University Press, 2 edn. (2004)

[Hei06] HEIKKILÄ, Marko and PIETIKÄINEN, Matti: A Texture-Based Method for Modeling the Background and Detecting Moving Objects. *IEEE Transactions on Pattern Analysis and Machine Intelligence* (2006), vol. 28(4):pp. 657–662

[Hei07a] HEINTZ, Fredrik; RUDOL, Piotr and DOHERTY, Patrick: From images to traffic behavior – A UAV tracking and monitoring application, in: *Proceedings of the 2007 International Conference on Information Fusion (FUSION)*

[Hei08] HEINZE, Norbert; ESSWEIN, Martin; KRÜGER, Wolfgang and SAUR, Günter: Automatic image exploitation system for small UAVs, in: *Airborne intelligence, surveillance, reconnaissance (ISR) systems and applications V*, vol. 6946 of *Proceedings of SPIE (2008)*

[Hei09] HEIKKILÄ, Marko; PIETIKÄINEN, Matti and SCHMID, Cordelia: Description of Interest Regions with Local Binary Patterns. *Pattern Recognition* (2009), vol. 42(3):pp. 425–436

[Hei12] HEINLY, Jared; DUNN, Enrique and FRAHM, Jan-Michael: Comparative evaluation of binary features, in: Andrew Fitzgibbon; Svetlana Lazebnik; Pietro Perona; Yoichi Sato and Cordelia Schmid (Editors) *Computer Vision – ECCV 2012 (Part II)*, vol. 7573 of *Lecture Notes in Computer Science (LNCS)*, Springer (2012), pp. 759–773

[Hen12] HENG, Cher Keng; YOKOMITSU, Sumio; MATSUMOTO, Yuichi and TAMURA, Hajime: Shrink Boost for Selecting Multi-LBP Histogram Features in Object Detection, in: *Proceedings of the 2012 IEEE International Conference on Computer Vision and Pattern Recognition (CVPR)*

[Hil07] HILL, Thomas and LEWICKI, Paul: *Statistics: Methods and Applications*, StatSoft, Inc. (2007)

[Hos12] HOSEINNEZHAD, Reza; VO, Ba-Ngu; VO, Ba-Tuong and SUTER, David: Visual tracking of numerous targets via multi-Bernoulli filtering of image data. *Pattern Recognition* (2012), vol. 45:pp. 3625–3635

[Hou02] HOU, Zujun J. and WEI, Guo-Wei: A new approach to edge detection. *Pattern Recognition* (2002), vol. 35(7):pp. 1559–1570

[Hyv01] HYVÄRINEN, Aapo; KARHUNEN, Juha and OJA, Erkki: *Independent Component Analysis*, Wiley (2001)

[Ibr10] IBRAHIM, Aryo Wiman Nur; CHING, Pang Wee; SEET, Gerald; LAU, Michael and CZAJEWSKI, Witold: Moving Objects Detection and Tracking Framework for UAV-based Surveillance, in: *Proceedings of the 2010 Fourth Pacific-Rim Symposium on Image and Video Technology*

[Iwa10] IWASHITA, Yumi; STOICA, Adrian and KURAZUME, Ryo: People identification using shadow dynamics, in: *Proceedings of the 2010 IEEE International Conference on Image Processing (ICIP)*

[Jai95] JAIN, Ramesh; KASTURI, Rangachar and SCHUNCK, Brian G.: *Machine Vision*, McGraw-Hill Inc. (1995)

[Jap11] JAPKOWICZ, Natalie and SHAH, Mohak: *Evaluating Learning Algorithms: A Classification Perspective*, Cambridge University Press (2011)

[Jon05] JONES, Ronald; RISTIC, Branko; REDDING, Nicholas J. and BOOTH, David M.: Moving Target Indication and Tracking from Moving Sensors, in: *Proceedings of the 2005 International Conference on Digital Image Computing: Techniques and Applications (DICTA)*

[Kal60] KALMAN, Rudolf Emil: A new approach to linear filtering and prediction problems. *Transactions of the ASME - Journal of Basic Engineering* (1960), vol. 82(1):pp. 35–45

[Kan05] KANG, Jinman; COHEN, Isaac; MEDIONI, Gérard and YUAN, Chang: Detection and tracking of moving objects from a moving platform in presence of strong parallax, in: *Proceedings of the 2005 IEEE International Conference on Computer Vision (ICCV)*

[Kas09] KASTURI, Rangachar; GOLDGOF, Dmitry; SOUNDARARAJAN, Padmanabhan; MANOHAR, Vasant; GAROFOLO, John; BOONSTRA, Matthew; KORZHOVA, Valentina and ZHANG, Jing: Framework for Performance Evaluation of Face, Text, and Vehicle Detection and Tracking in Video: Data, Metrics, and Protocol. *IEEE Transactions on Pattern Analysis and Machine Intelligence* (2009), vol. 31(2):pp. 319–336

[Kec13] KECK, Mark A.; GALUP, Luis and STAUFFER, Chris: Real-time tracking of low-resolution vehicles for wide-area persistent surveillance, in: *Proceedings of the 2013 IEEE Workshop on Application of Computer Vision (WACV)*

[Kim10] KIM, In Su; CHOI, Hong Seok; YI, Kwang Moo; CHOI, Jin Young and KONG, Seong G.: Intelligent Visual Surveillance - A Survey. *International Journal of Control, Automation, and Systems* (2010), vol. 8(5):pp. 926–939

[Kim13] KIM, Joosung; GWON, Ryu-Hyeok; PARK, Jin-Tak; KIM, Hakil and KIM, Yoo-Sung: A Semi-Automatic Video Annotation Tool to Generate Ground Truth for Intelligent Video Surveillance Systems, in: *Proceedings of the 2013 International Conference on Advances in Mobile Computing & Multimedia (MoMM)*, pp. 509–513

[Kit87] KITAGAWA, Genshiro: Non-Gaussian State-Space Modeling of Nonstationary Time Series. *Journal of the American Statistical Association* (1987), vol. 82(400):pp. 1032–1041

[Kle94] KLEIHORST, Richard Petrus: *Noise Filtering of Image Sequences*, Dissertation, Delft University of Technology, Netherlands (1994)

[Kru99] KRUEGER, Wolfgang: Robust real-time ground plane motion compensation from a moving vehicle. *Machine Vision and Applications* (1999), vol. 11:pp. 203–212

[Kuh55] KUHN, Harold W.: The Hungarian method for solving the assignment problem. *Naval Research Logistics Quarterly* (1955), vol. 2:pp. 83–97

[Kul51] KULLBACK, Solomon and LEIBLER, Richard A.: On information and sufficiency. *Annals of Mathematical Statistics* (1951), vol. 22:pp. 79–86

[Kum01] KUMAR, Rakesh; SAWHNEY, Herpreet; SAMARASEKERA, Supun; HSU, Steve; TAO, Hai; GUO, Yanlin; HANNA, Keith; POPE, Arthur; WILDES, Richard; HIRVONEN, David; HANSEN, Michael and BURT, Peter:

Aerial video surveillance and exploitation. *Proceedings of the IEEE* (2001), vol. 89(10):pp. 1518–1539

[Kum06] KUMAR, Pankaj; RANGANATH, Surendra; SENGUPTA, Kuntal and WEIMIN, Huang: Cooperative Multitarget Tracking With Efficient Split and Merge Handling. *IEEE Transactions on Circuits and Systems for Video Technology* (2006), vol. 16(12):pp. 1477–1490

[Kyd06] KYDD, Andrew H. and WALTER, Barbara F.: The Strategies of Terrorism. *International Security* (2006), vol. 31(1):pp. 49–79

[Lan11] LANDAU, Susan: *Surveillance or Security? The Risks Posed by New Wiretapping Technologies*, The MIT Press (2011)

[Lav10] LAVIGNE, Daniel; SAHLI, Samir; OUYANG, Yueh and SHENG, Yunlong: Unsupervised classification and clustering of image features for vehicle detection in large scale aerial images, in: *Proceedings of the 2010 International Conference on Information Fusion (FUSION)*

[Lee87] LEE, James S. J.; HARALICK, Robert M. and SHAPIRO, Linda G.: Morphologic edge detection. *IEEE Journal of Robotics and Automation* (1987), vol. 3(2):pp. 142–156

[Lee05] LEE, Dar-Shyang: Effective Gaussian mixture learning for video background subtraction. *IEEE Transactions on Pattern Analysis and Machine Intelligence* (2005), vol. 27(5):pp. 827–832

[Lei08] LEIBE, Bastian; LEONARDIS, Aleš and SCHIELE, Bernt: Robust object detection with interleaved categorization and segmentation. *International Journal of Computer Vision* (2008), vol. 77:pp. 259–289

[Let08] LETIENNE, Antoine; CHAMPAGNAT, Frédéric; KULCSÁR, Caroline; BESNERAIS, Guy Le and DE LESEGNO, Patrick Viaris: Fast Super-Resolution on Moving Objects in Video Sequences, in: *Proceedings of the 2008 European Signal Processing Conference (EUSIPCO)*

[Li09a] LI, Qingquan; LEI, Bo; YU, Yang and HOU, Rui: Real-time Highway Traffic Information Extraction Based on Airborne Video, in: *Proceedings of the 2009 International IEEE Conference on Intelligent Transportation Systems (ITSC)*

[Li09b] LI, Yuan; HUANG, Chang and NEVATIA, Ramakant: Learning to associate: HybridBoosted multi-target tracker for crowded scene, in: *Proceedings of the 2009 IEEE International Conference on Computer Vision and Pattern Recognition (CVPR)*

[Li14] LI, Huifang; ZHANG, Liangpei and SHEN, Huanfeng: An Adaptive Nonlocal Regularized Shadow Removal Method for Aerial Remote Sensing Images. *IEEE Transactions on Geoscience and Remote Sensing* (2014), vol. 52(1):pp. 106–120

[Lia12] LIANG, Pengpeng; TEODORO, Gregory; LING, Haibin; BLASCH, Erik; CHEN, Genshe and BAI, Li: Multiple Kernel Learning for Vehicle Detection in Wide Area Motion Imagery, in: *Proceedings of the 2012 International Conference on Information Fusion (FUSION)*

[Lin09] LIN, Renjun; CAO, Xianbin; XU, Yanwu; WU, Changxia and QIAO, Hong: Airborne moving vehicle detection for video surveillance of urban traffic, in: *Proceedings of the 2009 IEEE Intelligent Vehicles Symposium (IV)*

[Lin11] LIN, Albert Yu-Min; NOVO, Alexandre; HAR-NOY, Shay; RICKLIN, Nathan D. and STAMATIOU, Kostas: Combining GeoEye-1 Satellite Remote Sensing, UAV Aerial Imaging, and Geophysical Surveys in Anomaly Detection Applied to Archaeology. *IEEE Journal of Selected Topics in Applied Earth Observations and Remote Sensing (JSTARS)* (2011), vol. 4(4):pp. 870–876

[Liu05] LIU, Zhijun; CHEN, Chaoyang; SHEN, Xubang and ZOU, Xuecheng: Detection of small objects in image data based on the nonlinear principal component analysis neural network. *SPIE Optical Engineering* (2005), vol. 44

[Low04] LOWE, David G.: Distinctive Image Features from Scale-Invariant Keypoints. *Intern. Journal of Computer Vision* (2004), vol. 60(2):pp. 91–110

[Luc81] LUCAS, Bruce D. and KANADE, Takeo: An Iterative Image Registration Technique with an Application to Stereo Vision, in: *Proceedings of the 1981 International Joint Conference on Artificial Intelligence (IJCAI)*, pp. 674–679

[Luo12] LUO, Pingting; LIU, Fuqiang; LIU, Xiaofeng and YANG, Yingqian: Stationary Vehicle Detection in Aerial Surveillance with a UAV, in: *Proceedings of the 2012 International Conference on Information Science and Digital Content Technology (ICIDT)*

[Mäe03] MÄENPÄÄ, Topi: *The Local Binary Pattern Approach to Texture Analysis - Extensions and Applications*, Dissertation, University of Oulu, Finland (2003)

[Mag11] MAGGIO, Emilio and CAVALLARO, Andrea: *Video tracking: theory and practice*, Wiley (2011)

[Mar02] MARIANO, Vladimir Y.; MIN, Junghye; PARK, Jin-Hyeong; KASTURI, Rangachar; MIHALCIK, David; LI, Huiping; DOERMANN, David and DRAYER, Thomas: Performance evaluation of object detection algorithms, in: *Proceedings of the 2002 International Conference on Pattern Recognition (ICPR)*

[Mat02] MATAS, Jiri; CHUM, Ondrej; URBAN, Martin and PAJDLA, Tomas: Robust wide baseline stereo from maximally stable extremal regions, in: *Proceedings of the 2002 British Machine Vision Conference (BMVC)*

[May12] MAYHEW, Christopher A. and MAYHEW, Craig M.: Parallax visualization of UAV FMV and WAMI imagery, in: *Airborne Intelligence, Surveillance, Reconnaissance (ISR) Systems and Applications IX*, vol. 8360 of *Proceedings of SPIE (2012)*

[Meu13] MEUEL, Holger; RESO, Matthias; JACHALSKY, Jörn and OSTERMANN, Jörn: Superpixel-based Segmentation of Moving Objects for Low

Bitrate ROI Coding Systems, in: *Proceedings of the 2013 IEEE International Conference on Advanced Video and Signal-Based Surveillance (AVSS)*

[Mig05] MIGDAL, Joshua; IZO, Tomas and STAUFFER, Chris: Moving Object Segmentation Using Super-Resolution Background Models, in: *Proceedings of the 2005 IEEE International Conference on Computer Vision Workshops (ICCVW)*

[Mik05] MIKOLAJCZYK, Krystian and SCHMID, Cordelia: A performance evaluation of local descriptors. *IEEE Transactions on Pattern Analysis and Machine Intelligence* (2005), vol. 27:pp. 1615–1630

[Mil13] MILAN, Anton; SCHINDLER, Konrad and ROTH, Stefan: Challenges of Ground Truth Evaluation of Multi-Target Tracking, in: *Proceedings of the 2013 IEEE International Conference on Computer Vision and Pattern Recognition Workshops (CVPRW)*, pp. 735–742

[Mit97] MITCHELL, Thomas M.: *Machine Learning*, McGraw-Hill (1997)

[Mon11] MONARI, Eduardo: *Dynamische Sensorselektion zur auftragsorientierten Objektverfolgung in Kameranetzwerken*, Dissertation, Karlsruhe Institute of Technology, Germany (2011)

[Mor10] MORSE, Bryan S.; ENGH, Cameron H. and GOODRICH, Michael A.: UAV Video Coverage Quality Maps and Prioritized Indexing for Wilderness Search and Rescue, in: *Proceedings of the 2010 ACM/IEEE International Conference on Human-Robot Interaction (HRI)*

[Mül07] MÜLLER, Markus; KRÜGER, Wolfgang and SAUR, Günter: Robust image registration for fusion. *Information Fusion* (2007), vol. 8(4):pp. 347–353

[Mül10] MÜLLER, Thomas and MÜLLER, Markus: CART IV: Improving Camouflage Assessment With Assistance Methods, in: *Infrared Imaging Systems: Design, Analysis, Modeling, and Testing XXI*, vol. 7662 of *Proceedings of SPIE (2010)*

[Mun06] MUNDER, Stefan and GAVRILA, Dariu M.: An Experimental Study on Pedestrian Classification. *IEEE Transactions on Pattern Analysis and Machine Intelligence* (2006), vol. 28(11)

[Mun12] MUNDHENK, T. Nathan; NI, Kang-Yu; CHEN, Yang; KIM, Kyungnam and OWECHKO, Yuri: Detection of unknown targets from aerial camera and extraction of simple object fingerprints for the purpose of target reacquisition, in: *Intelligent Robots and Computer Vision XXIX: Algorithms and Techniques*, vol. 8301 of *Proceedings of SPIE (2012)*

[Nel72] NELDER, John and WEDDERBURN, Robert: Generalized Linear Models. *Journal of the Royal Statistical Society* (1972), vol. 135(3):pp. 370–384

[Net12] NETO, Jacy Montenegro M.; DA PAIXAO, Ronan A.; RODRIGUES, Luiz Renault L.; MOREIRA, Erick M.; DOS SANTOS, Joao Carlos Jose and ROSA, Paulo Fernando F.: A Surveillance Task for a UAV in a Natural Disaster Scenario, in: *Proceedings of the 2012 IEEE International Symposium on Industrial Electronics (ISIE)*

[Ngu07] NGUYEN, Thuy Thi; GRABNER, Helmut; BISCHOF, Horst and GRUBER, Barbara: On-line Boosting for Car Detection from Aerial Images, in: *Proceedings of the 2007 IEEE International Conference on Research, Innovation and Vision for the Future (RIVF)*

[Oja02] OJALA, Timo; PIETIKÄINEN, Matti and MÄENPÄÄ, Topi: Multiresolution Gray-Scale and Rotation Invariant Texture Classification with Local Binary Patterns. *IEEE Transactions on Pattern Analysis and Machine Intelligence* (2002), vol. 24(7):pp. 971–987

[Ore10] OREIFEJ, Omar; MEHRAN, Ramin and SHAH, Mubarak: Human identity recognition in aerial images, in: *Proceedings of the 2010 IEEE Conference on Computer Vision and Pattern Recognition (CVPR)*

[Ots79] OTSU, Nobuyuki: A threshold selection method from gray-level histograms. *IEEE Transactions on Systems, Man, and Cybernetics* (1979), vol. 9(1):pp. 62–66

[Pap00] PAPAGEORGIOU, Constantine and POGGIO, Tomaso: A Trainable System for Object Detection. *International Journal of Computer Vision* (2000), vol. 38:pp. 15–33

[Pap13] PAPI, Francesco; VO, Ba-Tuong; BOCQUEL, Mélanie and VO, Ba-Ngu: Multi-target Track-Before-Detect using Labeled Random Finite Set, in: *Proceedings of the 2013 International Conference on Control, Automation and Information Sciences (ICCAIS)*, pp. 116–121

[Pel12] PELAPUR, Rengarajan; CANDEMIR, Sema; BUNYAK, Filiz; POOSTCHI, Mahdieh; SEETHARAMAN, Guna and PALANIAPPAN, Kannappan: Persistent Target Tracking Using Likelihood Fusion in Wide-Area and Full Motion Video Sequences, in: *Proceedings of the 2012 International Conference on Information Fusion (FUSION)*, pp. 2420–2427

[Per06a] PERERA, A. G. Amitha; HOOGS, Anthony; SRINIVAS, Chukka; BROOKSBY, Glen and HU, Wensheng: Evaluation of Algorithms for Tracking Multiple Objects in Video, in: *Proceedings of the 2006 IEEE Applied Imagery and Pattern Recognition Workshop (AIPR)*

[Per06b] PERERA, A. G. Amitha; SRINIVAS, Chukka; HOOGS, Anthony; BROOKSBY, Glen and HU, Wensheng: Multi-Object Tracking Through Simultaneous Long Occlusions and Split-Merge Conditions, in: *Proceedings of the 2006 IEEE International Conference on Computer Vision and Pattern Recognition (CVPR)*

[Pic04] PICCARDI, Massimo: Background subtraction techniques: a review, in: *Proceedings of the 2004 IEEE International Conference on Systems, Man and Cybernetics*, pp. 3099–3104

[Pie11] PIETIKÄINEN, Matti; HADID, Abdenour; ZHAO, Guoying and AHONEN, Timo: *Computer Vision Using Local Binary Patterns*, Springer (2011)

[Pol10] POLAND, James M.: *Understanding Terrorism: Groups, Strategies, and Responses* , Prentice Hall (2010)

[Pol12] POLLARD, Thomas and ANTONE, Matthew: Detecting and Tracking All Moving Objects inWide-Area Aerial Video, in: *Proceedings of the 2012 IEEE International Conference on Computer Vision and Pattern Recognition Workshops (CVPRW)*

[Por03] PORTILLA, Javier; STRELA, Vasily; WAINWRIGHT, Martin J. and SIMONCELLI, Eero P.: Image Denoising Using Scale Mixtures of Gaussians in the Wavelet Domain. *IEEE Transactions on Pattern Analysis and Machine Intelligence* (2003), vol. 12(11):pp. 1338–1351

[Pri07] PRINZIE, Anita and VAN DEN POEL, Dirk: Random Multiclass Classification: Generalizing Random Forests to Random MNL and Random NB, in: Roland Wagner; Norman Revell and Günther Pernul (Editors) *Database and Expert Systems Applications*, vol. 4653 of *Lecture Notes in Computer Science (LNCS)*, Springer (2007), pp. 349–358

[Pro11] PROKAJ, Jan; DUCHAINEAU, Mark and MEDIONI, Gérard: Inferring tracklets for multi-object tracking, in: *Proceedings of the 2011 IEEE International Conference on Computer Vision and Pattern Recognition Workshops (CVPRW)*

[Pro12] PROKAJ, Jan; ZHAO, Xuemei and MEDIONI, Gérard: Tracking Many Vehicles in Wide Area Aerial Surveillance, in: *Proceedings of the 2012 IEEE International Conference on Computer Vision and Pattern Recognition Workshops (CVPRW)*

[Pro13] PROKAJ, Jan: *Exploitation of Wide Area Motion Imagery*, Dissertation, University of Southern California, Los Angeles, CA, USA (2013)

[Pro14] PROKAJ, Jan and MEDIONI, Gérard: Persistent Tracking for Wide Area Aerial Surveillance, in: *Proceedings of the 2014 IEEE International Conference on Computer Vision and Pattern Recognition (CVPR)*

[Pur08] PURI, Anuj: *Statistical profile generation of real-time UAV-based traffic data*, Dissertation, University of South Florida (2008)

[Qui92] QUINLAN, J. Ross: *C4.5: Programs for Machine Learning*, Morgan Kaufman Publishers Inc. (1992)

[Red12] REDDY, Kishore K.; CUNTOOR, Naresh; PERERA, Amitha and HOOGS, Anthony: Human Action Recognition in Large-Scale Datasets Using Histogram of Spatiotemporal Gradients, in: *Proceedings of the 2012 IEEE International Conference on Advanced Video and Signal-Based Surveillance (AVSS)*

[Rei10a] REILLY, Vladimir; IDREES, Haroon and SHAH, Mubarak: Detection and Tracking of Large Number of Targets in Wide Area Surveillance, in: Kostas Daniilidis; Petros Maragos and Nikos Paragios (Editors) *Computer Vision – ECCV 2010 (Part III)*, vol. 6313 of *Lecture Notes in Computer Science (LNCS)*, Springer (2010), pp. 186–199

[Rei10b] REILLY, Vladimir; SOLMAZ, Berkan and SHAH, Mubarak: Geometric constraints for human detection in aerial imagery, in: Kostas Daniilidis; Petros Maragos and Nikos Paragios (Editors) *Computer Vision – ECCV 2010 (Part VI)*, vol. 6316 of *Lecture Notes in Computer Science (LNCS)*, Springer (2010), pp. 252–265

[Ris04] RISTIC, Branko; ARULAMPALAM, Sanjeev and GORDON, Neil: *Beyond the Kalman Filter: Particle Filters for Tracking Applications*, Artech House Inc (2004)

[Roe00] ROERDINK, Jos B.T.M. and MEIJSTER, Arnold: The Watershed Transform: Definitions, Algorithms and Parallelization Strategies. *Fundamenta Informaticae* (2000), vol. 41(1,2):pp. 187–228

[Rud08] RUDOL, Piotr and DOHERTY, Patrick: Human Body Detection and Geolocalization for UAV Search and Rescue Missions Using Color and Thermal Imagery, in: *Proceedings of the 2008 IEEE Aerospace Conference*

[Rus03] RUSSELL, Stuart J. and NORVIG, Peter: *Artificial Intelligence: A Modern Approach*, Prentice Hall, 2 edn. (2003)

[Sah11] SAHLI, Samir; DUVAL, Pierre-Luc; SHENG, Yunlong and LAVIGNE, Daniel A.: Robust vehicle detection in aerial images based on salient region selection and superpixel classification, in: *Airborne Intelligence, Surveillance, Reconnaissance (ISR) Systems and Applications VIII*, vol. 8050 of *Proceedings of SPIE (2011)*

[Sal13] SALEEMI, Imran and SHAH, Mubarak: Multiframe Many-Many Point Correspondence for Vehicle Tracking in High Density Wide Area Aerial Videos. *International Journal of Computer Vision (IJCV)* (2013), vol. 104(2):pp. 198–219

[Sch14] SCHICK, Alexander: *Human Pose Estimation with Supervoxels*, Dissertation, Karlsruhe Institute of Technology, Germany (2014)

[Sha05a] SHAFIQUE, Khurram and SHAH, Mubarak: A noniterative greedy algorithm for multiframe point correspondence . *IEEE Transactions on Pattern Analysis and Machine Intelligence* (2005), vol. 27(1):pp. 51–65

[Sha05b] SHASTRY, Anand C. and SCHOWENGERDT, Robert A.: Airborne Video Registration and Traffic-Flow Parameter Estimation. *IEEE Transactions on Intelligent Transportation Systems* (2005), vol. 6(4):pp. 391–405

[Sha14] SHAO, Ling; YAN, Ruomei; LI, Xuelong and LIU, Yan: From Heuristic Optimization to Dictionary Learning: A Review and Comprehensive Comparison of Image Denoising Algorithms. *IEEE Transactions on Cybernetics* (2014), vol. 44(4):pp. 1001–1013

[She13a] SHEN, Hao; LI, Shuxiao; ZHANG, Jinglan and CHANG, Hongxing: Tracking-Based Moving Object Detection, in: *Proceedings of the 2013 IEEE International Conference on Image Processing (ICIP)*

[She13b] SHEN, Hao; LI, Shuxiao; ZHU, Chengfei; CHANG, Hongxing and ZHANG, Jinglan: Moving object detection in aerial video based on spatiotemporal saliency. *Chinese Journal of Aeronautics* (2013), vol. 26(5):pp. 1211–1217

[Shi94] SHI, Jianbo and TOMASI, Carlo: Good features to track, in: *Proceedings of the 1994 IEEE International Conference on Computer Vision and Pattern Recognition (CVPR)*

[Shi10] SHIH, Frank Y.: *Image Processing and Pattern Recognition: Fundamentals and Techniques*, Wiley (2010)

[Shi12] SHI, Xinchu; LING, Haibin; BLASCH, Erik and HU, Weiming: Context-Driven Moving Vehicle Detection in Wide Area Motion Imagery, in: *Proceedings of the 2012 International Conference on Pattern Recognition (ICPR)*

[Shr12] SHRIDHAR, Malayappan and WATTA, Paul: Pattern Recognition, in: Bruce G. Batchelor (Editor) *Machine Vision Handbook*, vol. 2, Springer (2012), pp. 1079–1102

[Sia12a] SIAM, Mennatullah and ELHELW, Mohamed: Robust Autonomous Visual Detection and Tracking of Moving Targets in UAV Imagery, in: *Proceedings of the 2012 IEEE International Conference on Signal Processing (ICSP)*

[Sia12b] SIAM, Mennatullah; ELSAYED, Ramy and ELHELW, Mohamed: On-board Multiple Target Detection and Tracking on Camera-Equipped Aerial Vehicles, in: *Proceedings of the 2012 IEEE International Conference on Robotics and Biomimetics (ROBIO)*

[Sme13] SMEULDERS, Arnold W. M.; CHU, Dung M.; CUCCHIARA, Rita; CALDERARA, Simone; DEGHGHAN, Afshin and SHAH, Mubarak: Visual Tracking: an Experimental Survey. *IEEE Transactions on Pattern Analysis and Machine Intelligence* (2013)

[Son14] SONG, Huihui; HUANG, Bo and ZHANG, Kaihua: Shadow Detection and Reconstruction in High-Resolution Satellite Images via Morphological Filtering and Example-Based Learning. *IEEE Transactions on Geoscience and Remote Sensing* (2014), vol. 52(5):pp. 2545–2554

[Sta99] STAUFFER, Chris and GRIMSON, W. Eric L.: Adaptive background mixture models for real-time tracking, in: *Proceedings of the 1999 International Conference on Computer Vision and Pattern Recognition (CVPR)*

[Ste08] STEPANOVA, Ekaterina: *Terrorism in Asymmetrical Conflict: Ideological and Structural Aspects*, SIPRI Research Report no. 23, Oxford University Press (2008)

[Sun06] SUN, Zehang; BEBIS, George and MILLER, Ronald: On-Road Vehicle Detection: A Review. *IEEE Transactions on Pattern Analysis and Machine Intelligence* (2006), vol. 28(5):pp. 694–711

[Sut98] SUTTON, Richard S. and BARTO, Andrew G.: *Reinforcement Learning: An Introduction*, MIT Press, Cambridge, MA, USA (1998)

[Sze11] SZELISKI, Richard: *Computer Vision: Algorithms and Applications*, Springer (2011)

[Taj09] TAJ, Murtaza and CAVALLARO, Andrea: Multi-camera track-before-detect, in: *Proceedings of the 2009 ACM/IEEE International Conference on Distributed Smart Cameras (ICDSC)*

[Tan01] TANG, Chi-Keung; MEDIONI, Gérard and LEE, Mi-Suen: N-Dimensional Tensor Voting and Application to Epipolar Geometry Estimation. *IEEE Transactions on Pattern Analysis and Machine Intelligence* (2001), vol. 23(8):pp. 829–844

[Tan06] TANAKA, Kensuke and SAJI, Hitoshi: Detection of parallelograms using hough transform. *The Transactions of the Institute of Electronics, Information and Communication Engineers D* (2006), vol. J89-D(3):pp. 606–612

[Tan07] TANAKA, Kensuke and SAJI, Hitoshi: Vehicle Extraction from Aerial Images Using Voting Process and Frame Matching, in: *Proceedings of the 2007 IEEE Intelligent Vehicles Symposium (IV)*

[Tib08] TIBSHIRANI, Ryan J.: Fast median calculation method. *arXiv* (2008), vol. 0806.3301

[Tin03] TING, Kai Ming and ZHENG, Zijian: A Study of AdaBoost with Naïve Bayesian Classifiers: Weakness and Improvement. *Computational Intelligence* (2003), vol. 19(2):pp. 186–200

[Tom91] TOMASI, Carlo and KANADE, Takeo: Detection and Tracking of Point Features, Tech. Rep. CMU-CS-91-132, Carnegie Mellon University, Pittsburgh, PA, USA (1991)

[Tor06] TORRALBA, Antonio; MURPHY, Kevin P. and FREEMAN, William T.: Shared Features for Multiclass Object Detection, in: Jean Ponce; Martial Hebert; Cordelia Schmid and Andrew Zisserman (Editors) *Toward Category-Level Object Recognition*, vol. 4170 of *Lecture Notes in Computer Science (LNCS)*, Springer (2006), pp. 345–361

[Tor11] TORRALBA, Antonio and EFRON, Alexey A.: Unbiased Look at Dataset Bias, in: *Proceedings of the 2011 IEEE International Conference on Computer Vision and Pattern Recognition (CVPR)*

[Tre10] TREIBER, Marco: *An Introduction to Object Recognition*, Advances in Computer Vision and Pattern Recognition (ACVPR), Springer (2010)

[Tsa06] TSAI, Victor J.D.: A Comparative Study on Shadow Compensation of Color Aerial Images in Invariant Color Models. *IEEE Transactions on Geoscience and Remote Sensing* (2006), vol. 44(6):pp. 1661–1671

[Tsa07] TSAI, Luo-Wei; HSIEH, Jun-Wei and FAN, Kuo-Chin: Vehicle detection using normalized color and edge map. *IEEE Transactions on Image Processing* (2007), vol. 16(3):pp. 850–864

[Tür13] TÜRMER, Sebastian; KURZ, Franz; REINARTZ, Peter; and STILLA, Uwe: Airborne Vehicle Detection in Dense Urban Areas Using HoG Features and Disparity Maps. *IEEE Journal of Selected Topics in Applied Earth Observations and Remote Sensing (JSTARS)* (2013), vol. 6(6):pp. 2327–2337

[Uki01] UKITA, Norimichi: *Real-time cooperative multi-target tracking by communicating active vision agents*, Dissertation, Kyoto University, Japan (2001)

[USA06] USAF RESEARCH LABORATORY: Columbus Large Image Format (CLIF) dataset, `https://www.sdms.afrl.af.mil/index.php?collection=clif2006` (2006)

[USA07] USAF RESEARCH LABORATORY: Columbus Large Image Format (CLIF) dataset, `https://www.sdms.afrl.af.mil/index.php?collection=clif2007` (2007)

[USA09] USAF RESEARCH LABORATORY: Wright-Patterson Air Force Base (WPAFB) dataset, `https://www.sdms.afrl.af.mil/index.php?collection=wpafb2009` (2009)

[van10] VAN EEKEREN, Adam W. M.; SCHUTTE, Klamer and VAN VLIET, Lucas J.: Multiframe Super-Resolution Reconstruction of Small Moving Objects. *IEEE Transactions on Image Processing* (2010), vol. 19(11):pp. 2901–2912

[Vap98] VAPNIK, Vladimir: *Statistical Learning Theory*, Wiley (1998)

[Vio01] VIOLA, Paul and JONES, Michael: Rapid object detection using a boosted cascade of simple features, in: *Proceedings of the 2001 IEEE International Conference on Computer Vision and Pattern Recognition (CVPR)*

[Vio04] VIOLA, Paul and JONES, Michael: Robust Real-time Face Detection. *International Journal of Computer Vision* (2004), vol. 57(2):pp. 137–154

[Vio05] VIOLA, Paul; JONES, Michael and SNOW, Daniel: Detecting Pedestrians Using Patterns of Motion and Appearance. *International Journal of Computer Vision* (2005), vol. 63(2):pp. 153–161

[Wan11] WANG, Sheng: Vehicle Detection on Aerial Images by Extracting Corner Features for Rotational Invariant Shape Matching, in: *Proceedings of the 2011 IEEE International Conference on Computer and Information Technology (CIT)*

[Wat04] WATKINSON, John: *The MPEG Handbook*, Focal Press, 2 edn. (2004)

[Wei98] WEICKERT, Joachim: *Anisotropic Diffusion in Image Processing*, Teubner-Verlag (1998)

[Wei10] WEI, Yichen and TAO, Litian: Efficient Histogram-Based Sliding Window, in: *Proceedings of the 2010 IEEE International Conference on Computer Vision and Pattern Recognition (CVPR)*

[Wu06] WU, Bo and NEVATIA, Ramakant: Tracking of multiple, partially occluded humans based on static body part detection, in: *Proceedings of the 2006 IEEE International Conference on Computer Vision and Pattern Recognition (CVPR)*

[Wu09] WU, Shunguang; TAN, Yi; DAS, Subhodev; BROADDUS, Christopher and CHIU, Ming-Yee: Multiple-Target Tracking via Kinematics, Shape and Appearance Based Data Association, in: *Signal and Data Processing of Small Targets*, vol. 7445 of *Proceedings of SPIE (2009)*

[Wu10] WU, Changxia; CAO, Xianbin; LIN, Renjun and WANG, Fei: Registration-based Moving Vehicle Detection for Low-altitude Urban Traffic Surveillance, in: *Proceedings of the 2010 World Congress on Intelligent Control and Automation (WCICA)*

[Xia08] XIAO, Jiangjian; CHENG, Hui; FENG, Han and YANG, Changjiang: Object Tracking and Classification in Aerial Videos, in: *Automatic Target Recognition XVIII*, vol. 6967 of *Proceedings of SPIE (2008)*

[Xia10] XIAO, Jiangjian; CHENG, Hui; SAWHNEY, Harpreet and HAN, Feng: Vehicle Detection and Tracking in Wide Field-of-View Aerial Video, in: *Proceedings of the 2010 IEEE Conference on Computer Vision and Pattern Recognition (CVPR)*

[Yal05] YALCIN, Hulya; HEBERT, Martial; COLLINS, Robert and BLACK, Michael J.: A flow-based approach to vehicle detection and background mosaicking in airborne video, in: *Proceedings of the 2005 IEEE International Conference on Computer Vision and Pattern Recognition (CVPR)*

[Yao08] YAO, Fenghui; SEKMEN, Ali and MALKANI, Mohan J.: Multiple moving target detection, tracking, and recognition from a moving observer, in: *Proceedings of the 2008 IEEE International Conference on Information and Automation (ICIA)*

[Yil06] YILMAZ, Alper; JAVED, Omar and SHAH, Mubarak: Object Tracking: A Survey. *ACM Computing Surveys (CSUR)* (2006), vol. 38(4)

[Yip94] YIP, R. K. K.: Line Patterns Hough Transform for Line Segment Detection, in: *Proceedings of the 1994 IEEE Region 10's Ninth Annual International Conference (TENCON'94)*, pp. 319–323

[Yu09] YU, Qian and MEDIONI, Gérard: Motion Pattern Interpretation and Detection for Tracking Moving Vehicles in Airborne Video, in: *Proceedings of the 2009 IEEE International Conference on Computer Vision and Pattern Recognition (CVPR)*

[Yua07] YUAN, Chang; MEDIONI, Gérard; KANG, Jinman and COHEN, Isaac: Detecting Motion Regions in the Presence of a Strong Parallax from a Moving Camera by Multiview Geometric Constraints. *IEEE Transactions on Pattern Analysis and Machine Intelligence* (2007), vol. 29(9):pp. 1627–1641

[Zas08] ZASS, Ron and SHASHUA, Amnon: Probabilistic Graph and Hypergraph Matching, in: *Proceedings of the 2008 IEEE International Conference on Computer Vision and Pattern Recognition (CVPR)*

[Zeh06] ZEHANG, Sun; BEBIS, George and MILLER, Ronald: [Monocular Precrash Vehicle Detection: Features and Classifiers. *IEEE Transactions on Image Processing* (2006), vol. 15(7):pp. 2019–2034

[Zha01] ZHAO, Tao and NEVATIA, Ram: Car Detection in Low Resolution Aerial Image, in: *Proceedings of the 2001 IEEE International Conference on Computer Vision (ICCV)*

[Zha13] ZHANG, Haichao; WIPF, David and ZHANG, Yanning: Multi-Image Blind Deblurring Using a Coupled Adaptive Sparse Prior, in: *Proceedings of the 2013 IEEE International Conference on Computer Vision and Pattern Recognition (CVPR)*

[Zhe13] ZHENG, Zezhong; ZHOU, Guoqing; WANG, Yong; LIU, Yalan; LI, Xiaowen; WANG, Xiaoting and JIANG, Ling: A Novel Vehicle Detection

Method With High Resolution Highway Aerial Image. *IEEE Journal of Selected Topics in Applied Earth Observations and Remote Sensing (JSTARS)* (2013), vol. 6(6):pp. 2338–2343

[Zhu10] ZHU, Linlin; FAN, Baojie; DU, Yingkui and TANG, Yandong: A tracking and locating method for UAVs Vision System, in: *Proceedings of the 2010 IEEE International Conference Information and Automation (ICIA)*

[Zhu14] ZHU, Jiejie; JAVED, Omar; LIU, Jingen; YU, Qian; CHENG, Hui and SAWHNEY, Harpreet: Pedestrian Detection in Low-resolution Imagery by Learning Multi-scale Intrinsic Motion Structures (MIMS), in: *Proceedings of the 2014 IEEE International Conference on Computer Vision and Pattern Recognition (CVPR)*

[Zit03] ZITOVÁ, Barbara and FLUSSER, Jan: Image registration methods: a survey. *Image and Vision Computing* (2003), vol. 21:pp. 977–1000

[Zit14] ZITNICK, C. Lawrence and DOLLÁR, Piotr: Edge Boxes: Locating Object Proposals from Edges, in: *Proceedings of the 2014 European Conference on Computer Vision (ECCV)*

Publications

[Bek13] BEKELE, Dagmawi; TEUTSCH, Michael and SCHUCHERT, Tobias: Evaluation of Binary Keypoint Descriptors, in: *Proceedings of the 2013 IEEE International Conference on Image Processing (ICIP)*

[Sau10] SAUR, Günter and TEUTSCH, Michael: SAR signature analysis for TerraSAR-X-based ship monitoring, in: *Image and Signal Processing for Remote Sensing XVI*, vol. 7830 of *Proceedings of SPIE (2010)*

[Sau11] SAUR, Günter; ESTABLE, Stephane; TEUFEL, Frank; KNABE, Stefan; TEUTSCH, Michael and GABEL, Matthias: Detection and Classification of man-made Offshore Objects in TerraSAR-X and RapidEye Imagery: Selected Results of the DeMarine-DEKO Project, in: *Proceedings of 2011 IEEE OCEANS*

[Teu10] TEUTSCH, Michael and KRÜGER, Wolfgang: Classification of small Boats in Infrared Images for maritime Surveillance, in: *Proceedings of the 2010 NURC WaterSide Security Conference (WSS)*

[Teu11a] TEUTSCH, Michael; KRÜGER, Wolfgang and BEYERER, Jürgen: Fusion of Region and Point-Feature Detections for Measurement Reconstruction in Multi-Target Kalman Tracking, in: *Proceedings of the 2011 International Conference on Information Fusion (FUSION)*

[Teu11b] TEUTSCH, Michael; KRÜGER, Wolfgang and HEINZE, Norbert: Detection and classification of moving objects from UAVs with optical sensors, in: *Signal Processing, Sensor Fusion, and Target Recognition XX*, vol. 8050 of *Proceedings of SPIE (2011)*

[Teu11c] TEUTSCH, Michael and SAUR, Günter: Comparison of using single- or multi-polarimetric TerraSAR-X images for segmentation and classification of man-made maritime objects, in: *Image and Signal Processing for Remote Sensing XVII*, vol. 8180 of *Proceedings of SPIE (2011)*

[Teu11d] TEUTSCH, Michael and SAUR, Günter: Segmentation and Classification of Man-made Maritime Objects in TerraSAR-X Images, in: *Proceedings of the 2011 IEEE International Geoscience and Remote Sensing Symposium (IGARSS)*

[Teu11e] TEUTSCH, Michael and SCHAMM, Thomas: Fast Line and Object Segmentation in Noisy and Cluttered Environments Using Relative Connectivity, in: *Proceedings of the 2011 International Conference on Image Processing, Computer Vision, and Pattern Recognition (IPCV)*

[Teu12a] TEUTSCH, Michael and KRÜGER, Wolfgang: Detection, Segmentation, and Tracking of Moving Objects in UAV Videos, in: *Proceedings of the 2012 IEEE International Conference on Advanced Video and Signal-Based Surveillance (AVSS)*

[Teu12b] TEUTSCH, Michael and KRÜGER, Wolfgang: Spatio-Temporal Fusion of Object Segmentation Approaches for Moving Distant Targets, in: *Proceedings of the 2012 International Conference on Information Fusion (FUSION)*

[Teu13a] TEUTSCH, Michael and BEYERER, Jürgen: Noise Resistant Gradient Calculation and Edge Detection using Local Binary Patterns, in: Jong-Il Park and Junmo Kim (Editors) *Computer Vision – ACCV 2012 Workshops*, vol. 7728 of *Lecture Notes in Computer Science (LNCS)*, Springer (2013), pp. 1–14

[Teu13b] TEUTSCH, Michael and MÜLLER, Thomas: Hot spot detection and classification in LWIR videos for person recognition, in: *Automatic Target Recognition XXIII*, vol. 8744 of *Proceedings of SPIE (2013)*

[Teu13c] TEUTSCH, Michael; TRANTELLE, Patrick and BEYERER, Jürgen: Adaptive Real-Time Image Smoothing Using Local Binary Patterns and Gaussian Filters, in: *Proceedings of the 2013 IEEE International Conference on Image Processing (ICIP)*

[Teu14a] TEUTSCH, Michael; KRÜGER, Wolfgang and BEYERER, Jürgen: Evaluation of Object Segmentation to Improve Moving Vehicle Detection in Aerial Videos, in: *Proceedings of the 2014 IEEE International Conference on Advanced Video and Signal-Based Surveillance (AVSS)*

[Teu14b] TEUTSCH, Michael; MÜLLER, Thomas; HUBER, Marco and BEYERER, Jürgen: Low Resolution Person Detection with a Moving Thermal Infrared Camera by Hot Spot Classification, in: *Proceedings of the 2014 IEEE International Conference on Computer Vision and Pattern Recognition Workshops (CVPRW)*

List of Figures

1.1 Luna UAV with a VIS camera and one aerial image. 4
1.2 Challenges of moving object detection and tracking. 9

2.1 Example images taken from the VIVID and the WPAFB dataset. 14
2.2 Comparison of background learning and difference images. . . 21
2.3 Motion vector clustering vs. difference images [Sia12b]. 23
2.4 Appearance of persons in top view aerial videos. 29

3.1 Concept of the processing chain. 34
3.2 Object segmentation vs. object detection. 36

4.1 Concept of independent motion detection. 40
4.2 Motion vector clustering vs. difference images. 42
4.3 Examples for independent motion detection and clustering. . 44
4.4 Distribution of motion vector magnitudes for an example image. 45
4.5 Problems of independent motion detection and clustering. . . 46

5.1 Motivation for object detection and segmentation. 49
5.2 Concept of object detection and segmentation. 50
5.3 Motivation for image stacking. 52
5.4 Concept of image stacking. 54
5.5 Image stacks for two vehicles with small relative velocity. . . . 55
5.6 Association of motion vectors to master vectors. 58

5.7 Image stack update. 59
5.8 Replacement of motion clusters by image stacks. 61
5.9 Examples for successful application of image stacking. 63
5.10 Concept of gradient based object segmentation. 66
5.11 Calculation and interpretation of LBP [Mäe03]. 68
5.12 Image noise models visualized by LBP distributions. 69
5.13 Noise resistant gradient calculation using LBP. 71
5.14 Different gradient calculation methods for object segmentation. 74
5.15 From gradients to objects. 76
5.16 Calculation of quantile based thresholding. 77
5.17 Gradient based object segmentation vs. relative connectivity. . 78
5.18 Proposed algorithm for calculating relative connectivity. 83
5.19 Concept of object segmentation using relative connectivity. . . 84
5.20 From relative connectivity to objects. 85
5.21 Concept of object detection using local sliding window. 86
5.22 Example for object detection using local sliding window. 87
5.23 Image rescaling for detection of differently sized objects. . . . 89
5.24 Average gradient magnitudes for person and vehicle samples. . 90
5.25 Influence of image rescaling and T_{dov} to sliding window. . . . 91
5.26 Calculation of integral channel features. 94
5.27 Example for removal of duplicate detections. 98
5.28 Example for removal of outlier detections. 100

6.1 Concept of multiple object tracking. 103
6.2 Association of detections to tracks. 105
6.3 Association of motion vectors to tracks. 106
6.4 Lifetime and association time of motion vectors. 107
6.5 Example for reconstuction of detections by using motion vectors.108
6.6 Flowchart of the multiple object tracking algorithm. 110

7.1 Visualization of GT, TP, FP, FN, and TN. 112
7.2 Examples for the evaluation of object detection. 114
7.3 Aerial videos used for the experiments. 121
7.4 Samples used for classifier training and evaluation. 122
7.5 Samples used for classifier training and evaluation. 123
7.6 Parameter optimization for gradient based segmentation. . . . 125

7.7 Parameter optimization for relative connectivity. 128
7.8 Parameter optimization for local sliding window. 131
7.9 Decision values of different classifiers for sliding window. . . . 133
7.10 Parameter optimization for image stacking. 135
7.11 Parameter optimization for outlier removal. 136
7.12 Parameter optimization for multiple object tracking. 137
7.13 Concepts of the implemented algorithms from the literature. . 140
7.14 f-score evaluation of object detection and segmentation. . . . 141
7.15 Qualitative evaluation for object detection and segmentation. 146
7.16 Qualitative evaluation for object detection and segmentation. 147
7.17 Imprecise image stacking for turning vehicles. 149
7.18 Qualitative evaluation for image stacking. 152
7.19 Qualitative evaluation for image stacking. 153
7.20 Qualitative evaluation for multiple object tracking. 158
7.21 Evaluation of the entire processing chain. 162
7.22 Some examples for the local sliding window approach. 163

List of Tables

2.1 Related work overview (first part). 15
2.2 Related work overview (second part). 16

7.1 Statistics of the aerial video datasets. 119
7.2 Statistics of the aerial images used for classifier training. 120
7.3 Gradient based segmentation after parameter optimization. . 127
7.4 AUC comparison for 5 descriptors and 6 classifiers. 130
7.5 Evaluation of different scale levels for object detection. 134
7.6 Quantitative evaluation for object detection and segmentation. 144
7.7 Quantitative evaluation for object detection and segmentation. 145
7.8 Quantitative evaluation for image stacking. 151
7.9 Quantitative evaluation for multiple object tracking. 156
7.10 Quantitative evaluation for multiple object tracking. 157
7.11 Evaluation of the proposed methods' processing time. 160

Acronyms

AUC Area Under the Curve 115

BN Bayesian Network 26

CC-ICA Class-Conditional Independent Component Analysis 95

ChnFtrs Integral Channel Features 92

CLIF Columbus Large Image Format 13

DARPA Defense Advanced Research Projects Agency 13

DBN Dynamic Bayesian Network 27

DBT Detect-Before-Track 21

DCT Discrete Cosine Transform 92

DEM Digital Elevation Model 39

DPM Deformable Part Model 27

EM Expectation Maximization 31

FBPDA Feature-Based Probabilistic Data Association 107

FM track fragmentation 117

FN False Negative 8

FP False Positive 8

FPR False Positive Rate 115

GIS Geographic Information System 24

GLM Generalized Linear Model 31

GMKL Generalized Multiple Kernel Learning 28

GMM Gaussian Mixture Model 24

GPU Graphics Processing Unit 67

GSD Ground Sampling Distance 33

GT Ground Truth 8

gPb global Probability of boundary 48

HOG Histogram of Oriented Gradients 27

HSV Hue Saturation Value 19

ICA Independent Component Analysis 95

ID identifier 106

IR infrared 11

ISM Implicit Shape Model 27

IoU Intersection over Union 30

JI Jaccard index 30

JPDAF Joint Probabilistic Data Association Filter 30

KL Kullback-Leibler divergence 31

KLT Kanade-Lucas-Tomasi 17

k-NN k-Nearest Neighbors 28

LBP Local Binary Pattern 10

LDA Linear Discriminant Analysis 96

LMedS Least Median Of Squares 17

LoFT Likelihood of Features Tracking 32

LPHT Line Patterns Hough transform 79

LWIR long wave infrared 93

MAP maximum a posteriori probability 31

MHT Multiple Hypothesis Tracking 30

MIMS Multi-Scale Intrinsic Motion Structure 28

MLT mostly lost 117

MOTA Multiple Object Tracking Accuracy 117

MOTP Multiple Object Tracking Precision 117

MSER Maximally Stable Extremal Regions 50

MT mostly tracked 117

N-MODA Normalized Multiple Object Detection Accuracy 116

N-MODP Normalized Multiple Object Detection Precision 116

NB Naïve Bayes 93

NMS Non-Maximum Suppression 27

OOB Out-Of-Bag 95

OWT Oriented Watershed Transform 48

PSNR Peak-Signal-To-Noise Ratio 70

PT partially tracked 117

RANSAC Random Sample Consensus 17

RBF Radial Basis Function 29

RF Random Forest 26

RNB Random Naïve Bayes 93

ROC Receiver Operating Characteristic 115

ROI Region of Interest 28

SAR Synthetic Aperture Radar 10

SFM Structure From Motion 18

SFS Sequential Forward Selection 96

SIFT Scale Invariant Features Transform 17

SLIC Simple Linear Iterative Clustering 48

SURF Speeded Up Robust Features 17

SVM Support Vector Machine 26

TBD Track-Before-Detect 21

TN True Negative 112

TP True Positive 112

TPR True Positive Rate 114

UAPC Unsupervised Affinity Propagation Clustering 26

UAV Unmanned Aerial Vehicle 2

UCM Ultrametric Contour Map 48

VIS visual-optical 2

WAMI Wide Area Motion Imagery 3

WAS Wide Area Surveillance 3

WPAFB Wright-Patterson Air Force Base 13

Karlsruher Schriftenreihe zur Anthropomatik
(ISSN 1863-6489)

Herausgeber: Prof. Dr.-Ing. Jürgen Beyerer

Die Bände sind unter www.ksp.kit.edu als PDF frei verfügbar
oder als Druckausgabe bestellbar.

Band 1 Jürgen Geisler
Leistung des Menschen am Bildschirmarbeitsplatz. 2006
ISBN 3-86644-070-7

Band 2 Elisabeth Peinsipp-Byma
Leistungserhöhung durch Assistenz in interaktiven Systemen zur Szenenanalyse. 2007
ISBN 978-3-86644-149-1

Band 3 Jürgen Geisler, Jürgen Beyerer (Hrsg.)
Mensch-Maschine-Systeme. 2010
ISBN 978-3-86644-457-7

Band 4 Jürgen Beyerer, Marco Huber (Hrsg.)
Proceedings of the 2009 Joint Workshop of Fraunhofer IOSB and Institute for Anthropomatics, Vision and Fusion Laboratory. 2010
ISBN 978-3-86644-469-0

Band 5 Thomas Usländer
Service-oriented design of environmental information systems. 2010
ISBN 978-3-86644-499-7

Band 6 Giulio Milighetti
Multisensorielle diskret-kontinuierliche Überwachung und Regelung humanoider Roboter. 2010
ISBN 978-3-86644-568-0

Band 7 Jürgen Beyerer, Marco Huber (Hrsg.)
Proceedings of the 2010 Joint Workshop of Fraunhofer IOSB and Institute for Anthropomatics, Vision and Fusion Laboratory. 2011
ISBN 978-3-86644-609-0

Band 8 Eduardo Monari
Dynamische Sensorselektion zur auftragsorientierten Objektverfolgung in Kameranetzwerken. 2011
ISBN 978-3-86644-729-5

Band 9 Thomas Bader
Multimodale Interaktion in Multi-Display-Umgebungen. 2011
ISBN 3-86644-760-8

Band 10 Christian Frese
Planung kooperativer Fahrmanöver für kognitive Automobile. 2012
ISBN 978-3-86644-798-1

Band 11 Jürgen Beyerer, Alexey Pak (Hrsg.)
Proceedings of the 2011 Joint Workshop of Fraunhofer IOSB and Institute for Anthropomatics, Vision and Fusion Laboratory. 2012
ISBN 978-3-86644-855-1

Band 12 Miriam Schleipen
Adaptivität und Interoperabilität von Manufacturing Execution Systemen (MES). 2013
ISBN 978-3-86644-955-8

Band 13 Jürgen Beyerer, Alexey Pak (Hrsg.)
Proceedings of the 2012 Joint Workshop of Fraunhofer IOSB and Institute for Anthropomatics, Vision and Fusion Laboratory. 2013
ISBN 978-3-86644-988-6

Band 14 Hauke-Hendrik Vagts
Privatheit und Datenschutz in der intelligenten Überwachung: Ein datenschutzgewährendes System, entworfen nach dem „Privacy by Design" Prinzip. 2013
ISBN 978-3-7315-0041-4

Band 15 Christian Kühnert
Data-driven Methods for Fault Localization in Process Technology. 2013
ISBN 978-3-7315-0098-8

Band 16 Alexander Bauer
Probabilistische Szenenmodelle für die Luftbildauswertung. 2014
ISBN 978-3-7315-0167-1

Band 17 Jürgen Beyerer, Alexey Pak (Hrsg.)
Proceedings of the 2013 Joint Workshop of Fraunhofer IOSB and Institute for Anthropomatics, Vision and Fusion Laboratory. 2014
ISBN 978-3-7315-0212-8

Band 18 Michael Teutsch
Moving Object Detection and Segmentation for Remote Aerial Video Surveillance. 2015
ISBN 978-3-7315-0320-0